IMAGES
of America

THE SAUQUOIT VALLEY

This book is dedicated to Nelson Gray,
who said I should write a book,
and to my husband, Melville Edwards,
who encouraged it.

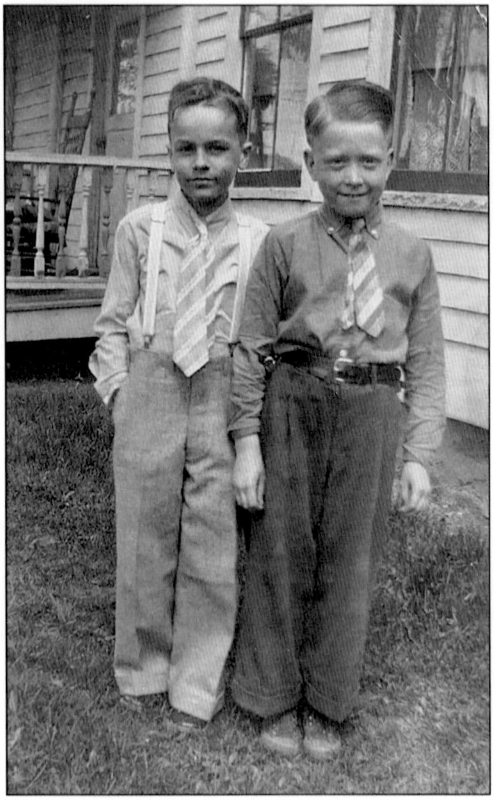

Shown are Nelson Gray and Melville Edwards, c. 1936.

IMAGES
of America

THE SAUQUOIT VALLEY

Evelyn R. Edwards

ARCADIA
PUBLISHING

ISBN 978-0-7385-0286-1

Published by Arcadia Publishing
Charleston, South Carolina

Printed in the United States of America

Library of Congress Catalog Card Number: 00106407

For all general information contact Arcadia Publishing at:
Telephone 843-853-2070
Fax 843-853-0044
E-mail sales@arcadiapublishing.com
For customer service and orders:
Toll-Free 1-888-313-2665

Visit us on the Internet at www.arcadiapublishing.com

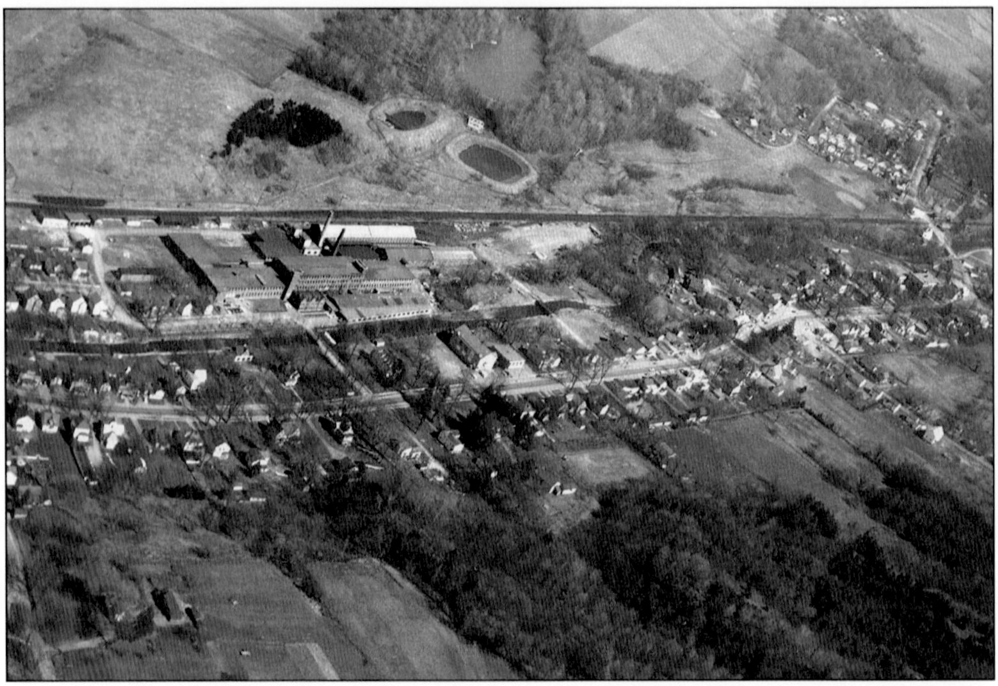

This aerial view of Willowvale and Chadwicks, looking eastward, is from c. 1955. At the top of the photograph are two reservoirs that supplied water to the Willowvale Bleachery. That factory is at the left in front of the Delaware, Lackawanna, and Western (DL&W) railroad tracks. Old Route 8 cuts through the center from left to right. The left three-quarters of the photograph is Willowvale. Chadwicks proceeds along Route 8 and then continues south to Sauquoit. Elm Street winds eastward at the right. The trees at the bottom center surround the entrance to the Willowvale Glen. (Photograph courtesy of Norma R. Clark.)

Contents

ACKNOWLEDGMENTS

Many people gave generously of their time, knowledge, and photographs to contribute to this book. I want to thank all those who so willingly and graciously told their stories and shared their memories of the Sauquoit Valley. The assistance and support of my husband, Melville Edwards, was also greatly appreciated. If I have forgotten anyone, it is not for lack of gratitude, but for lack of memory.

Mike Belowich, Polly Blunk, Norma R. Clark, Betty Crawford, John Ladd Crossley, Michael Crowe, Betty Flynn Dawes, Bob Dicker, Joyce Dougherty Donovan, Ken Hartzell, George and Dorothy Hotchkin, Marian R. Jones, Gordon Knapp, Angela Kress, Theo Lafferty, Doris M. Lamphear, Rollin Mallory, Barbara Munde, Bonny and Elmer Niles, Tom Parry, Sharon Puleo, June Rosborough, Jerry Schafer, Tom Schafer, Beatrice Seckner, Joyce and Martin Shephard, Lewis Smith, Helen Stanimer, Adelbert Stauring, Mike and Marcia Steiger, John Tabia, and Max Townsend.

Special recognition is due for the work of Utica photographer A.J. Manning and others like him, who for the first decades of the 20th century, photographed many of the area's small towns and villages, leaving a priceless record for future generations.

Any additions or corrections to this book are welcome. E-mail: *eveygram@aol.com*.

The photograph of the Sears Gas Station in New Hartford in chapter eight is used with the permission of Jeff Milstein of Paper House Productions.

INTRODUCTION

The Sauquoit Valley is a rural area in central New York. South of the more well-known Mohawk Valley, it has its own unique character. This book is a glimpse back at the Sauquoit Valley in the late 19th and early 20th centuries. It is not a comprehensive history of the valley, but glimpses of the people and villages as they once were. For the purposes of this book, the Sauquoit Valley covers Paris Hill, Paris Station, and Cassville at the southern end of the valley; Clayville, Holman City, and Sauquoit in the town of Paris; and Chadwicks, Willowvale, Washington Mills, and New Hartford in the town of New Hartford. At this point, the Sauquoit and Mohawk Valleys overlap. The Sauquoit Creek continues from New Hartford through the villages of New York Mills, Yorkville, and Whitesboro, ending its journey when it tumbles into the Mohawk River at Whitesboro.

The early 1900s was a period of many changes: automobiles were a novelty; mass transit was available with trolleys and trains; and many people walked to work at adjacent businesses or nearby mills. It was a time when children ran outside to look up at the sky if an airplane flew over. The community life revolved around the mills, stores, and churches. One-room schoolhouses dotted the rural landscape.

In the 1800s and the first half of the 1900s, the Sauquoit Valley was the site of many industries: lumber mills, textile mills, gristmills, tanneries, and tool factories. By the 1950s, many of these mills had closed their doors or left the area to head for the southern United States. The residents looked for employment with the large corporations that remained, such as General Electric, Utica Drop Forge, Bendix Corporation, Chicago Pneumatic Tool Company, and Rome's Griffiss Air Base. When, in turn, many of these facilities left the area, insurance companies, banks, and service industries provided employment. Although still recovering from this upheaval, the area will always be considered home to many longtime inhabitants of the Sauquoit Valley. This volume is written with past, present, and future residents of the valley in mind, with the hope that they will enjoy this journey through the past, and that vintage postcard lovers will enjoy the view.

The maps at the beginning of each chapter are provided to give a general idea of the layout of each village. Although these maps have been reduced to fit the format of the book, a good magnifying glass will reveal names and details. The maps were first published in the *New Century Atlas of Oneida County, New York* in 1907 by the Century Map Company of Philadelphia.

Generally, the images in the book have been arranged geographically from south to north, with excursions down the side streets, then backtracking to the main routes. The majority of the scenes illustrated are from vintage postcards from the collection of Melville and Evelyn Edwards. Some photographs and postcards are from private collections or historical societies. Photographs have been used—especially in Paris Station and Holman City—to supplement the meager postcard record of these small hamlets.

BIBLIOGRAPHY

Cookinham, Henry J. *History of Oneida County, New York, Vol. 2*. Chicago: The S.J. Clarke Publishing Company, 1912.

Durant, Samuel, ed. *History of Oneida County, New York*. Philadelphia: Everts & Fariss, 1878.

Jones, Pomroy. *Annals and Recollections of Oneida County*. Utica, NY: published by author, 1851.

Rogers, Henry C. *History of the Town of Paris and the Valley of the Sauquoit*. Utica, NY: White & Floyd, printers, 1881.

Wager, Daniel E., ed. *Our County and its People, Oneida County, New York*. Boston: Boston Publishing Company, 1896.

Beers Atlas of Oneida County, 1874.

New Century Atlas of Oneida County, 1907.

Files and Resources:

Kirkland Town Library; Davies Family Museum at Paris Station; New Hartford Historical Society; Town of Paris Historical Society; Utica Public Library; Oneida County Historical Society; various unpublished informal papers from local historical societies.

One

Paris Hill and Paris Station

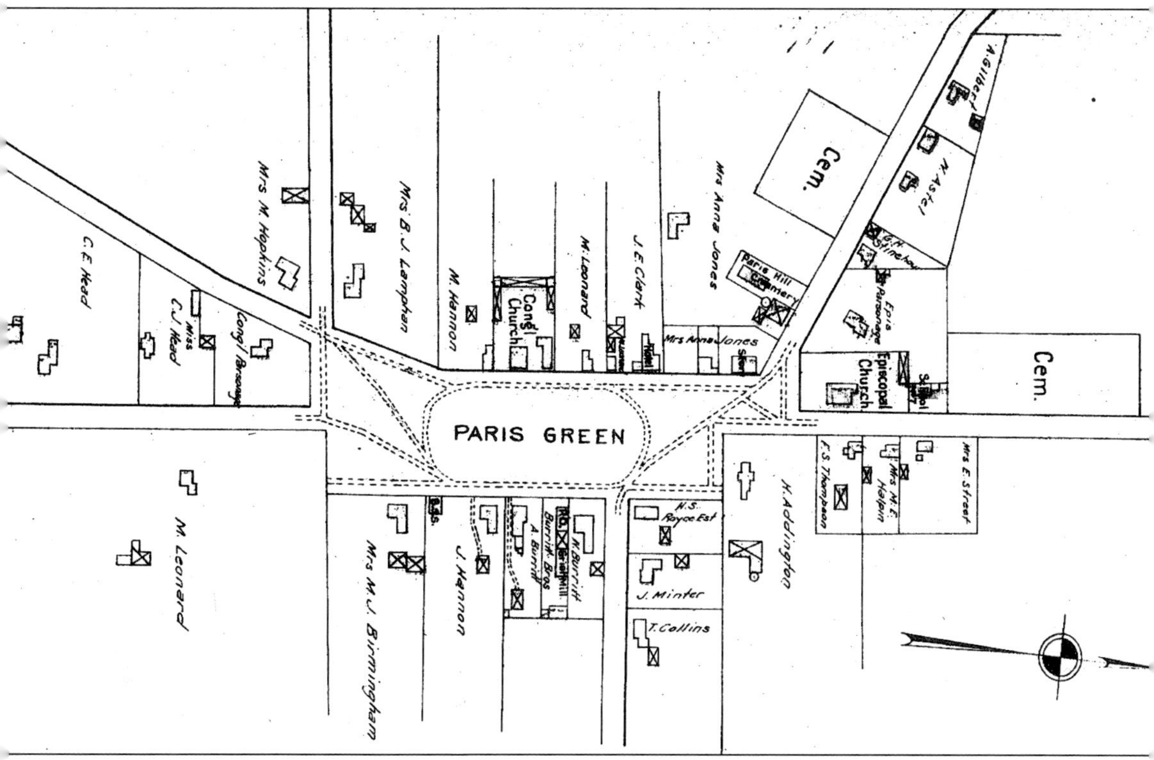

According to Henry Rogers, the Native Americans called Paris "Ganundoglee," meaning "hills shrunk together." Major Amaziah Royce, arriving in 1789, was the first settler near Paris Hill, but Colonel Timothy Tuttle was the first settler in the village proper. Paris is 1,660 feet above sea level, and was the first settlement in the township. In 1789 Paris, or Paris Hill as it came to be called, was in the town of Whitestown, then a part of Herkimer County. Oneida County was formed in 1798, making Paris a part of the new county. The town of Paris was organized in 1792.

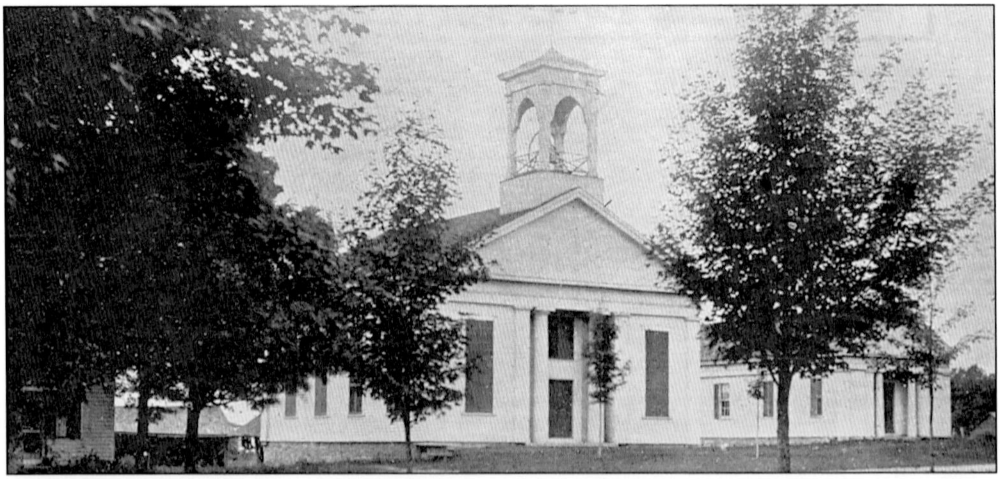

The Paris Congregational Church dates from 1791, when the famous Reverend Jonathan Edwards organized it. Edwards was well known in New England and Massachusetts as a pious and benevolent teacher. During his 1791 Paris Hill visit, Reverend Edwards organized Churches in Clinton and New Hartford. The Paris church replaced an earlier one that had burned. The first frame church building was erected in the center of the village green more than 200 years ago, in 1796.

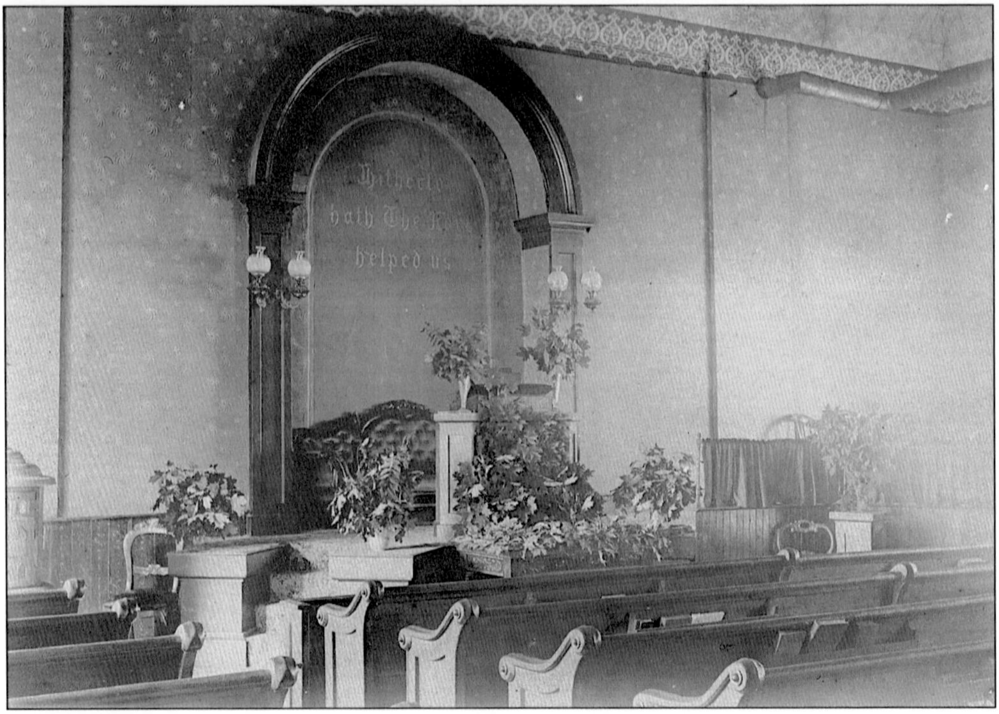

At the time of its inception by Rev. Jonathan Edwards, the Paris Congregational Church employed Rev. Eliphalet Steele as their first pastor. However, Rev. Asahel Norton, pastor of the Church in Clinton in 1792, officiated at the Paris church until Reverend Steele's arrival in 1795. Its interior has not changed much from its early days. The stained glass windows were installed through the efforts of Miss Jennie C. Jones, an active parishioner until 1943. The old bell is still perched atop the roof.

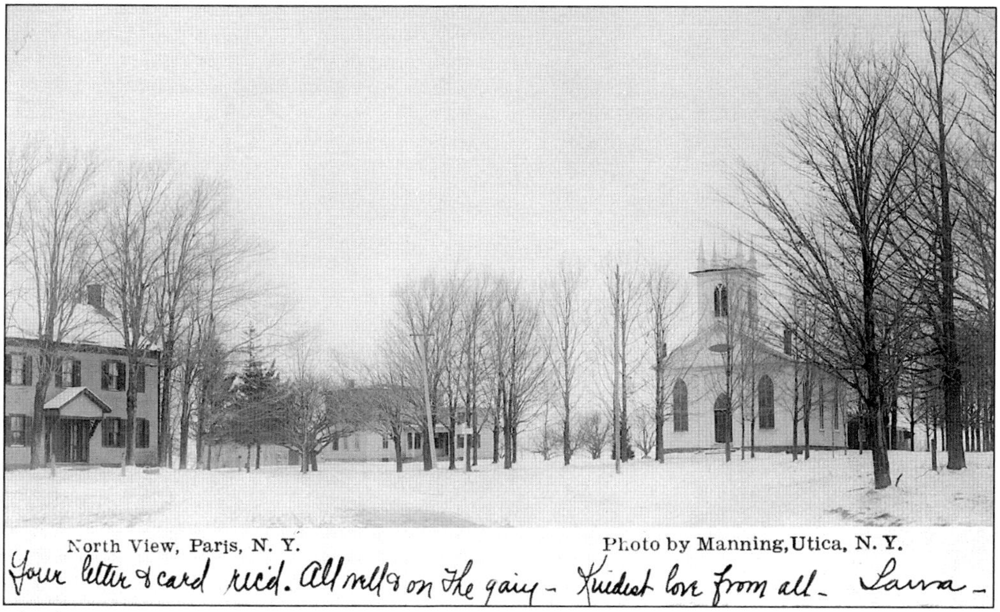

The first Episcopal Church at the north end of the village green was erected in 1797. It was later moved and remodeled for a parsonage and a school. A new church, St. Paul's Episcopal Church (pictured), was built in 1818 to replace the old one. Today, it is open only for an occasional service. Behind the church is the cemetery where Col. Isaac Paris, an early benefactor of the town of Paris, was reinterred from Fort Plain in 1880. A memorial service to mark the occasion was attended by more than 2,000 people.

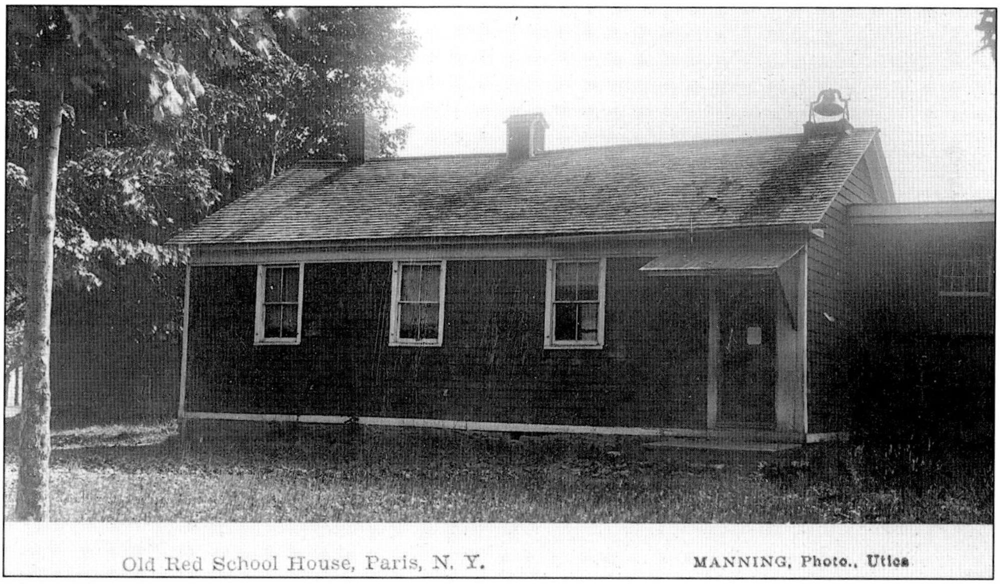

The Old Red Schoolhouse was located behind St. Paul's Episcopal Church between the church and the cemetery. When the school was removed, the cemetery was expanded. The schoolhouse was erected c. 1813. A school reunion was held there on June 30, 1896. About 700 people attended the festivities, which included a reading of the history of the school. A choir made up of people from two village churches performed, and the retelling of old tales was enjoyed by all.

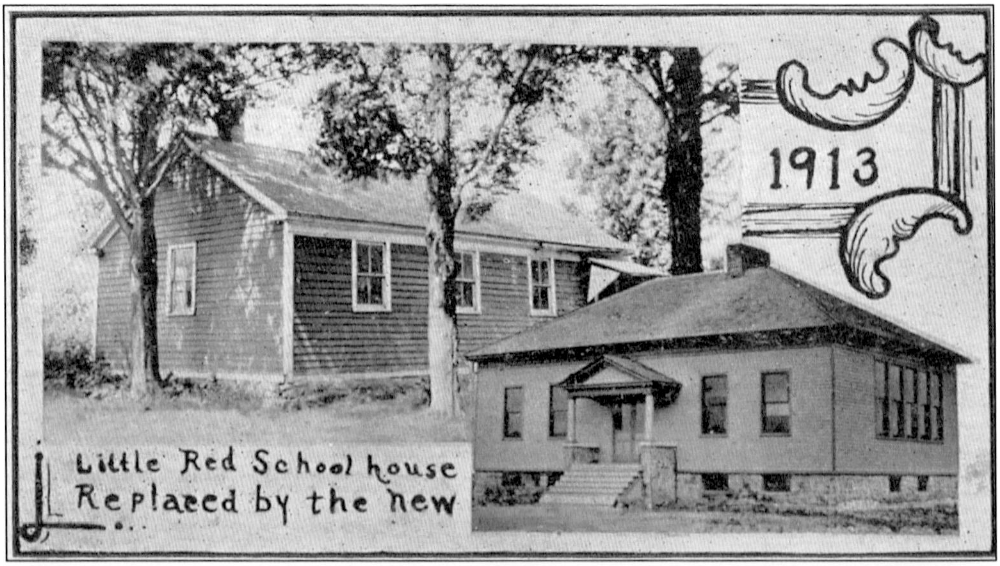

A larger school located just north of the village green on what is now Route 12 replaced the Old Red Schoolhouse. The school was built by 1913 to handle the increased enrollment. The school, which became a private residence in later years, was lost to fire in the early 1980s.

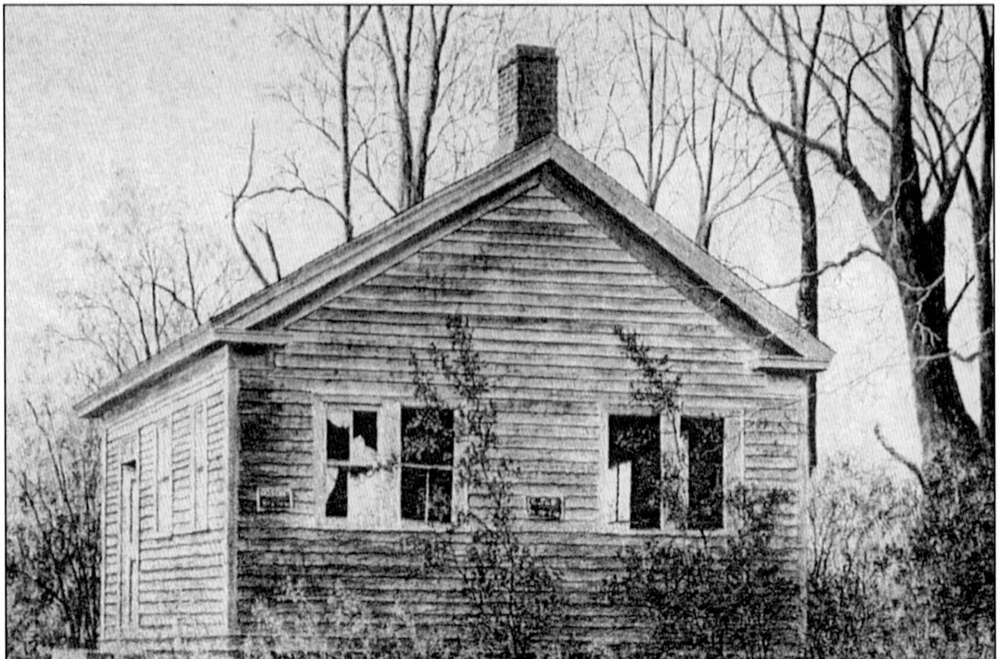

Approximately 140 years old, the Doolittle School had deteriorated by the late 1980s to look like this painting. Purchased by the town of Paris, it was restored by a dedicated group of volunteers and is open for tours. The one-room school was built c. 1850, and elementary students were taught there until 1951. Charles H. Smith, a longtime Holman City resident, was a teacher there in the early 1900s. Daniel Collins, a Doolittle teacher in 1945, now speaks to school groups who visit the site. (Print courtesy of Polly Blunk.)

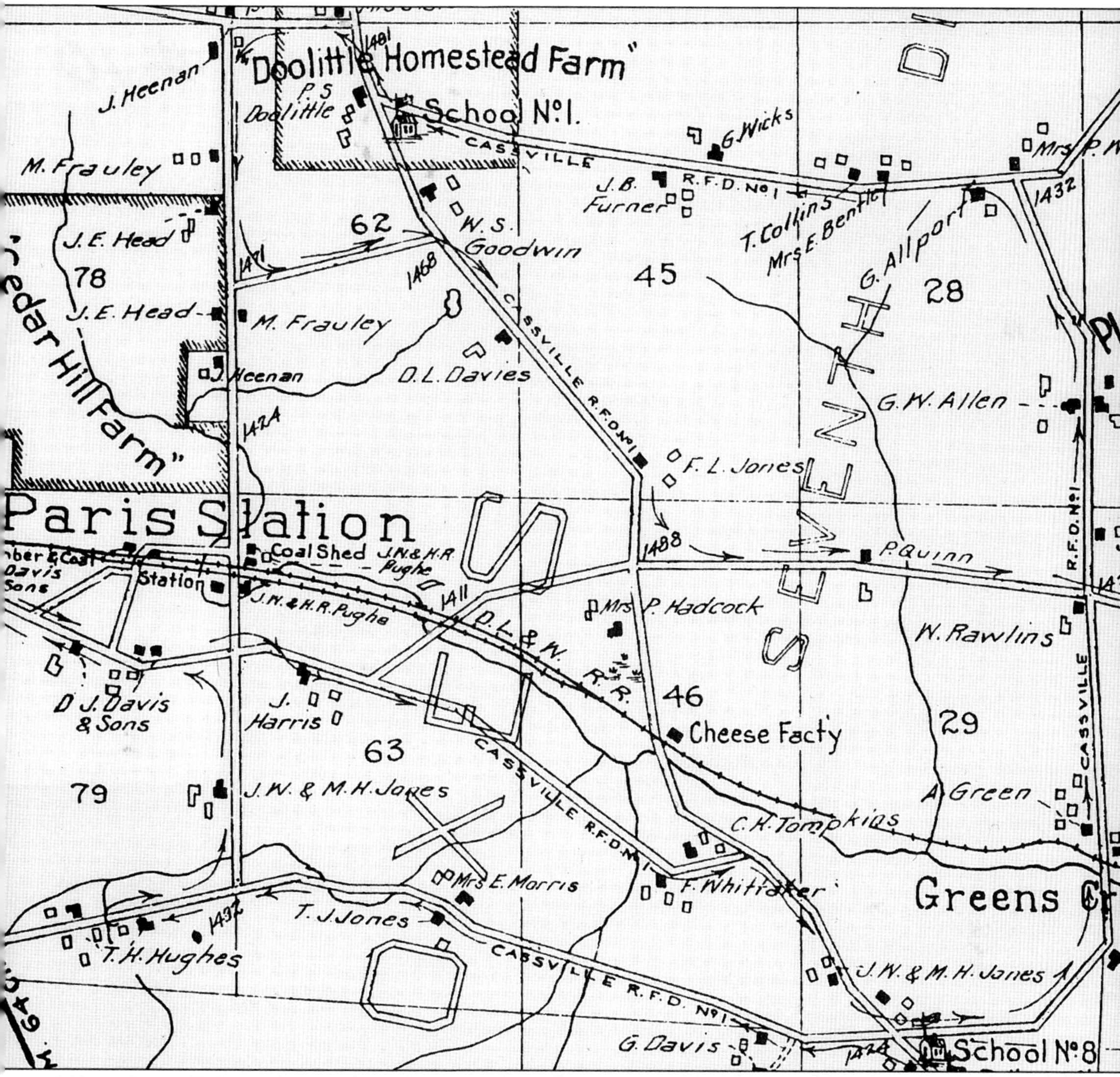

Although small, Paris Station has a big interest in history. Looming large in its history is David J. Davies, the original proprietor of the locally well-known Lincoln Davies Store. David was joined in business by his son Lincoln. Lincoln's oldest daughter Hazel preserved many family mementos; in 1973, a museum was built to house these items. Family pictures, scrapbooks full of news clippings, and numerous other artifacts are displayed there to transport visitors to an earlier time.

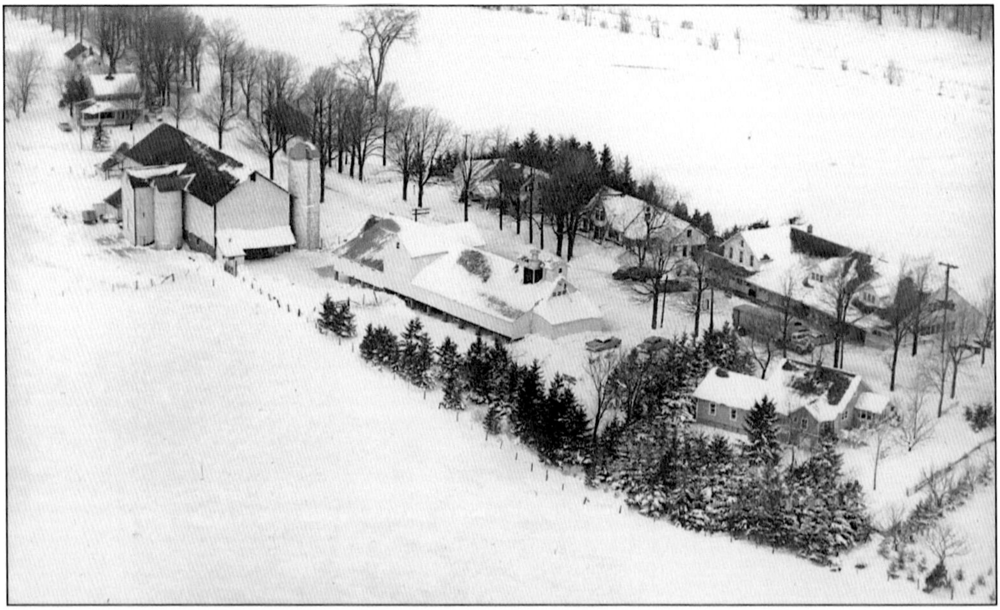

Taken *c.* 1955, this aerial photo postcard shows the hamlet of Paris Station nestled near the base of Tassel Hill, which is the highest point in Oneida County. (The elevation is 2,100 feet above sea level according to Rogers's history.) The Lincoln Davies Store is seen at the right. The former feed mill across the road is now used to stock doors and windows. The farm, once operated by Albert and Louise Davies Townsend, is at the left. The Davies Family Museum was erected across from the farm in 1973.

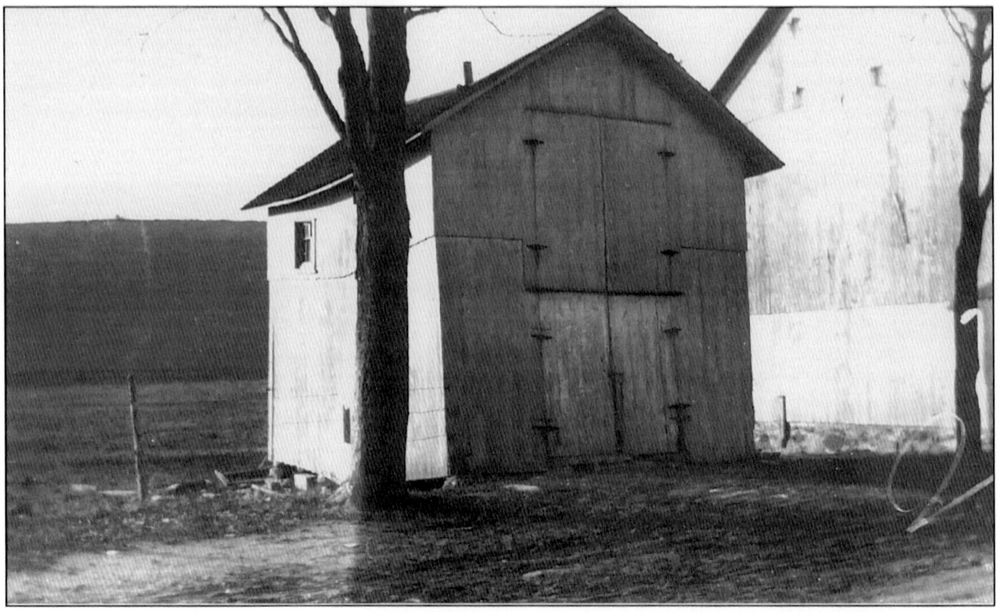

This small barnlike structure was the first Davies family store, built *c.* 1865. When David J. Davies died in 1908, his son Lincoln bought the business. Grain and coal was sold from this small building (no longer existing), which stood next to the farm and across the road from the present store. When Lincoln Davies died suddenly in 1917, his wife, May Head Davies, and her older children continued to operate it.

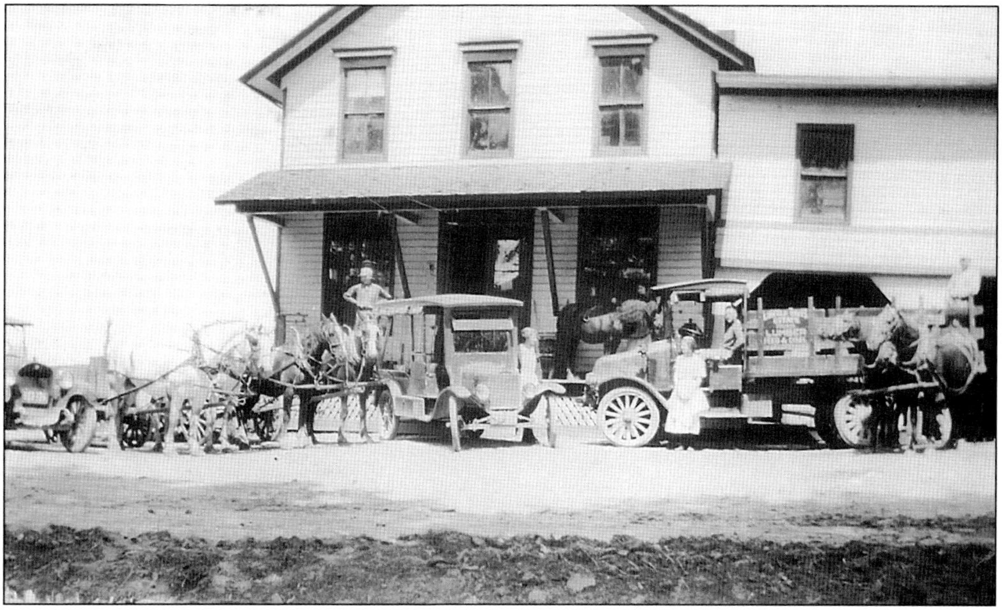

Family members take time for a photograph on a typical busy day at the Lincoln Davies Store in 1923. With an inventory of literally everything from "soup to nuts," the unique store flourished. Feed, grain, tools, groceries, lumber, and supplies are all available at the family store. Word-of-mouth advertising still attracts business from local farmers and their neighbors throughout the Sauquoit Valley and beyond.

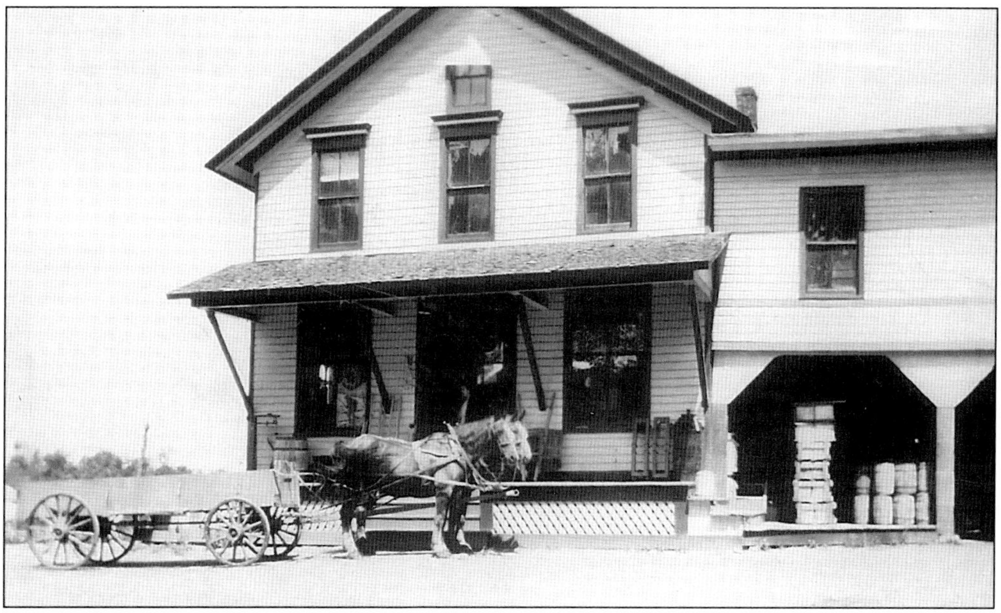

A horse-drawn wagon waits in front of the Lincoln Davies Store to be loaded with supplies for area customers, *c.* 1923. Horses and wagons were used for delivery in the years before motorized vehicles. Howard Davies was the deliveryman, and his job proved fruitful. He met his future wife, Ellen Wicks, on one of his stops. As an added service, the Davies's wives, Lena and Ellen—married to Ralph and Howard respectively—toured the countryside taking grocery orders.

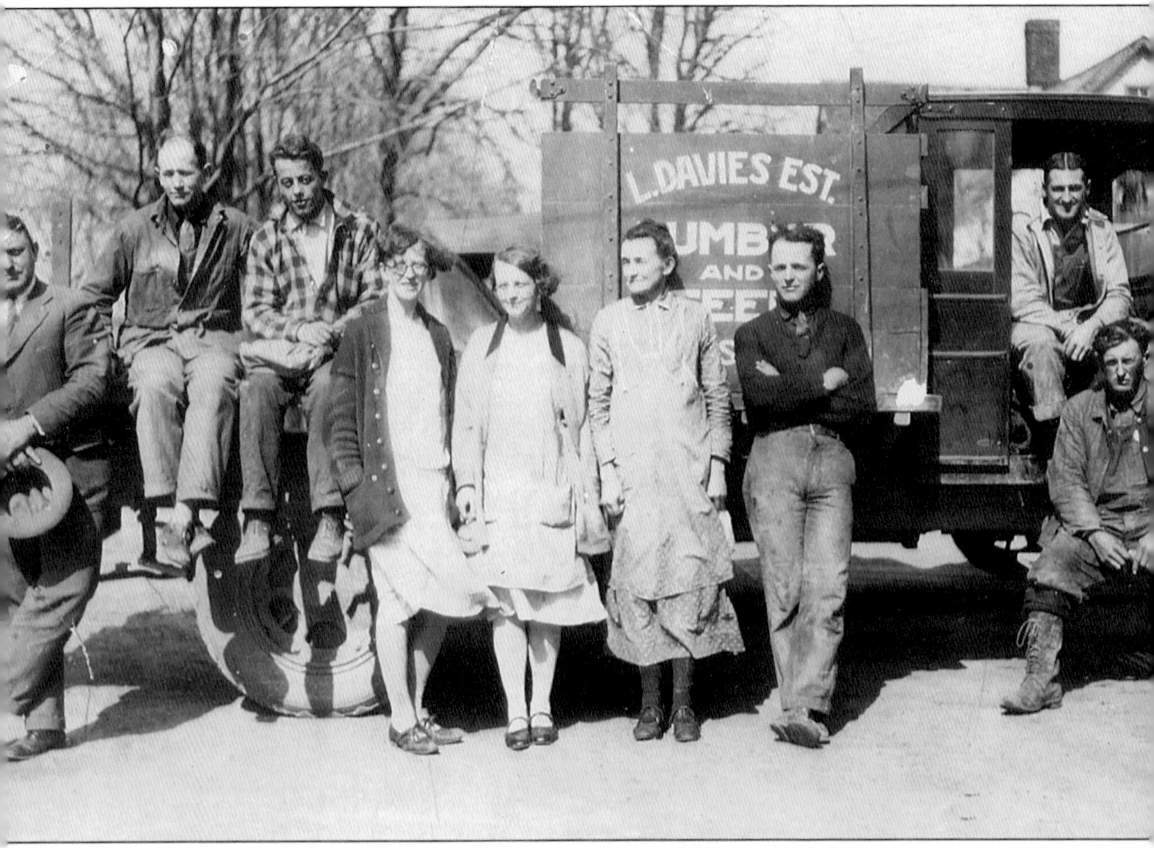

The Lincoln Davies family and the store's employees pose by their delivery truck. Shown are, from left to right, an unknown salesman, Ralph Davies, Emerson Brownell, Florence Davies Jones, Hazel Davies Woodin, May Head Davies (Lincoln's widow), and Howard Davies. The two men at right are Clifford Gallup (sitting in the truck) and Morelle Matteson (on the running board). David Davies started the first store after the railroad built tracks through the middle of his farm, thus providing ready access for receiving and shipping supplies. In 1890, the present store was built; Lincoln built many additions over the years. Lincoln took over the business after his father died in 1908. Later, the building was destroyed by fire after railroad workers dumped hot ashes near the coal and lumber. The store was consumed at a cost of $25,000. The coal continued to burn for six months. Presently, Florence Davies Jones's son and daughter-in-law, Ron and Judy Jones, carry on the family tradition at the Paris Station store. (All Paris Station photographs and the postcard are courtesy of Max Townsend.)

Two

Cassville

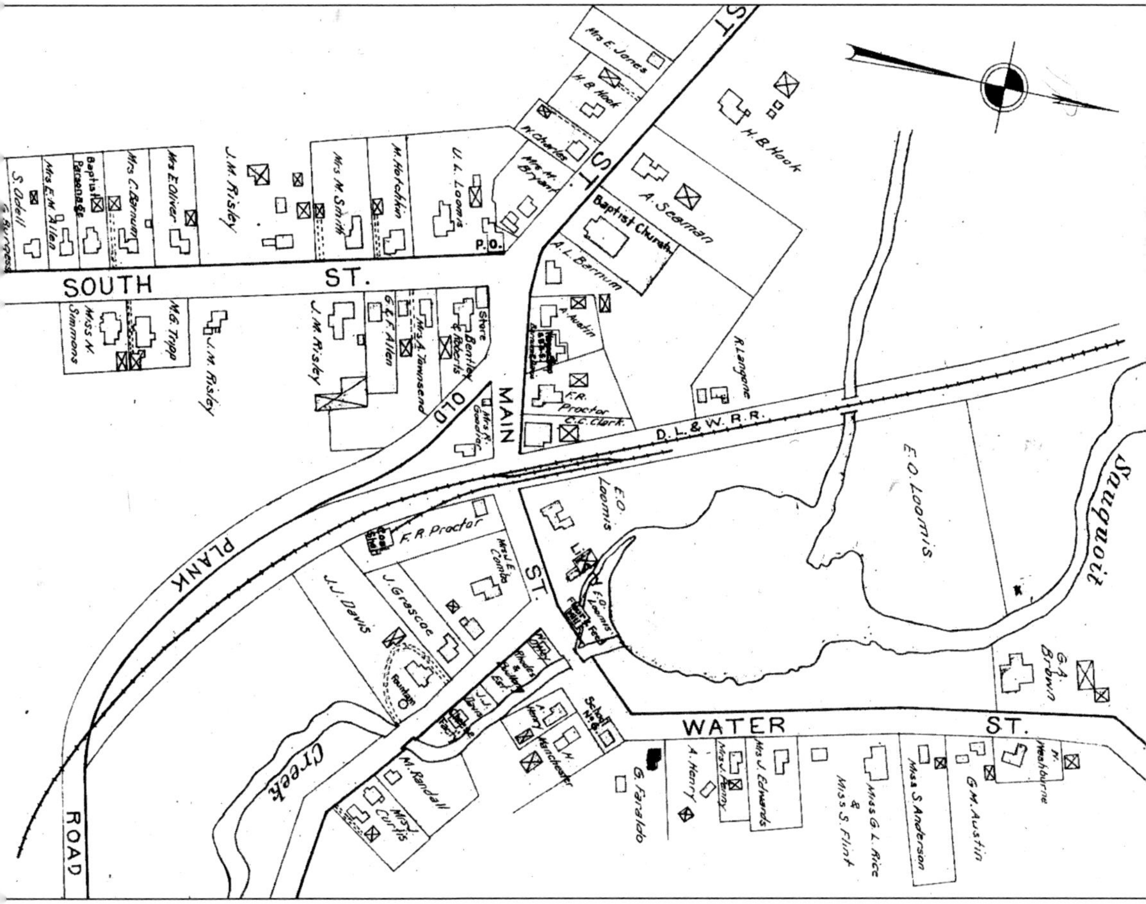

Although once the site of a railroad junction, a cheese factory, gristmills, sawmills, and a couple of general stores, Cassville has always been predominantly a residential village. (These businesses were not all active at the same time, but were spread out over many years.) Agriculture was a common occupation, but opportunities for employment were greater in larger towns. The rapid growth of Utica after construction of the Erie Canal left small villages like Cassville at a disadvantage. Cassville remains largely residential today.

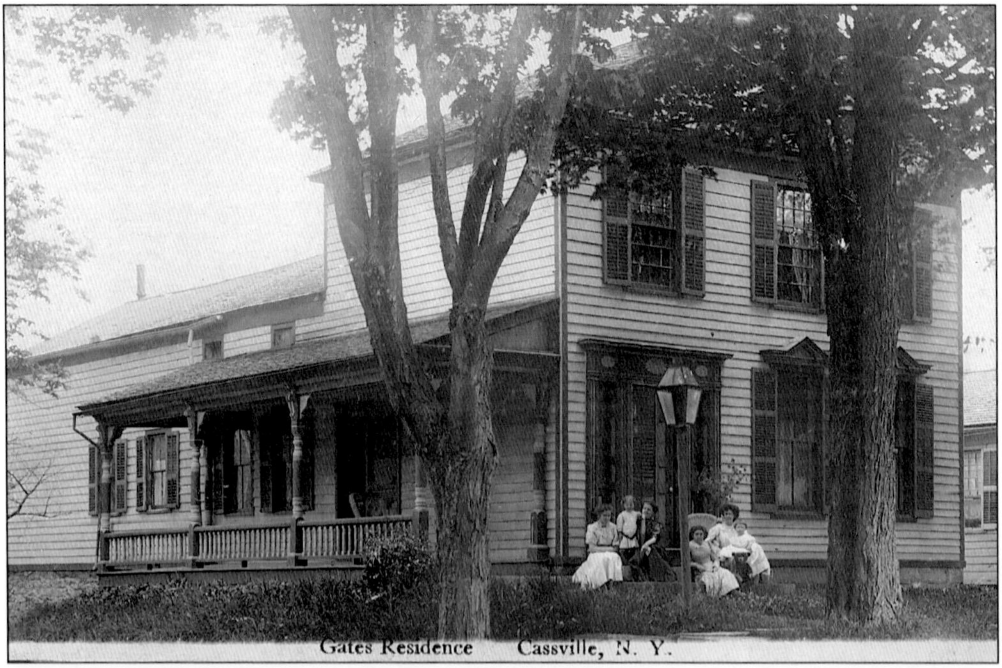

The Gates residence, located on the east side of Summit Road (then West Street), has been somewhat altered in appearance since this *c.* 1910 photograph. The door with side columns and window lights has been replaced, but the decorative lintels still adorn the remaining windows. The side porch has been removed. (Note that today, Summit Road is rather S-shaped. West Street was at the top of the S, and Water Street was at the bottom, continuing past the bottom of the S on what is now Reservoir Road).

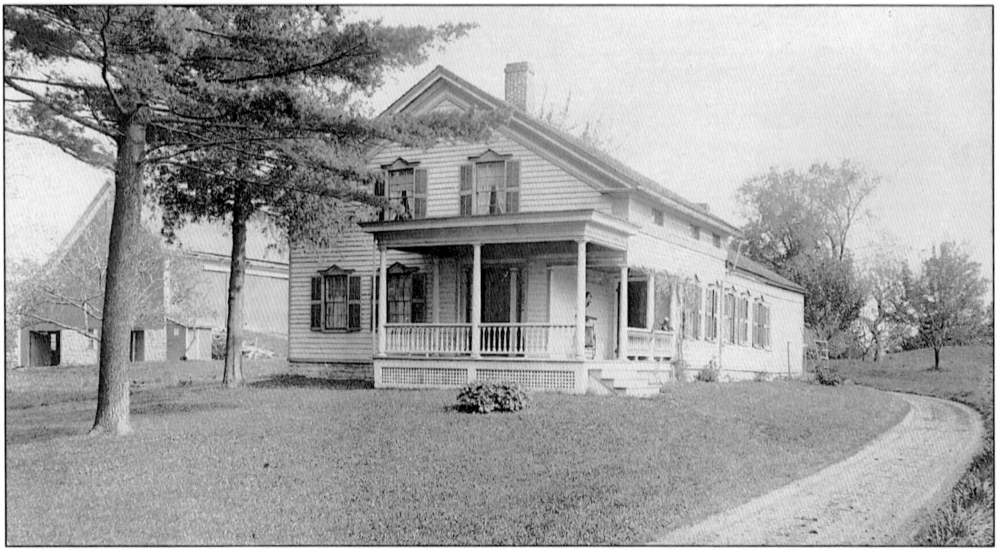

This home on Summit Road has been home to numerous Cassville families. In 1874, it was the G.W. Bagg property, and later the home of the Seegmuller, Hotchkin, Conover, Keehle, and Holderegger families. George Hotchkin, a Cassville resident, was born in this house in 1922. A barn is still behind the house, but the pine trees are gone, and the front porch has been enclosed. It is presently the residence of Bruce and Jayne Baran.

The Cassville Community Baptist Church, which was first organized in 1802, held early meetings in homes and barns. In 1815, the first house of worship was built on Upper Reservoir Road. In 1832, this church was replaced; a new church was erected on the site of the present Baptist Church. A fire on December 1, 1867 destroyed the uninsured building, but contributions from the congregation financed a new church, the present Cassville Community Baptist Church. In 1977, a room was added to house the Cassville Library.

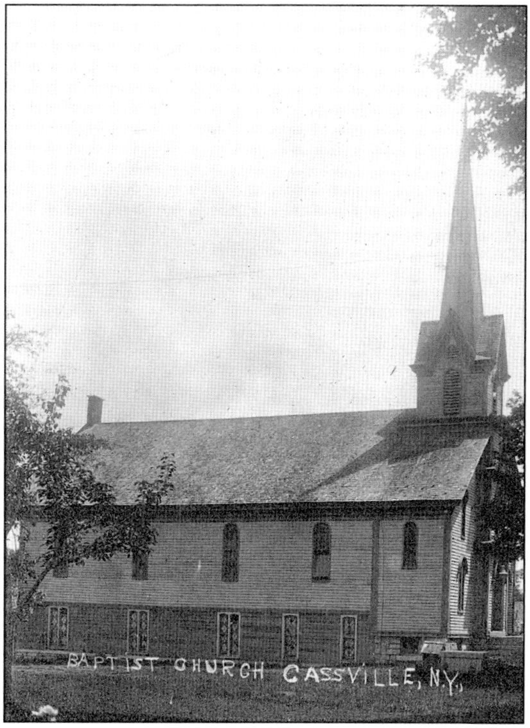

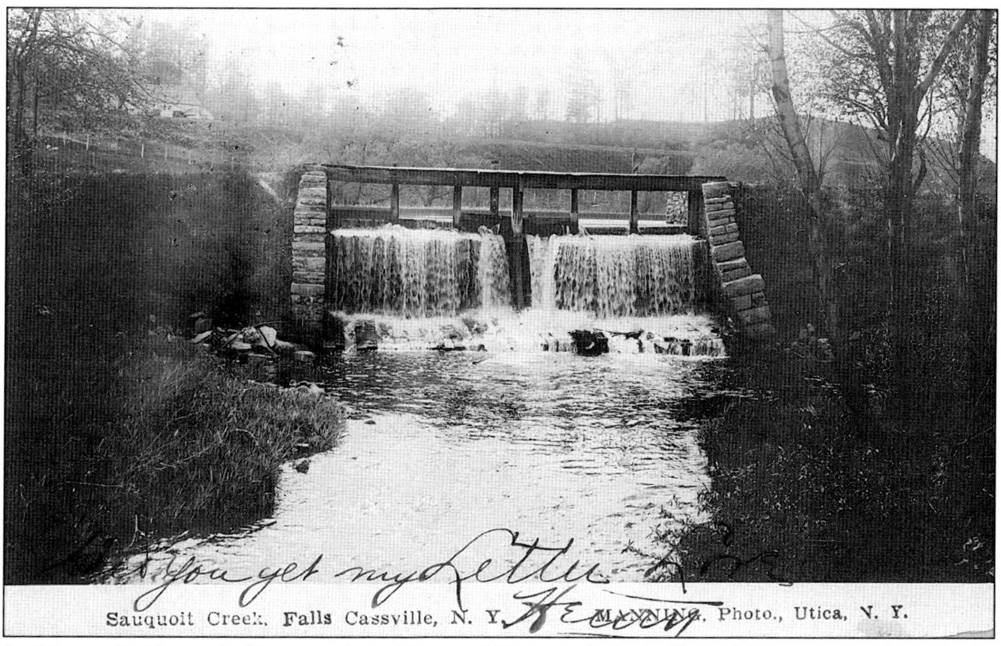

In Henry C. Rogers's *History of the Town of Paris and the Valley of the Sauquoit* (1881), he describes the route of the Sauquoit Creek. Rising at the base of Tassel Hill, it flows to the southeast for three miles, then turns sharply north at Cassville and continues through Clayville, Sauquoit, Chadwicks, Willowvale, Washington Mills, and New Hartford. It travels 17 miles and falls 1,014 feet. It crosses the Mohawk Valley at New York Mills, Yorkville, and Whitesboro.

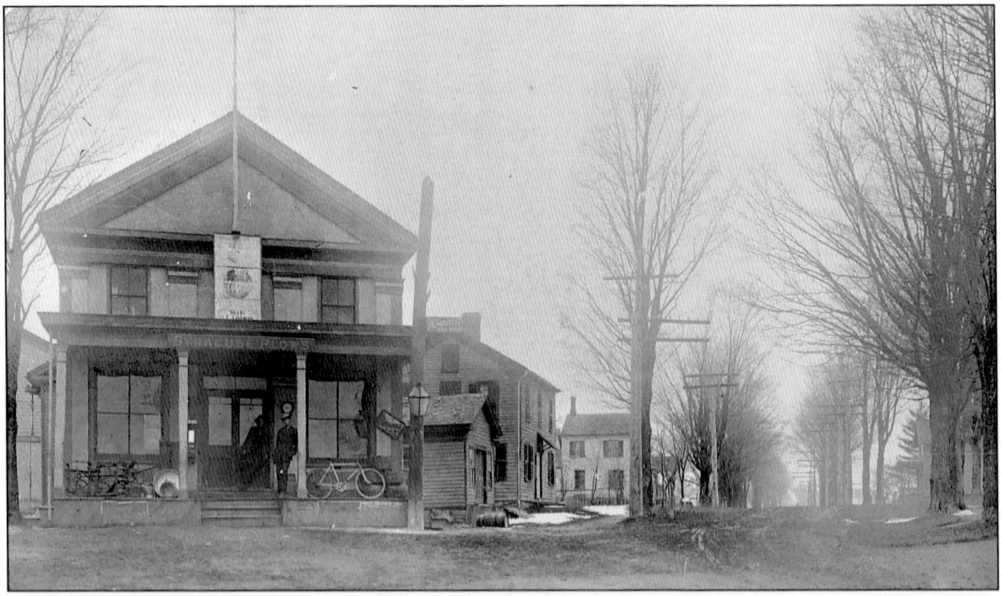

A view of West Street (now Summit Road) shows the U.L. Loomis Store on the corner of South Street (now Main Street). The second house up Summit Road, on the left, was the birthplace of Susie B. Charles (Parry), the mother of present valley resident, Tom Parry. His grandfather was Wallace Charles, a longtime Sauquoit Valley resident. The small building directly behind the store, recently destroyed by a fire, is next door to the Crowe residence.

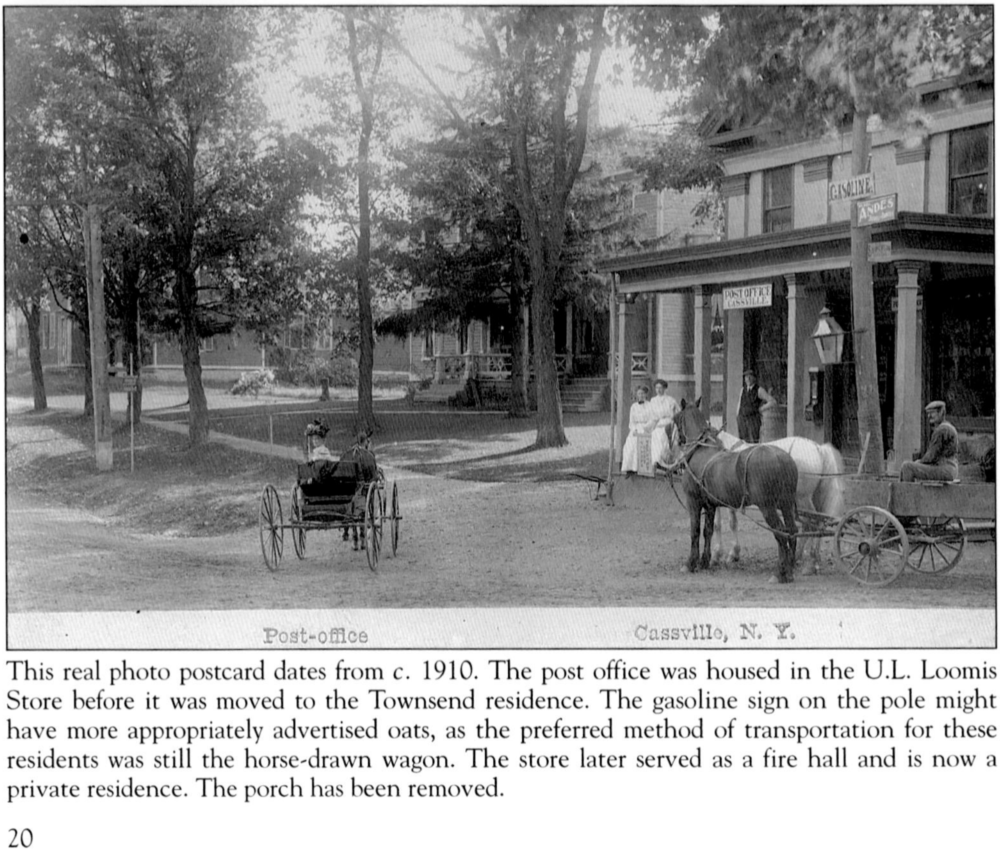

This real photo postcard dates from *c.* 1910. The post office was housed in the U.L. Loomis Store before it was moved to the Townsend residence. The gasoline sign on the pole might have more appropriately advertised oats, as the preferred method of transportation for these residents was still the horse-drawn wagon. The store later served as a fire hall and is now a private residence. The porch has been removed.

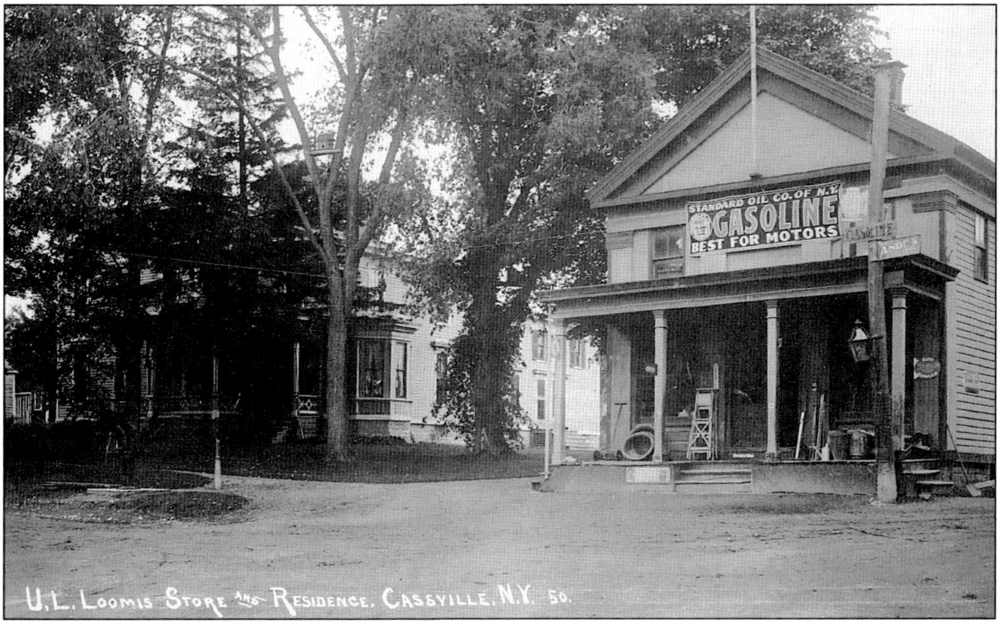

According to Henry G. Williams in his paper *A History of the Village of Cassville* (1951), this was the first general store in Cassville. Originally established by Calvin Budlong in 1824, the store was sold in 1859 to Norman Merrill, who operated it until 1889. It was then purchased by U.L. Loomis, who ran the store until 1925 and resided in the home next door. Its Victorian features having been recently removed, the house has been reduced in size, greatly altering its appearance. Note the Bell Telephone sign on the left porch column.

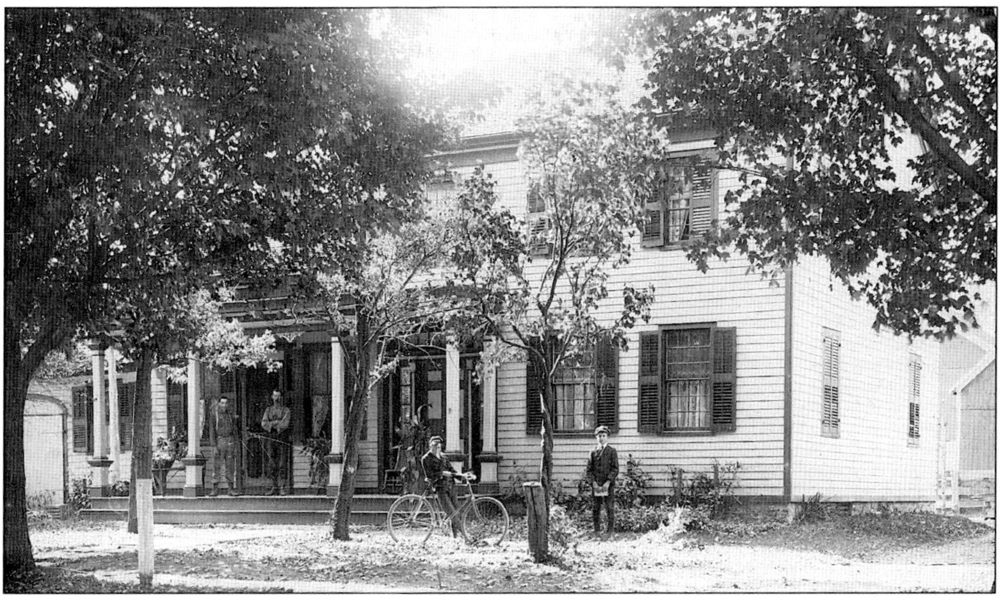

Perhaps built *c.* 1820, this house, without the porch, looks very different today. At times a tenant home, it has been owned by several related families: Eastman, Risley, Williams, and at one time Reginald and Marjorie Davies. Current owners Joseph and Faith Palmer plan to restore the home to its 1910 appearance. A garage and an addition on the left have been removed, and the barn on the right in back was recently razed.

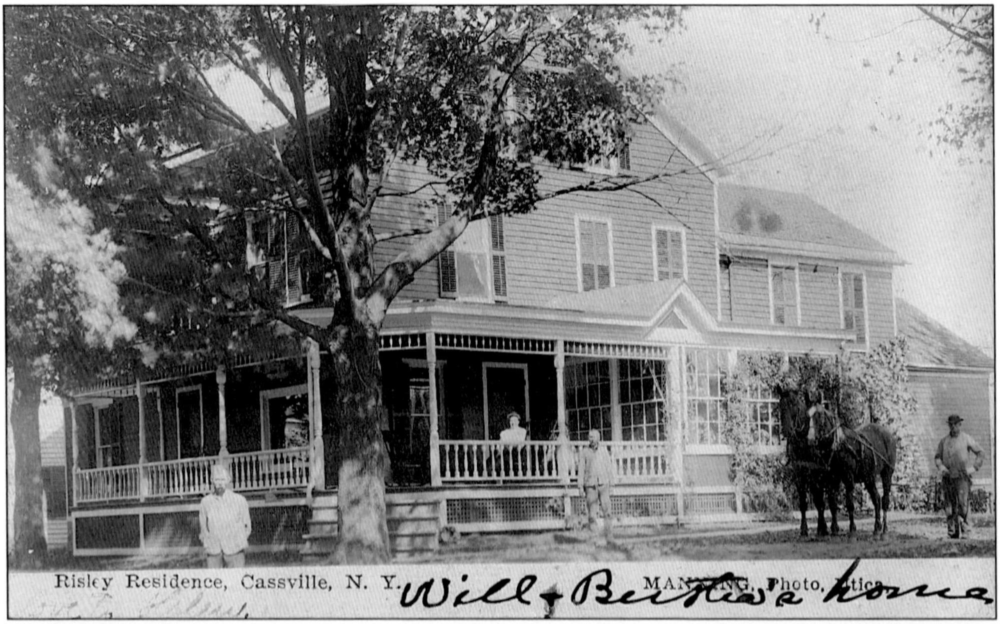

The Risley residence was a large two-and-one-half-story home. The present occupants—Mike and Marcia Steiger, who purchased the home in 1972—relate that the house, originally one and one half stories high, was jacked up and another story built underneath in 1906. As part of the Risley Farm, hops were grown on the land behind the house. After Prohibition, however, the crop was switched to hay and oats. Longtime area congressman William Williams, who married Bertha Risley, once lived here.

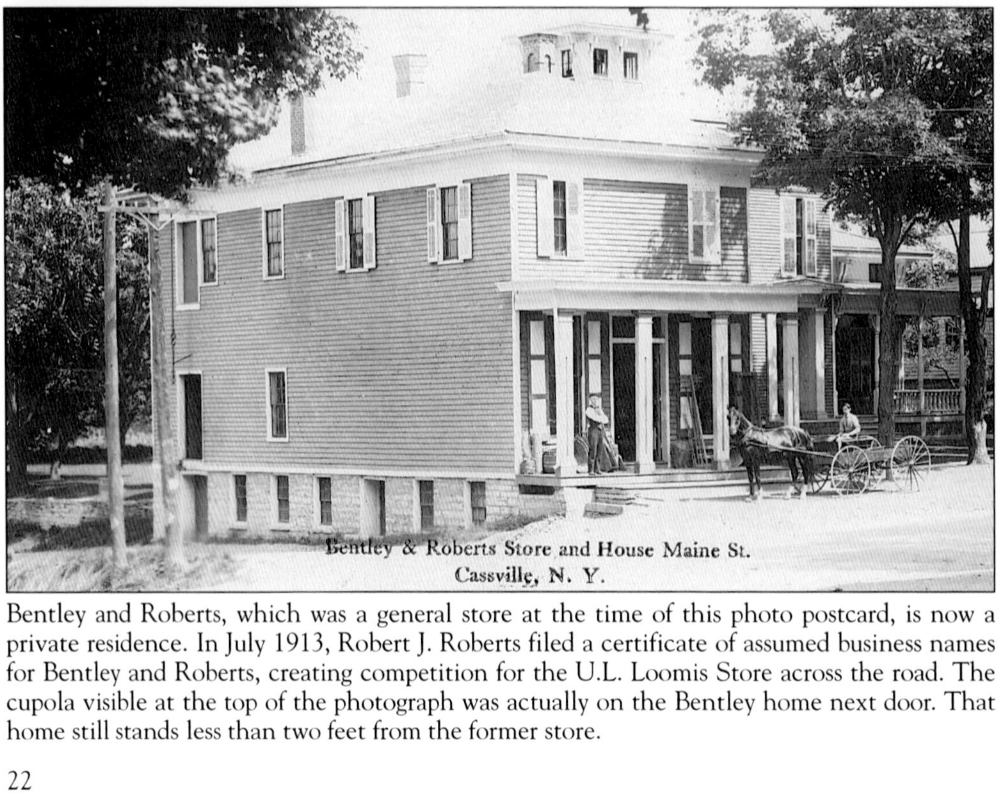

Bentley and Roberts, which was a general store at the time of this photo postcard, is now a private residence. In July 1913, Robert J. Roberts filed a certificate of assumed business names for Bentley and Roberts, creating competition for the U.L. Loomis Store across the road. The cupola visible at the top of the photograph was actually on the Bentley home next door. That home still stands less than two feet from the former store.

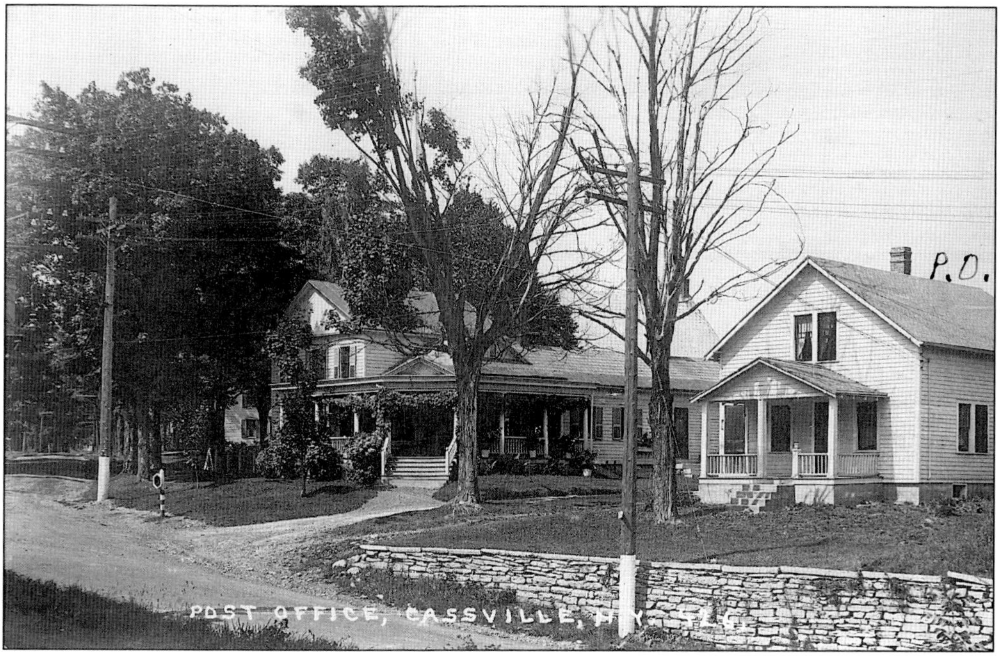

This former post office on the right is located on Summit Road opposite Main Street. During the 1920s and through the 1940s, this was also the home of Postmaster Aida Austin Townsend. Cassville—originally called Toad Hollow because of the noise of the frogs and toads in nearby swamps—was renamed Paris Hollow in 1830. In 1835, it was changed to Cassville in honor of Lewis Cass, a Michigan governor who had spoken in the area.

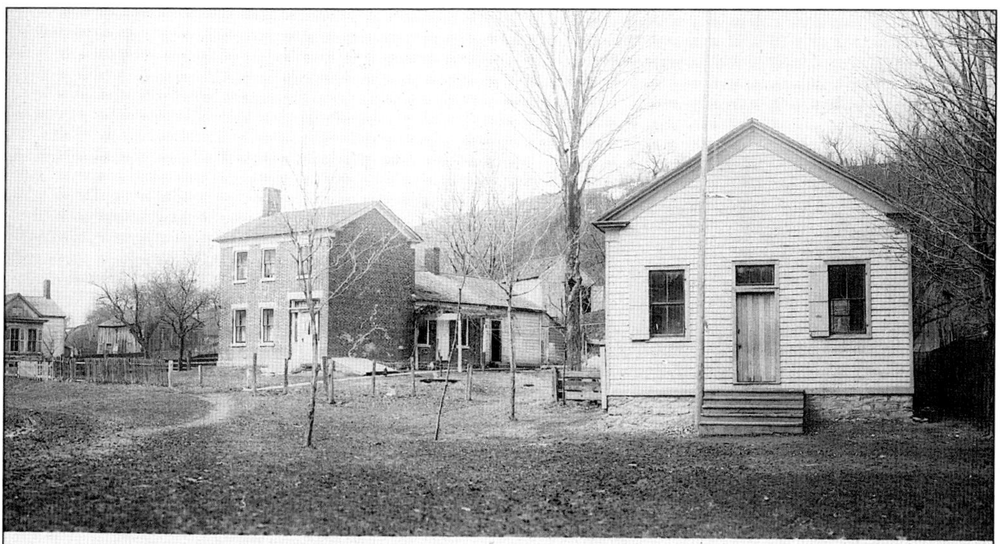

This A.J. Manning real photo postcard records the one-room schoolhouse just beyond the stone bridge on Reservoir Road. The schoolhouse is now a private residence. The brick house next door was, at one time, the home of Merwin and Mary Sherman Smith. The house west of that is where "Aunt Fannie died." (See the stone bridge postcard on page 24.)

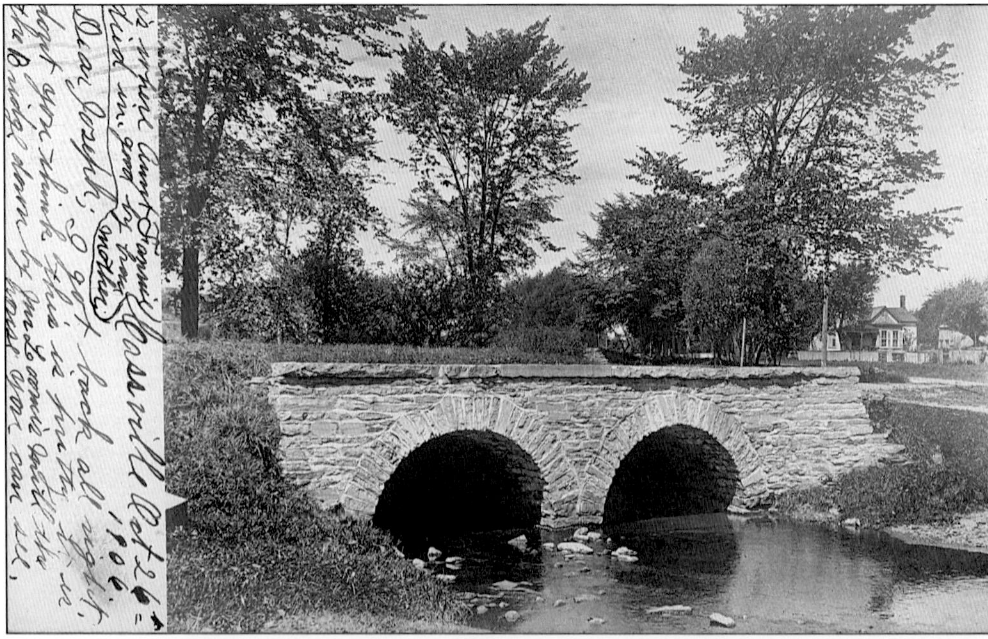

This picturesque stone bridge, c. 1906, is on Reservoir Road (once Water Street). The writer of the postcard relates that the house seen on the right is "where Aunt Fannie died, and it is down by Mr. Loomis' mill." Perhaps this is the same Mr. Loomis who ran the general store, since it was not uncommon for early businessmen to be involved in multiple enterprises.

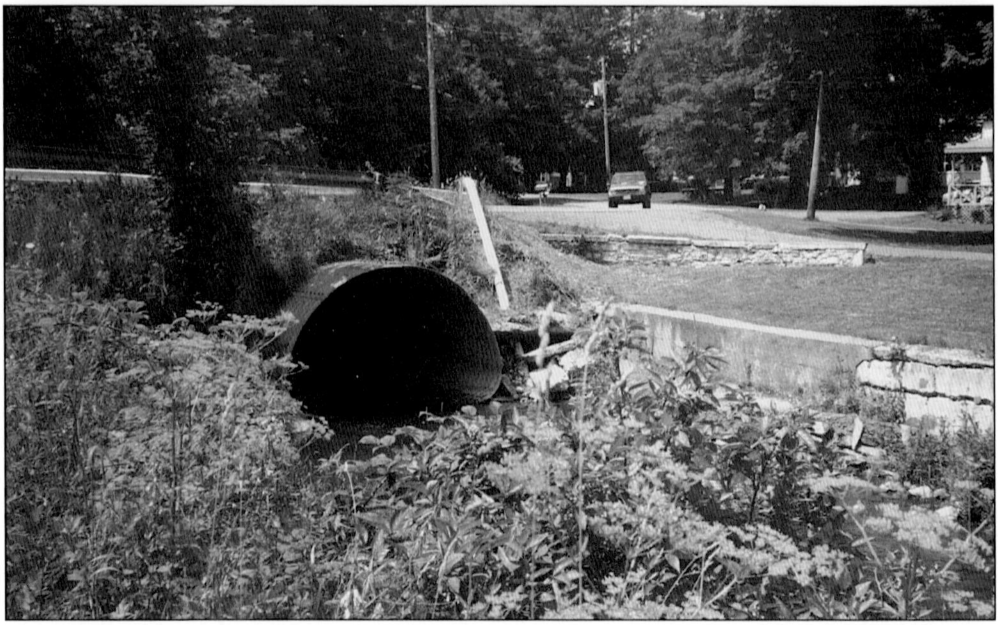

This 1996 photograph of the site of the stone bridge shows that the course of the stream has moved slightly to the left. Although traces of the old bridge are still visible, a utilitarian but less picturesque bridge now occupies the site. The corrugated iron pipe directs the flow of water, which was low and weed-choked at the time of this photograph. On 1874 and 1907 maps, the house seen on the right was a schoolhouse.

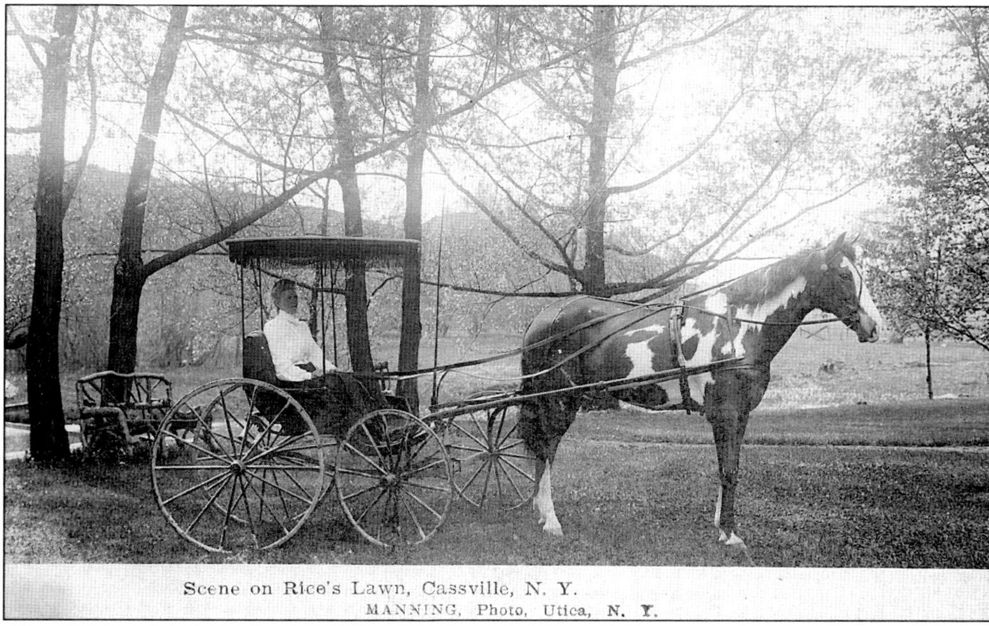

This scene across from the Rice's residence on Water Street features a handsome dappled horse pulling a stylish carriage. The rustic bench provided a place to enjoy the view of the Sauquoit Creek that flowed nearby. The driver appears to be the lady seated in the carriage in the next postcard.

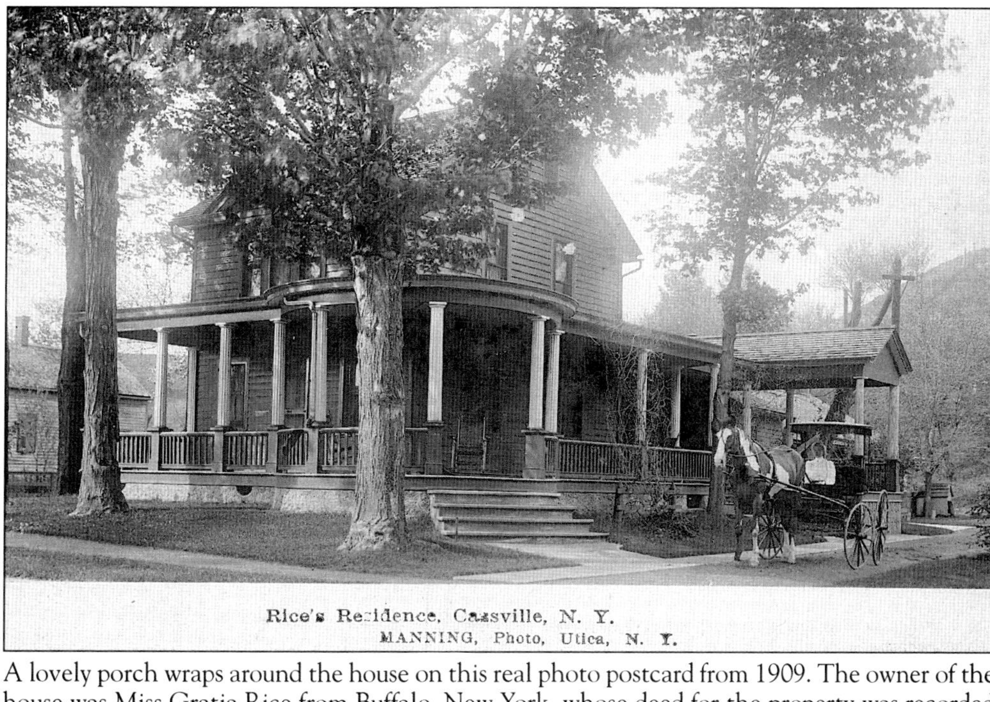

A lovely porch wraps around the house on this real photo postcard from 1909. The owner of the house was Miss Gratia Rice from Buffalo, New York, whose deed for the property was recorded on March 27, 1899. She lived in the house at the time of the photograph, having purchased it from Amos Anderson, who was the owner listed on an 1874 map. Currently occupied by the Jack Hollenbeck family, the porches on this residence remain intact.

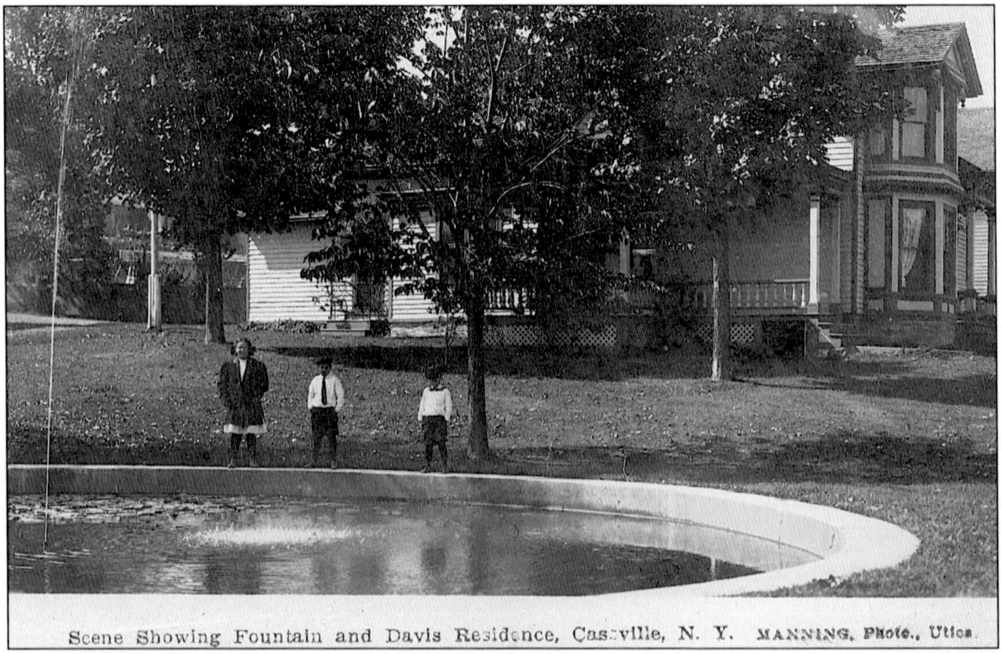

In 1907, J.J. Davis owned one of the oldest homes in Cassville—complete with a pond and a fountain. The home is located on what was once called Water Street, now Summit Road. The Davis acreage stretched all the way back to the railroad right-of-way. The property across the street next to a cheese factory was also owned by J.J. Davis. In later years, this home was the residence of Bill Rohl, an office administrator at the Utica Willowvale Bleachery.

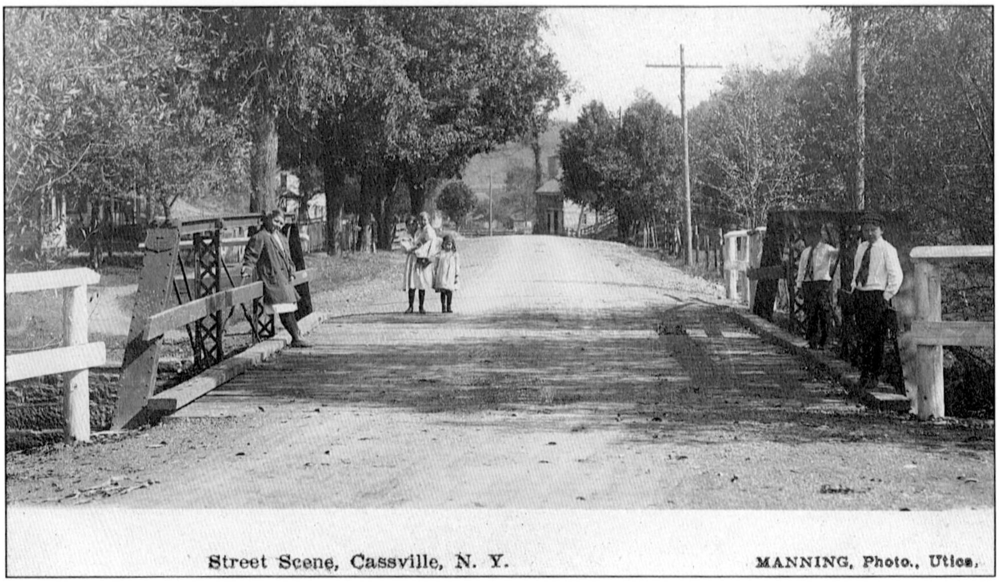

The boys and girls observing the photographer appear to be dressed up for church or perhaps school. They stand on a bridge over the Sauquoit Creek on Summit Road in the village, a short distance west of Route 8. Like the thousands of pictures taken by local photographers, this postcard by Utica cameraman A J. Manning is a precious record of the early days of the 20th century.

Three

Clayville and Holman City

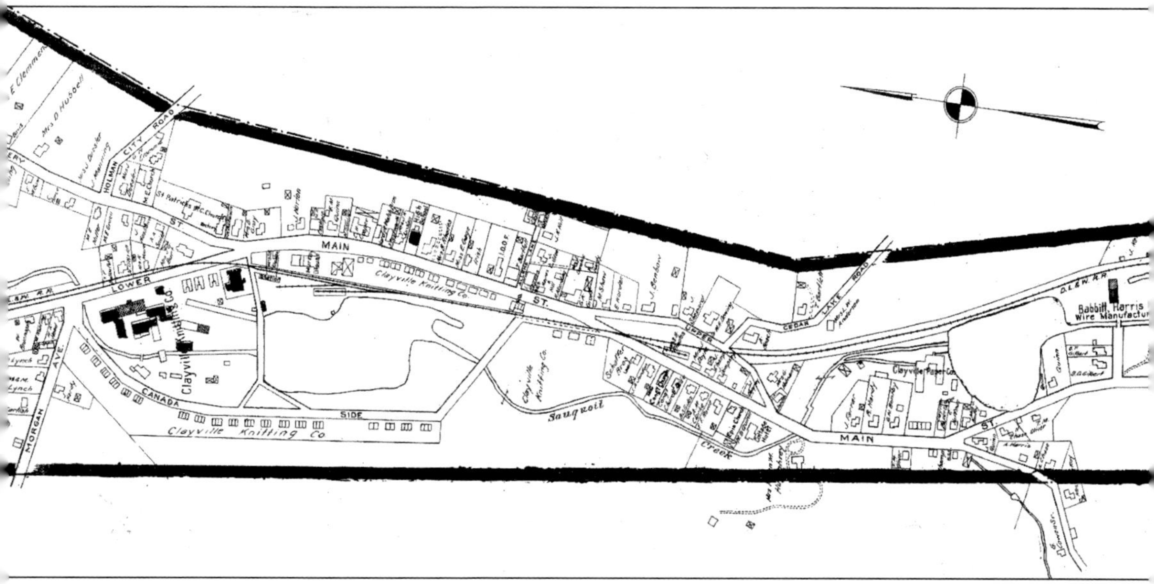

Clayville was initially called Paris Furnace for the iron ore furnace erected across from the D.J. Millard residence. Erected in 1801, it was one of the first manufacturing businesses in the valley. It was established by Judge Sanger (founder of New Hartford), Colonel Avery, and Judge Sweeting. The village's name was changed to Clayville to honor the great orator and statesman Henry Clay. The change was originally proposed in 1844, but was not officially made until 1849. In September 1849, on his way to the New York state fair in Syracuse, Clay visited the village that had been named after him. He addressed a large gathering from the front porch of the Millard home.

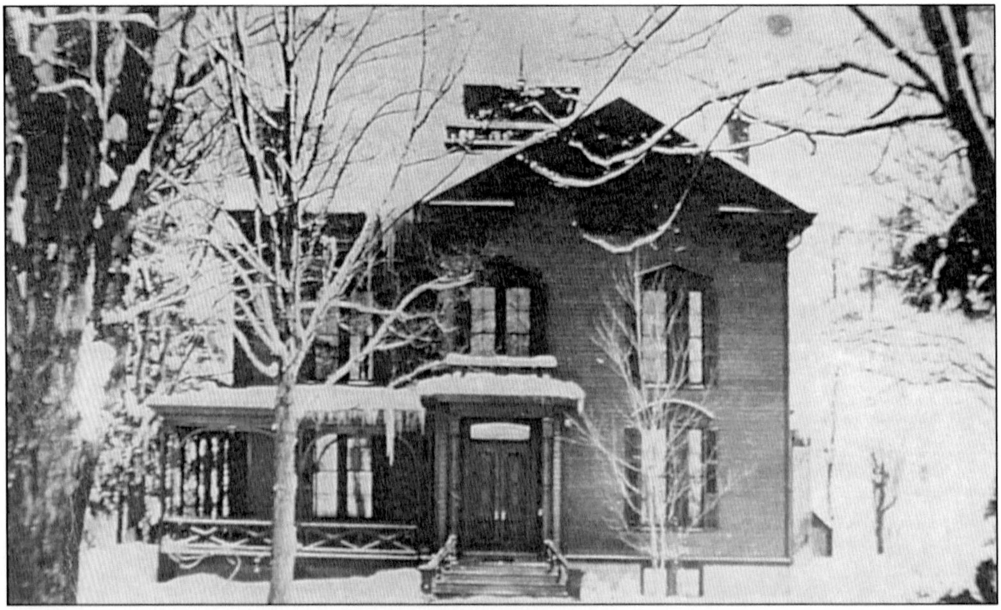

One of the Gilbert family homes (today the property of Don Moore) stands on the eastern side of Oneida Street, looking very much like it did in this *c.* 1910 picture. Hannah and Theodore Gilbert Sr. came to the Sauquoit Valley in 1789 from Connecticut with five daughters and two of their sons. One daughter, Harriet, married Solomon Rogers. They were parents of Henry C. Rogers, the author of *The History of the Town of Paris and the Valley of the Sauquoit*.

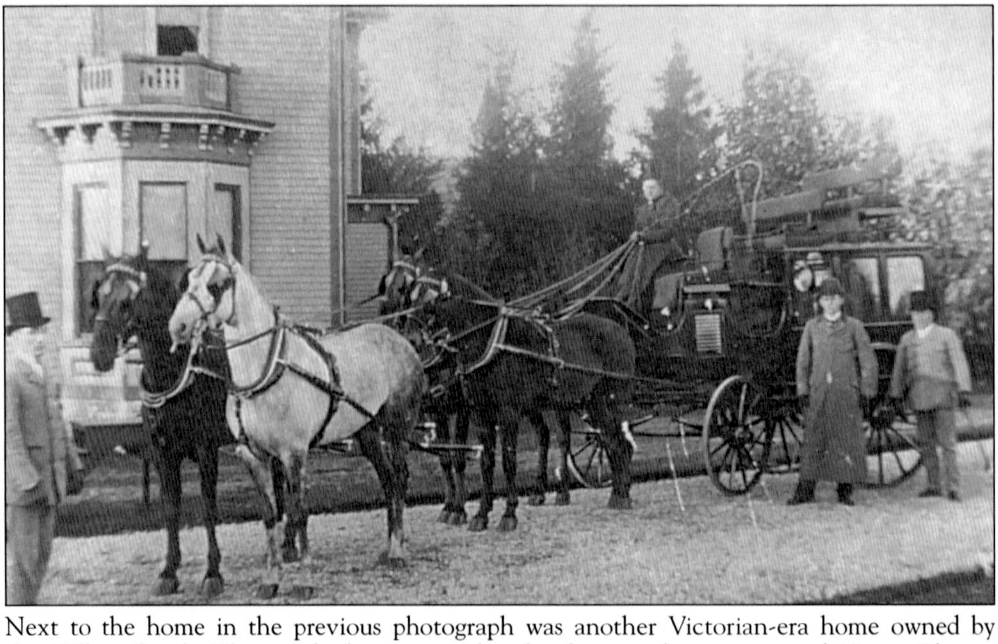

Next to the home in the previous photograph was another Victorian-era home owned by the Gilbert family. The coach shown is said to be the one that transported Henry Clay to the Millard Mansion on his 1849 visit. Although not mentioned in the *Utica Daily Gazette* report, the story has been told that when the coach made a stop at the Episcopal Church, some local boys unhitched the horses and manually pulled the coach, depositing Mr. Clay at the Millard doorstep.

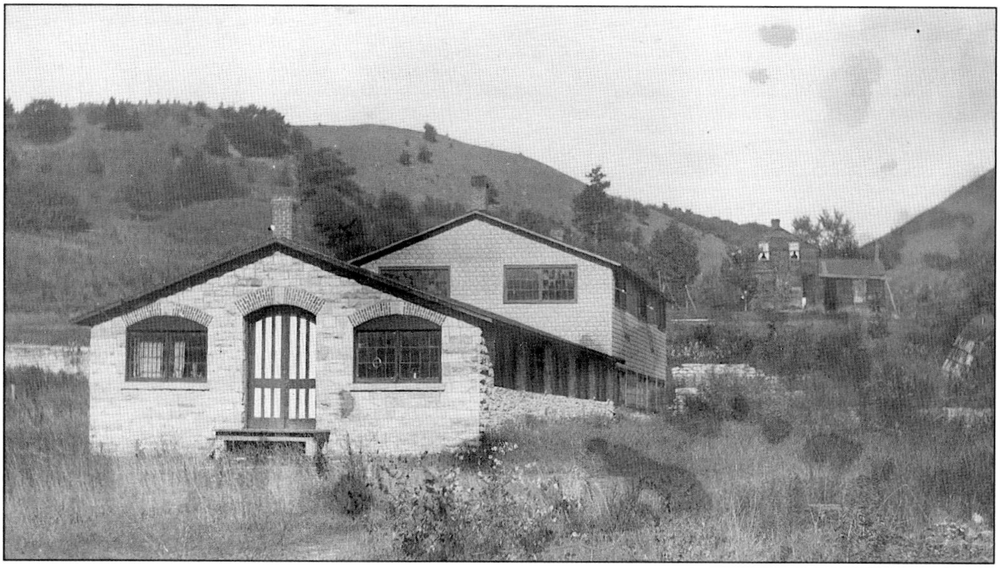

The wire mill at the southern end of Clayville—which once nestled against the village's eastern hills behind the Gilbert homes—no longer exists. The homes of the Gilbert family, who were early pioneers of the town of Paris, still stand nearby. A 1907 business directory lists the Babbitt Harris Company, wire manufacturers, in Clayville. It also lists B.T. Babbitt as its secretary and treasurer. He was likely a descendant of Benjamin Talbot Babbitt, an early 1800s entrepreneur born in Holman City.

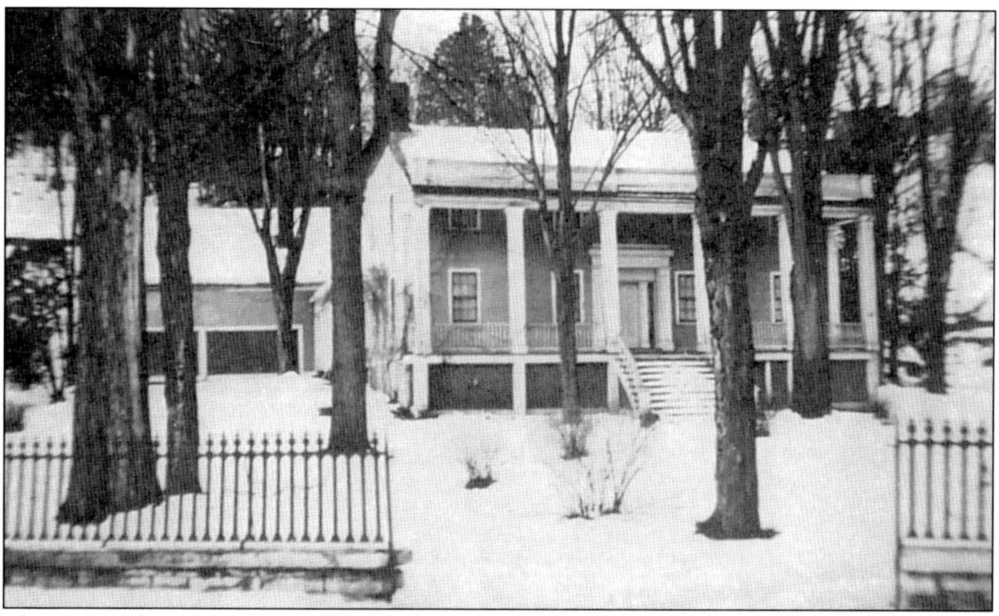

The Millard homestead on old Route 8 in Clayville is the oldest structure in the village. It was built in the early 1800s, although some believe it was built as early as 1775. First erected as a "posthouse" or inn, it was later Mr. Scollard's tavern. Howard Luce operated it as a hotel before it was converted into a residence for the family of David J. Millard. When Henry Clay visited in 1849 to show appreciation for the village being named in his honor, he spoke from the porch to a large gathering.

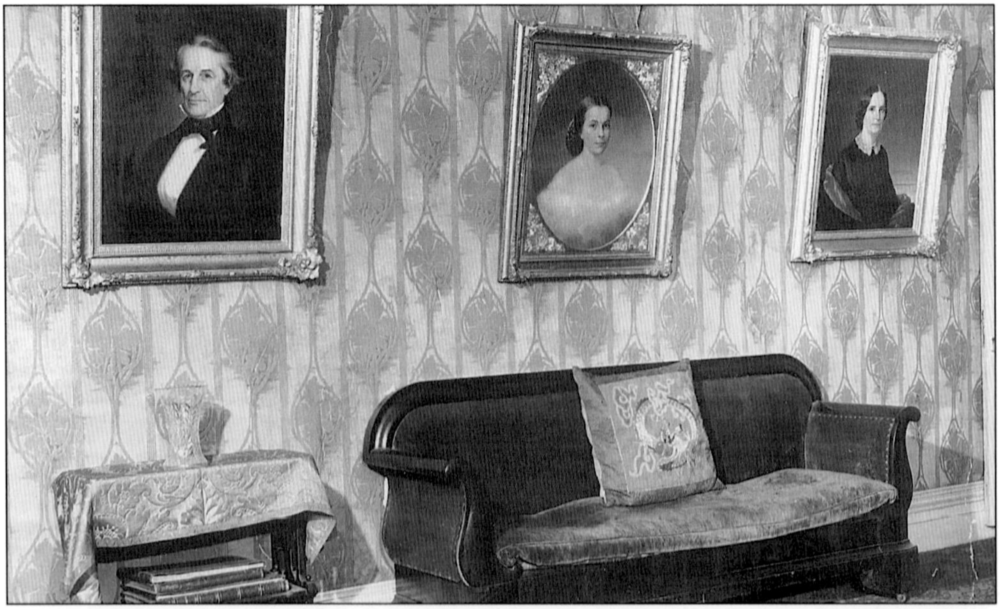

These interior views of the Millard home are from sepia photographs taken when the Millards lived there. Over the Victorian settee are the family's portraits. On the left is David J. Millard, a businessman who traveled all over the world, bringing furniture and mementos from China and other far-away spots. On the right is Mrs. Clarissa Millard, and in the center is their daughter, also named Clarissa. The house was a stop on the Underground Railroad.

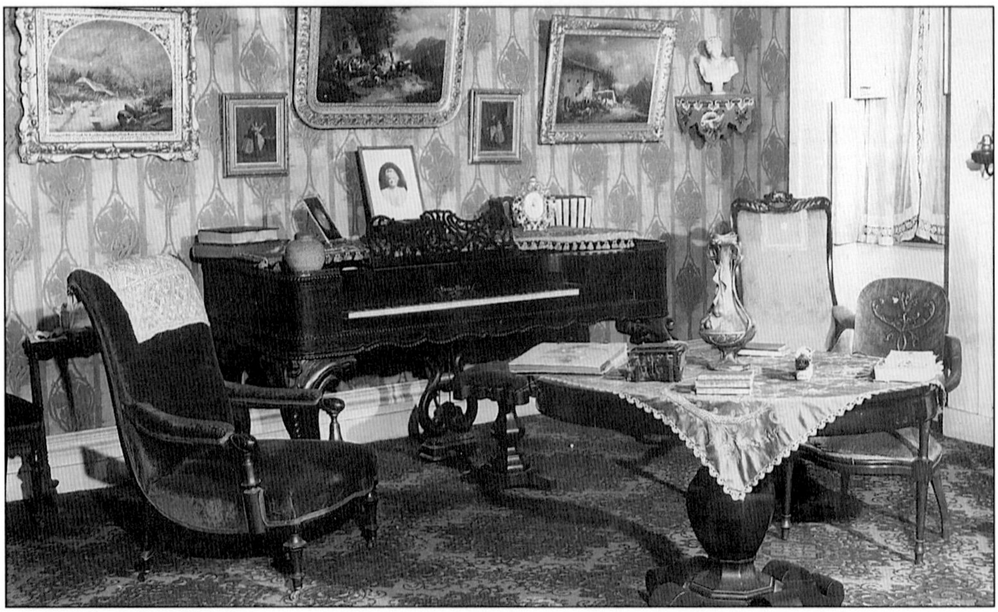

Although the Millard home once had 35 rooms, 13 were removed from a back portion of it because of deterioration that made it impractical to restore. Its present owners, Gordon and Elizabeth (Rusty) Knapp, have retained many interesting features of the historic mansion. This room still contains the piano purchased by the Millard family to entertain Henry Clay. The photograph on the piano is of Mrs. Millard. It now hangs in her former home. (Interior photographs of the Millard house are courtesy of Gordon Knapp.)

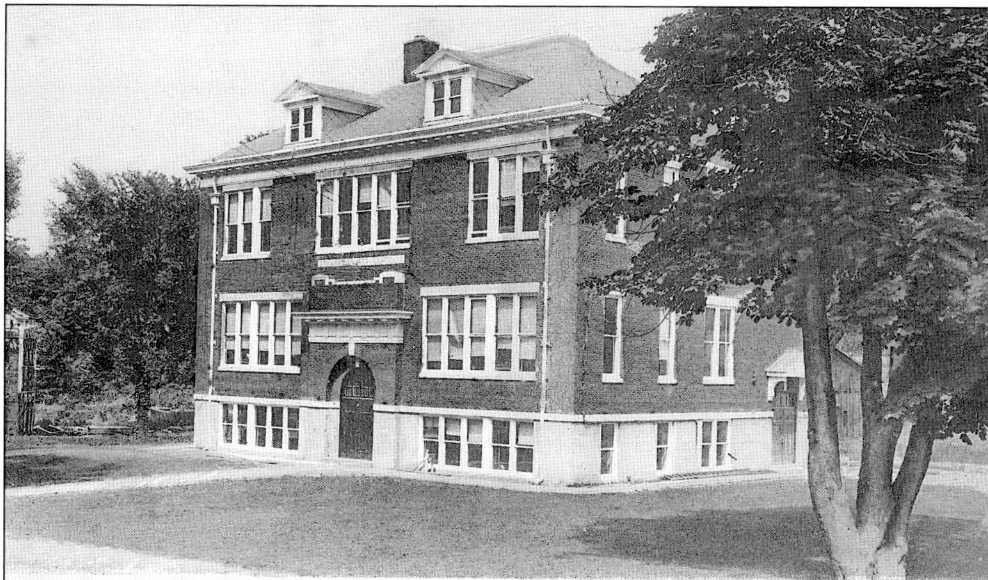

HIGH SCHOOL. - CLAYVILLE, N. Y.

Clayville High School replaced the two-story brick schoolhouse that later became a bank. This newer school, located on Old Route 8 (Oneida Street), was razed in the 1990s because it had not been used as a school for many years. Elementary students from the Sauquoit school district attended school here in the early 1970s.

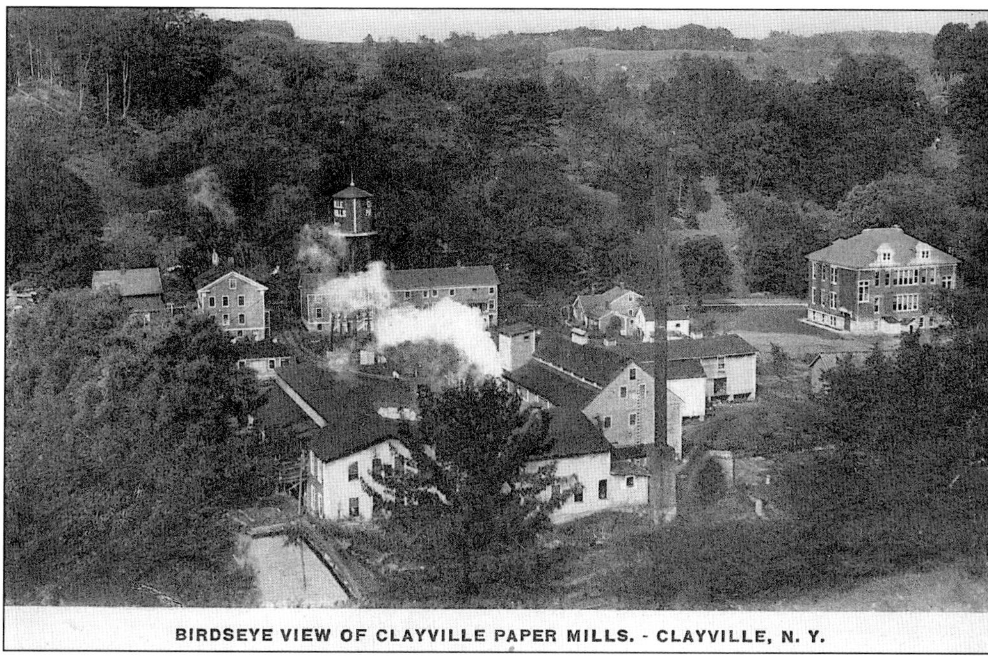

BIRDSEYE VIEW OF CLAYVILLE PAPER MILLS. - CLAYVILLE, N. Y.

A bird's-eye view shows the Clayville paper mill and the Clayville school that was built in the first decade of the 1900s. In later years, Concel Inc. operated a paper mill that closed in June 1972. Ruth Smith Richards attended the high school here (right), and met her future husband, George Richards, when he came from Otsego County to work in the mill.

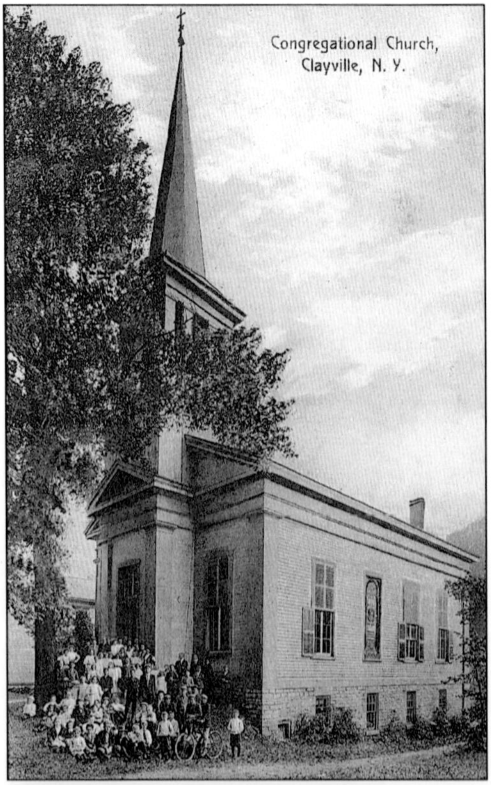

A final service on April 25, 1999 was a farewell to the Congregational Church of Clayville, leaving St. Patrick's Catholic the sole church in the village. The church had been a part of village life since 1856. A dwindling membership and economic problems led to its closing. The church building with its beautiful stained glass windows is being donated to the Clayville library. The Town of Paris Historical Society will relocate to the library's former home, once an Episcopal Church.

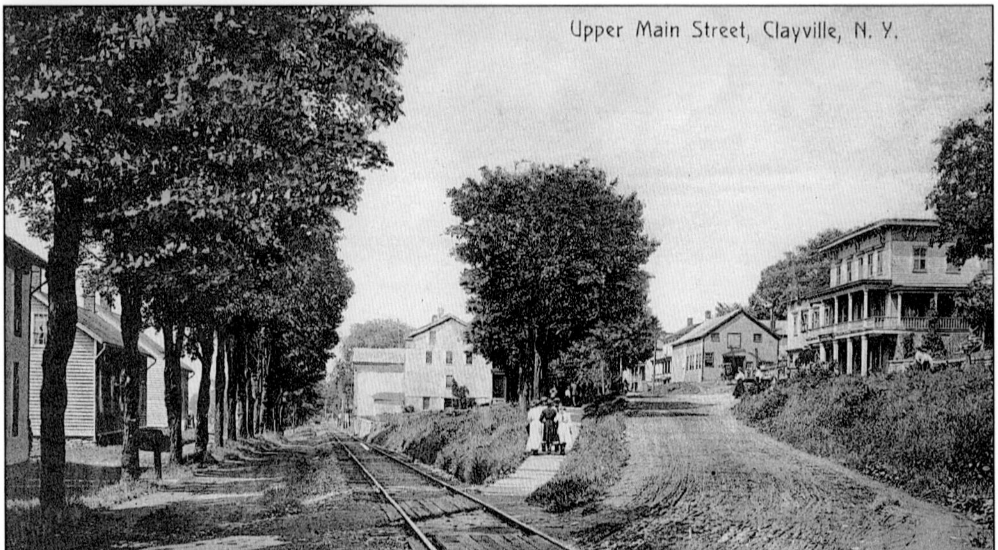

The large three-story building on the right was the Central Hotel. Owned by the Sweeney's until 1964, a new building was erected when this structure burned in 1931. Ted and Helen Stanimer purchased it and operated a tavern there for many years. In 1997, an addition was built to the left of the tavern for the Clayville Mini-Mart. Railroad Street, which was not paved at the time, ran along the tracks in this pre-World War I postcard. Today, the American Legion is located between the hotel and Railroad Street.

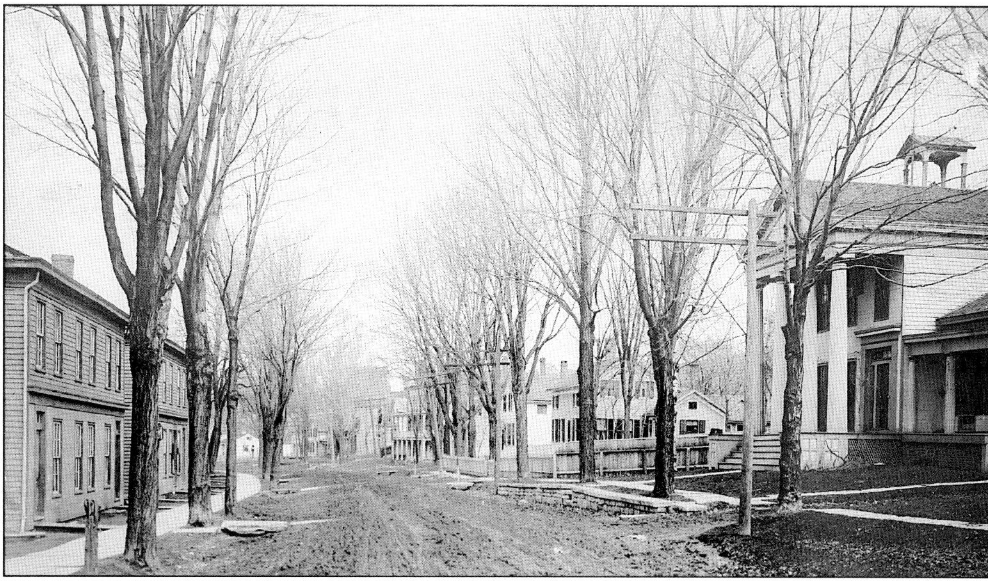

Main Street, *c.* 1909, is the site of a beautiful Greek Revival-style home, seen on the right. Over the roof is the bell tower of the school. The Cameron family, who lived there in the 1940s and 1950s, remodeled, reducing the number of rooms. Behind the house, early residents had built extensive servants quarters that were later made into apartments. The tenement houses that were built for mill employees, seen on the left, are still standing today.

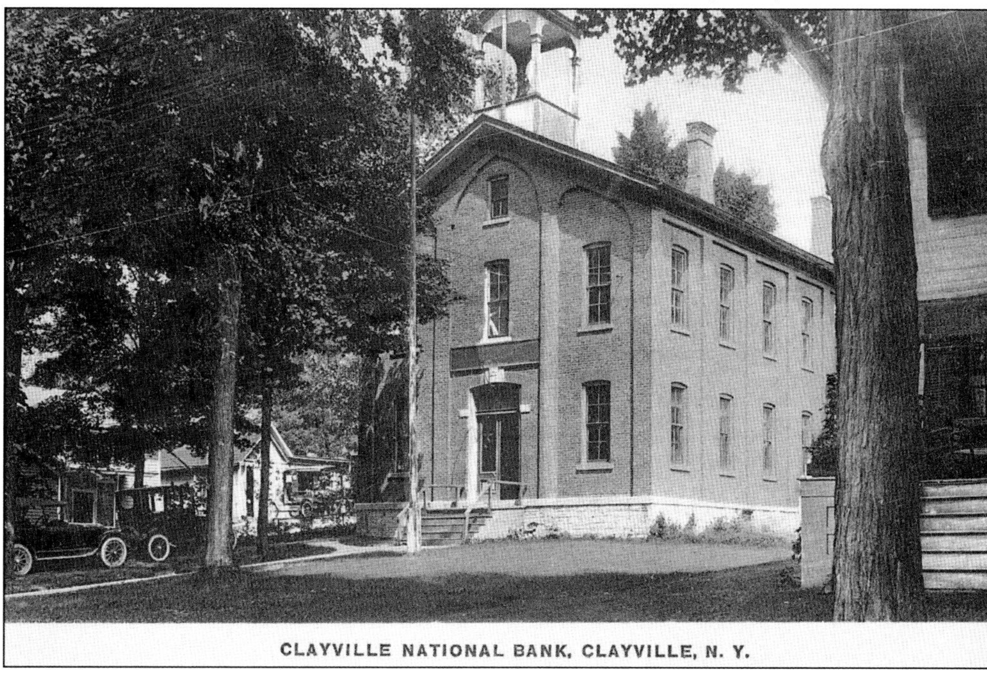

CLAYVILLE NATIONAL BANK, CLAYVILLE, N. Y.

Built in 1876 at a cost of $6,000, Clayville High School was replaced before 1914 by a new three-and-one-half-story brick school. The newer school (see page 31) was razed in the early 1990s. The building pictured here became the Clayville National Bank after its school days. Currently, the Town of Paris Historical Society uses the facility. An addition on the right front portion is occupied by the Clayville Fire Department.

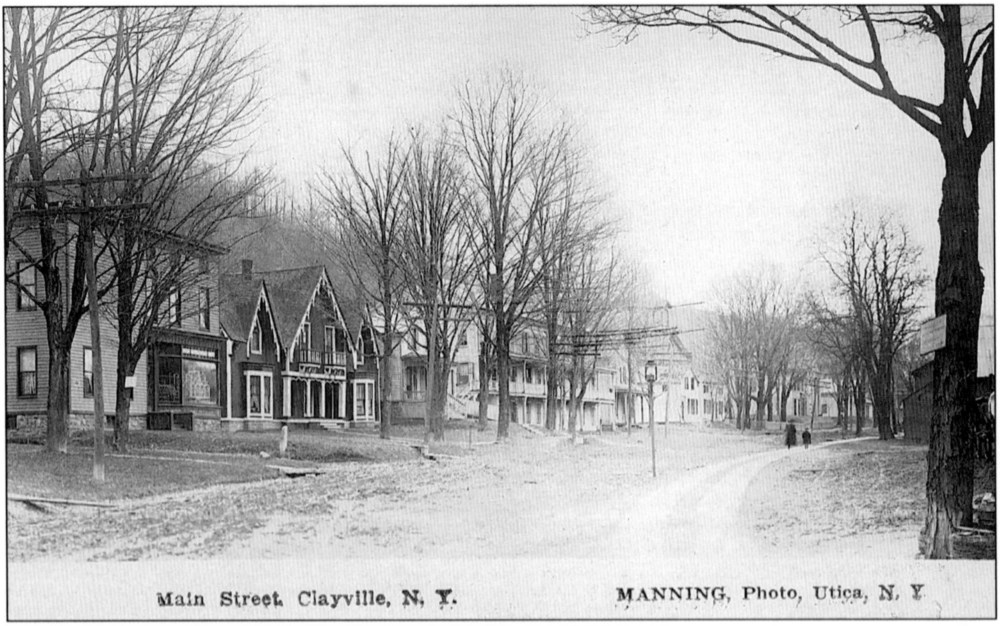

The Quinn's Gothic-style home, no longer in existence, was next to the family's store on Main Street, c. 1908. The former store currently houses the Clayville Post Office. Further down the street, four doors south, is the bell tower on the earlier school, which by this time was a bank. The bank succumbed to the stock market crash of 1929, and some depositors lost their savings.

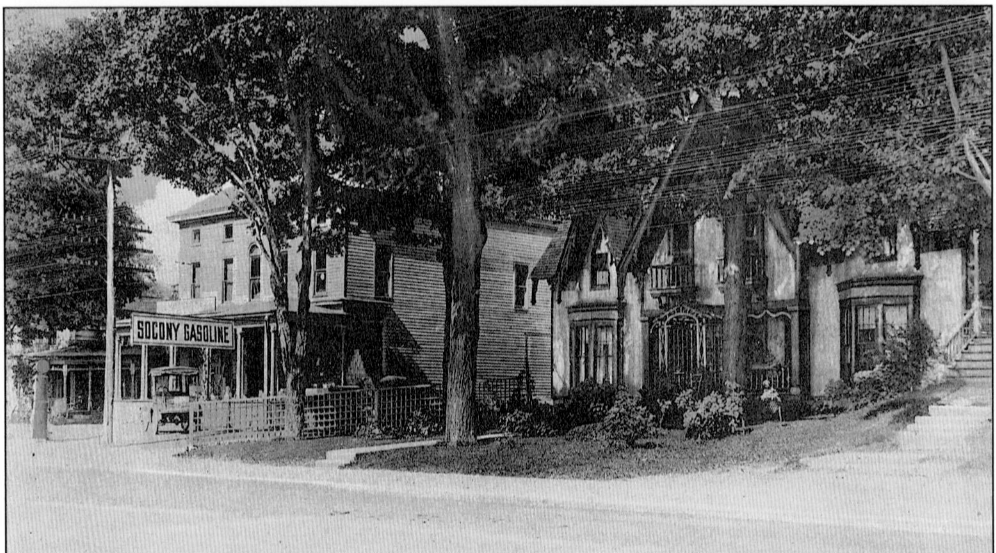

A c. 1925 view of the Quinn residence and store is shown here. With increasing use of automobiles, gas pumps were added. One of the Quinn daughters, Marjorie, was a pianist and a friend of Tom Parry's sister, Ruth Parry Baylis. The two friends provided the music for the West Winfield Catholic Church services; Marjorie played the piano while Ruth sang the mass in Latin.

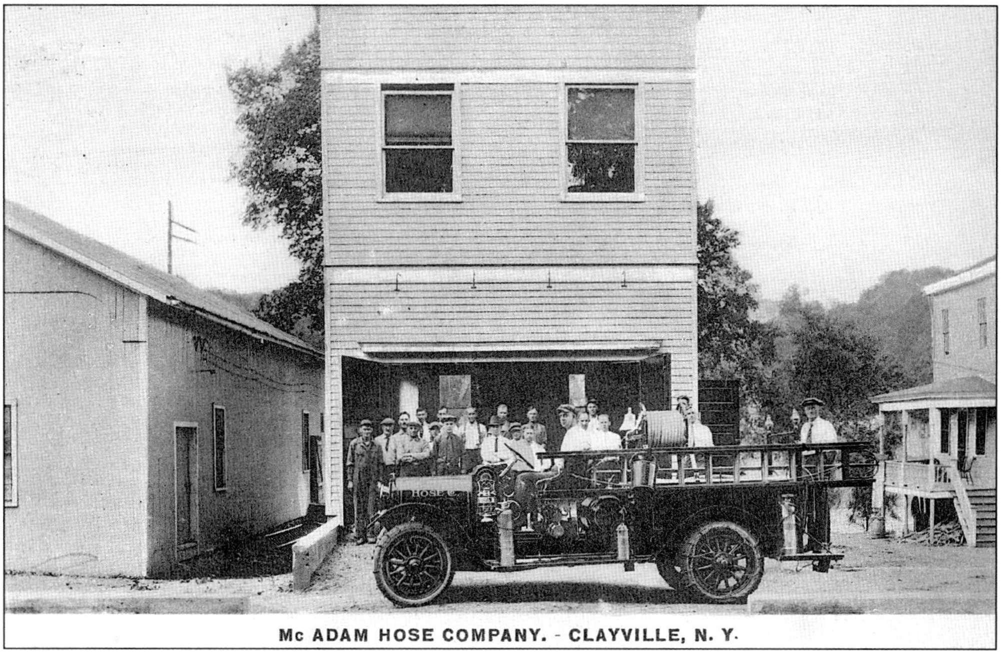

The McAdam Hose Company building, erected next to the Murray House, is now next to an empty lot. Frederick Hollister was instrumental in building the fire hall to house their hand engine, *c.* 1850. This view is *c.* 1922. The tall man standing at the rear of the truck was John D. Parry, the father of current Sauquoit Valley resident, Tom Parry. John was fond of telling people who asked about his height that he was "five feet, 18 inches" tall.

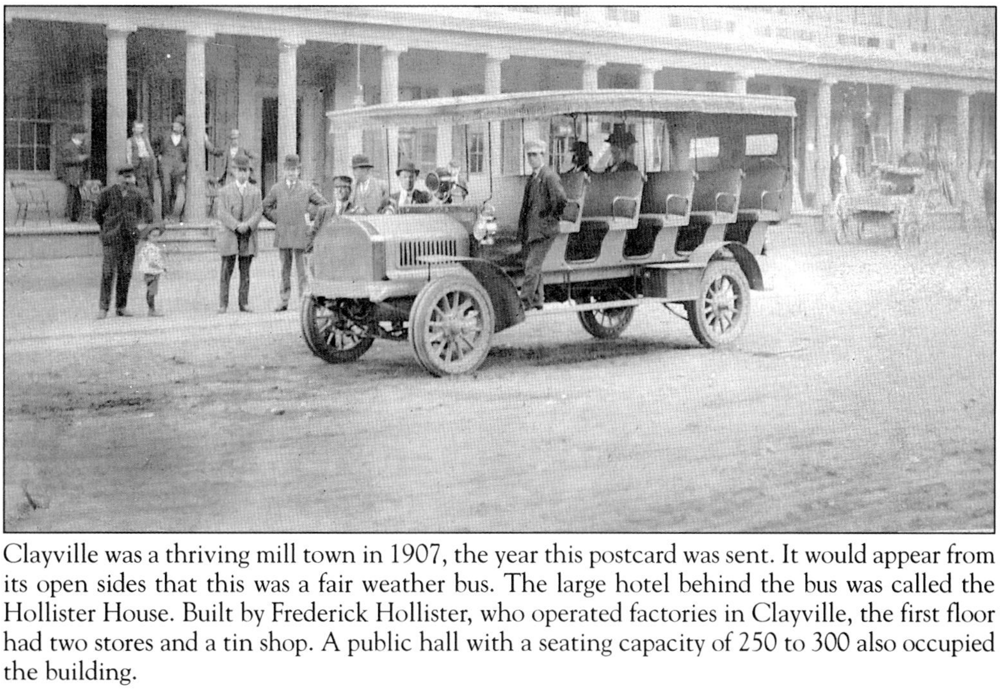

Clayville was a thriving mill town in 1907, the year this postcard was sent. It would appear from its open sides that this was a fair weather bus. The large hotel behind the bus was called the Hollister House. Built by Frederick Hollister, who operated factories in Clayville, the first floor had two stores and a tin shop. A public hall with a seating capacity of 250 to 300 also occupied the building.

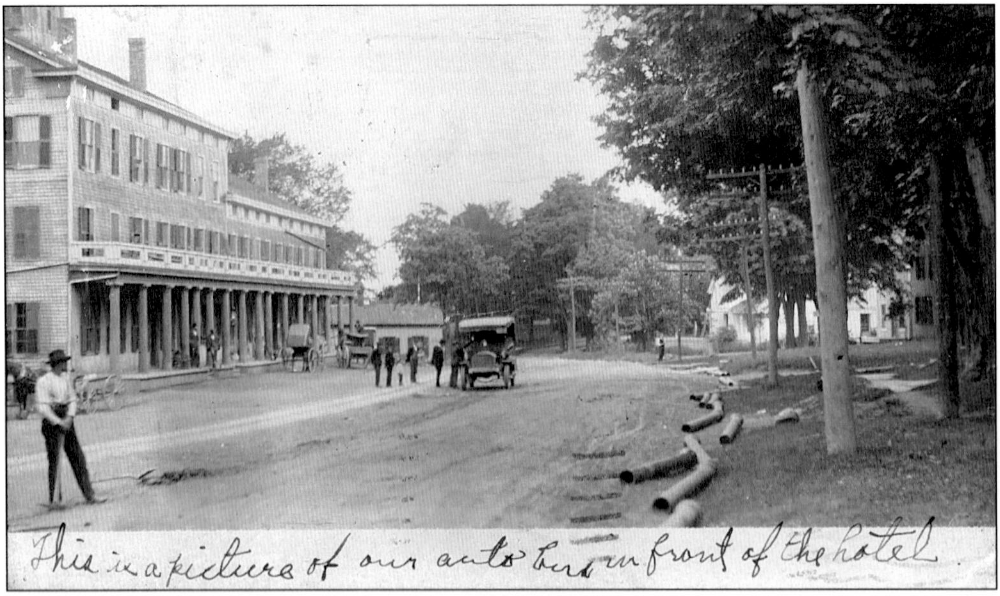

Formerly the Hollister House, this hotel became the Murray House in 1912. Frederick Hollister built the hotel in 1849. Along with D.J. Millard, Hollister was credited with building Clayville up from a small hamlet to the largest village in the town of Paris, and one of the most important manufacturing sites in the state. The workman with the pickax appears to be laying water or drainage pipes.

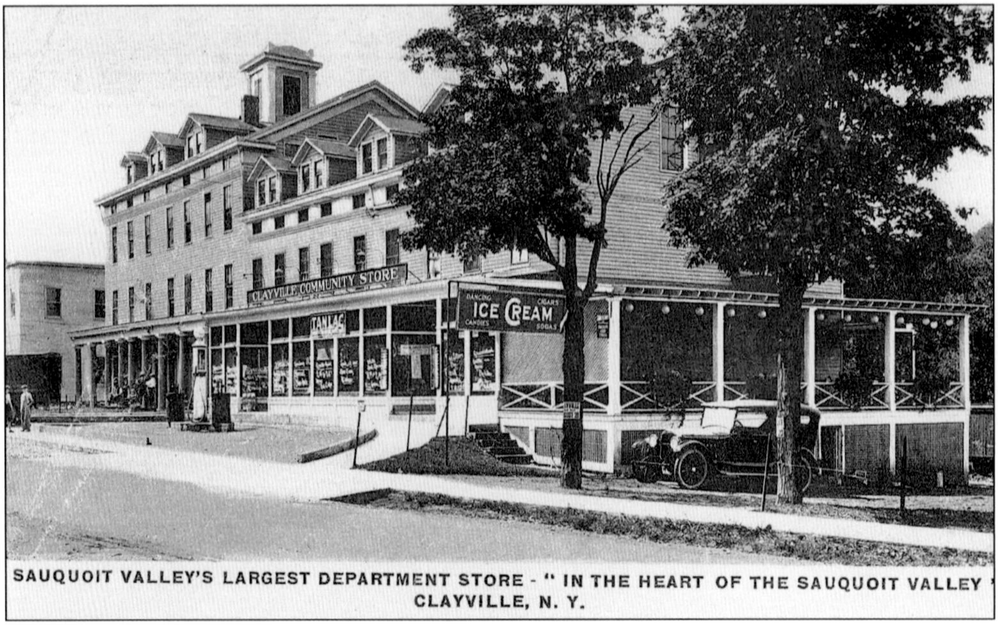

What had been the Hollister House and the Murray House became the Clayville Community Store, "Sauquoit Valley's Largest Department Store" in the 1920s. Ruth Smith (Richards) of nearby Holman City recalled enjoying ice cream on the large porch at the end of the building after going to the movies. As a teenager, Tom Parry was a soda jerk here. In 1935, C.G. Alberding bought the structure and converted it into a hardware store. The building was destroyed by an arsonist in the early 1970s.

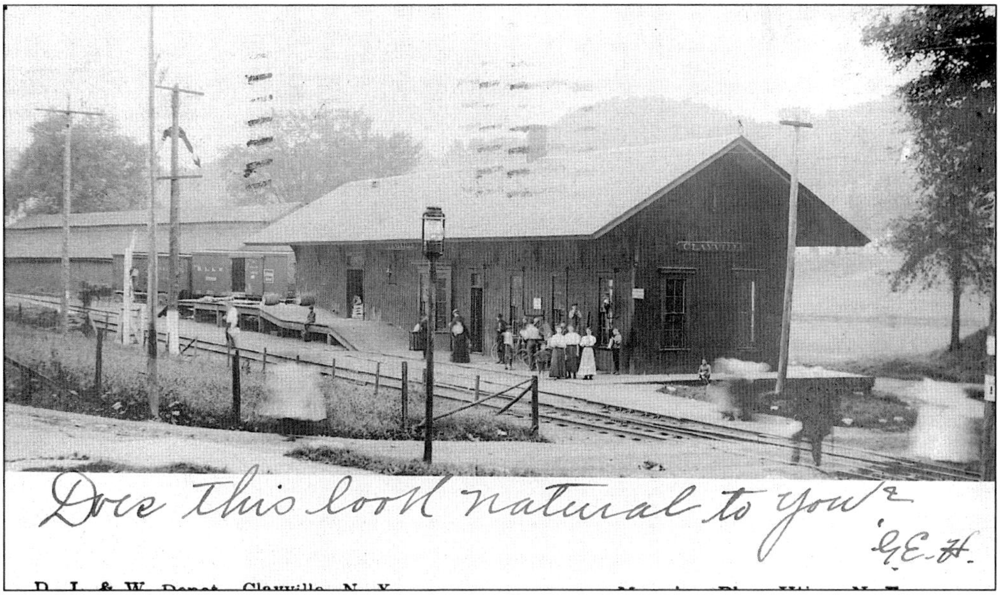

Passengers wait at the Delaware, Lackawanna, and Western Railroad depot in Clayville, *c.* 1907. The DL&W Railroad took passengers north to Utica and south toward Binghamton. The railroad also provided transport of goods to and from the mills. Richfield Junction at Cassville was a branch line to Richfield Springs, then a popular resort community. Constructed *c.* 1868, the railroad is still in use.

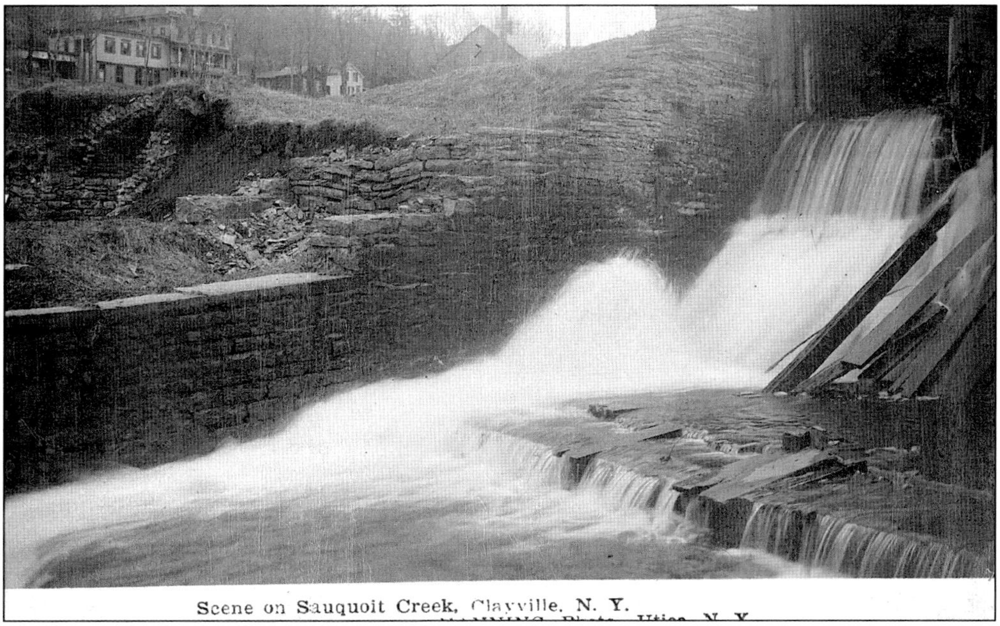

This *c.* 1909 scene on the Sauquoit Creek illustrates why so many mills sprang up along the waterway. Available waterpower was an inducement to manufacturers to build along its banks. Rising near Paris Station at Tassel Hill, the creek flows southeast, then turns north near Cassville before traversing the valley and tumbling into the Mohawk River at Whitesboro. The large three-story building second from the left on the top is believed to be the apartment house known as "The Battleship".

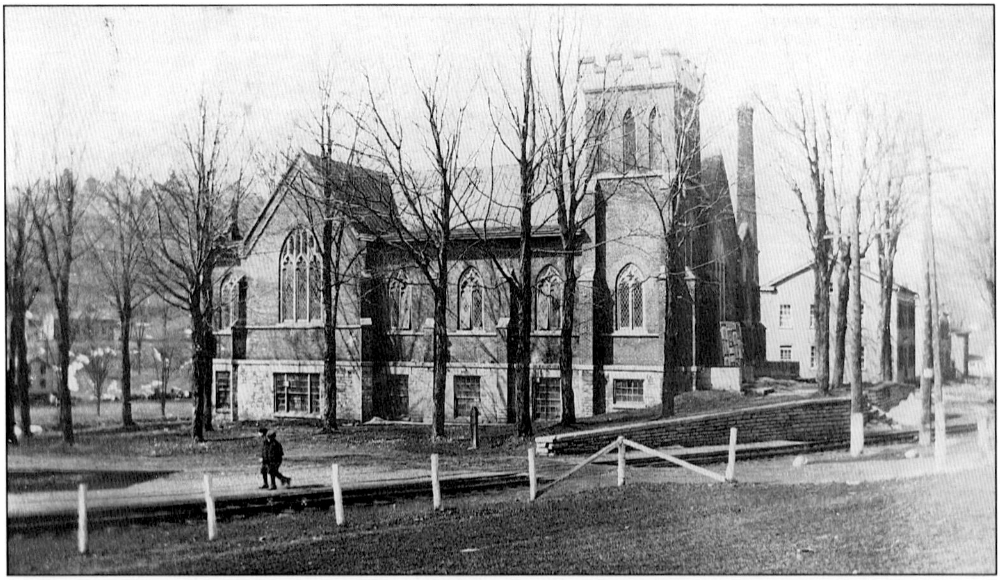

St. John's Episcopal Church was built in 1848–49 on a site deeded to the Episcopal Church by the Empire Mills Company. Costing about $20,000 to build, it was incorporated in 1849 with 21 members. In *c.* 1907, the building was damaged by fire, and the knitting mill purchased the property. The church moved down the street to a new frame edifice. The wooden church later became the village library until it was moved to larger quarters, the former Congregational Church, in November 1999.

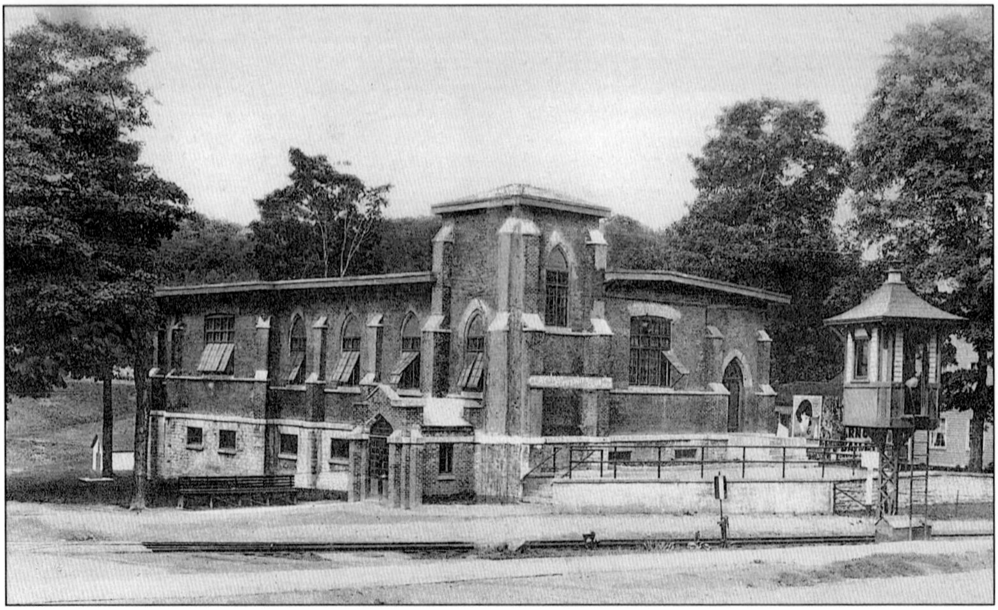

The former site of the Episcopal Church had become the men's club and opera house by *c.* 1910. For many years, it was a social center for the village with bowling alleys in the basement and a basketball court upstairs. Silent movies were shown here, accompanied on the violin by Bea Seckner, a longtime Clayville resident. In later years, the building was used for a youth center until the property was purchased by Homogenous Metals *c.* 1979 for expansion purposes. It was later razed.

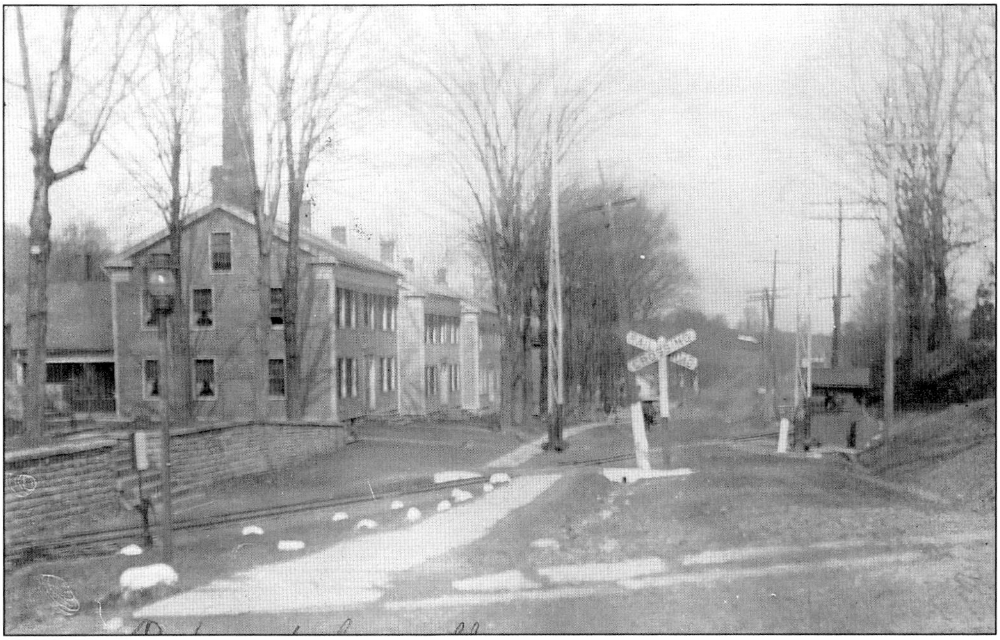

Next to the opera house and men's club were these tenement houses, built by mill owners to house employees. These houses are no longer standing. In 1890, the Clayville Manufacturing Company owned eight tenement houses. Frederick Hollister, an 1890s entrepreneur and owner of a woolen factory, built 17 double tenement houses on Canada Street, and about that many more on the west side of the old main road.

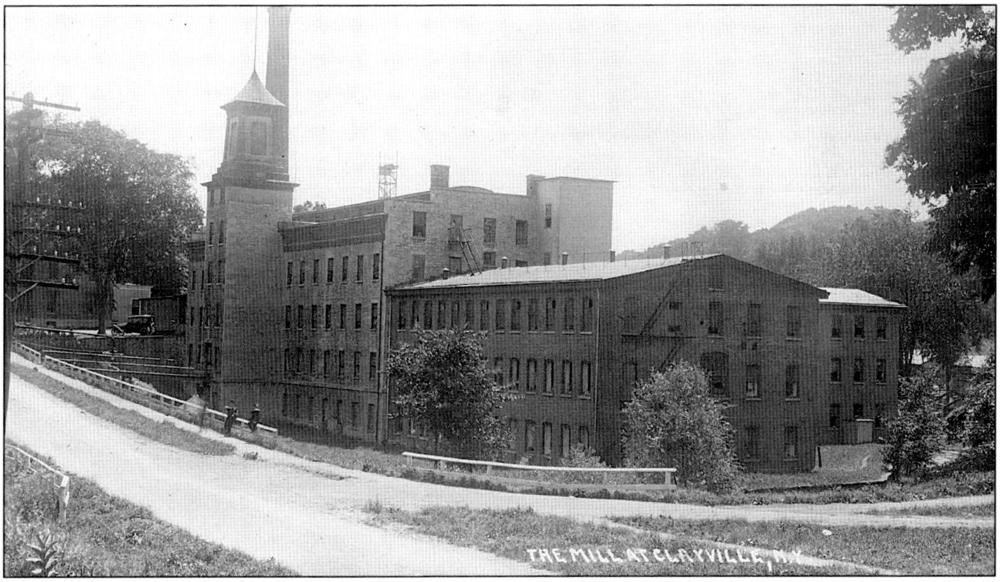

The Clayville Knitting Mill employed many Sauquoit Valley residents and attracted labor from surrounding counties. A number of mills flourished and waned during the 1800s and 1900s. This building, a part of the mill complex, was lost to an accidental fire. Once the home of Utica Drop Forge and Tool Company, the sole industrial resident today is Homogeneous Metals, which opened in 1979 in a remaining section of the vacant Clayville Knitting Mill. In 1982, they employed 125 people.

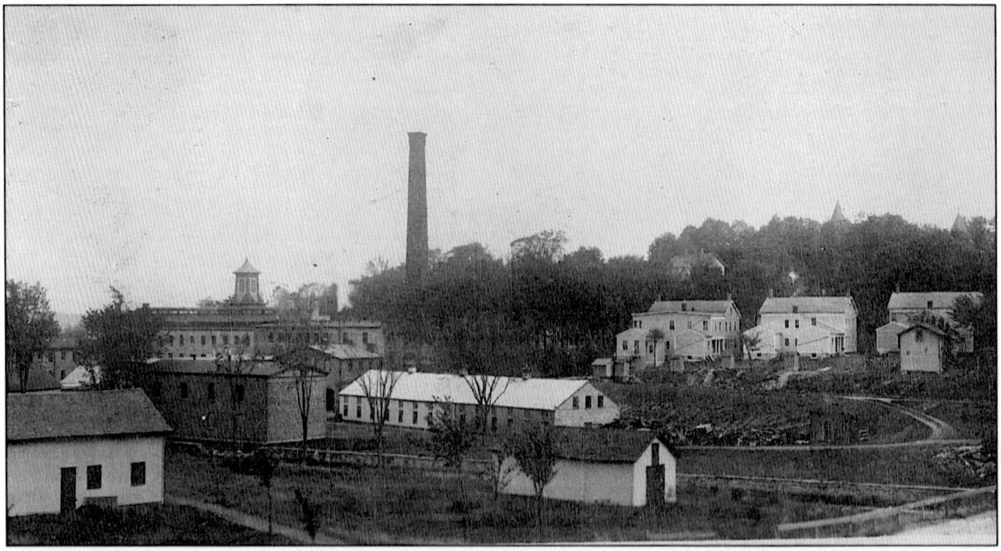

This *c.* 1910 bird's-eye view of Clayville shows the knitting mill on the left with several of the tenement houses, built for mill employees, on the right. The steeples of the Methodist and St. Patrick's Catholic Churches appear above the treetops on the right. One of the numerous millponds in the village was to the right out of the picture. Presently, many of the ponds in Clayville and the entire valley have been filled in.

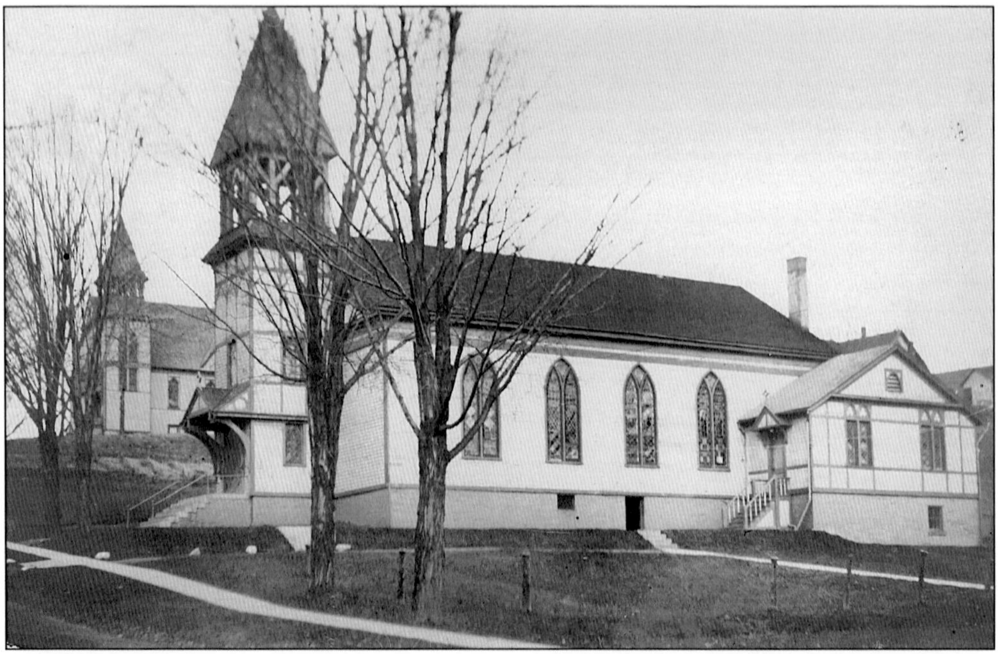

St. Patrick's Church is currently the only church remaining in Clayville. The Methodist Church on the hill behind it no longer stands. The lot of the Methodist Church now is overgrown with trees and weeds. Polly Blunk, a founding member of the Town of Paris Historical Society, visited the site in 1988. She found only the 1887 cornerstone marking the former home of Clayville's Methodists.

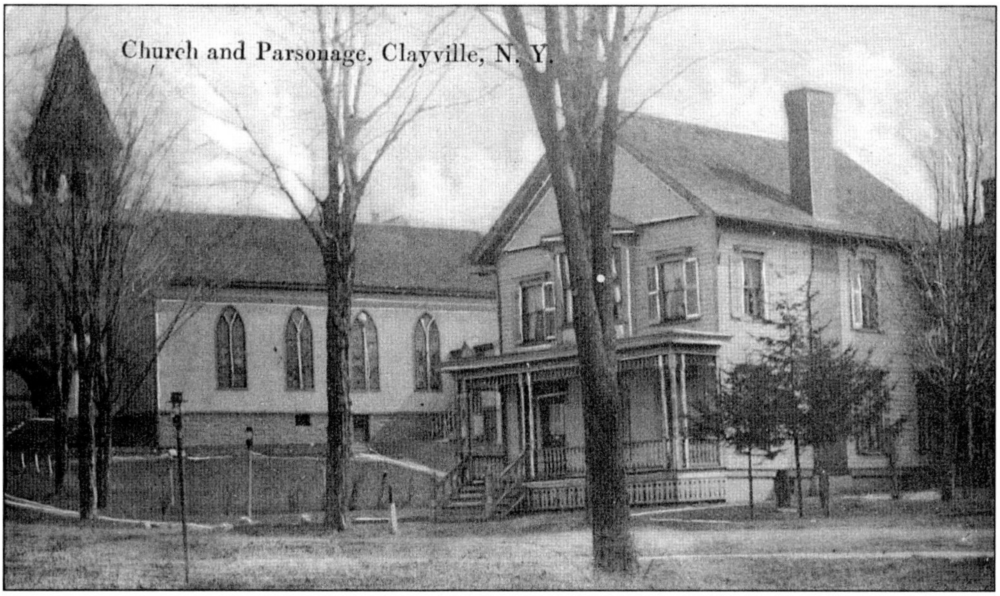

This view shows the St. Patrick's Church and Parsonage, *c.* 1918, which are both still in use. A *Utica Observer* article of July 30, 1906, describes a picnic for parish children held in Kuhn's Grove in Sauquoit. It featured a ball game between the "Clayville lads" and the Sauquoit and Chadwicks boys. The article relates that "after the stuffing had been almost knocked out of the ball," the Clayville boys were defeated 3 to 6. Also featured were a three-legged race, tug-of-war, and a potato race.

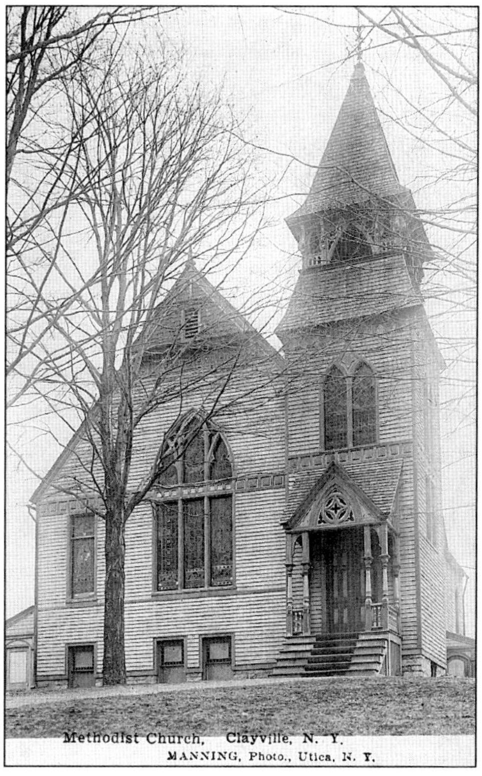

The Clayville Methodist Church that was organized "during the Rebellion" was built in 1887 on the steep hill beyond St. Patrick's Church. When the Methodist Church closed, the property was sold to neighboring St. Patrick's, who used it for social activities, bingo games, and wedding receptions until it was severely damaged by fire and razed in the late 1940s. Ken Hartzell, a current Clayville resident, remembers a teacher helping the students make kaleidoscopes from fragments of stained glass that were salvaged from the church site.

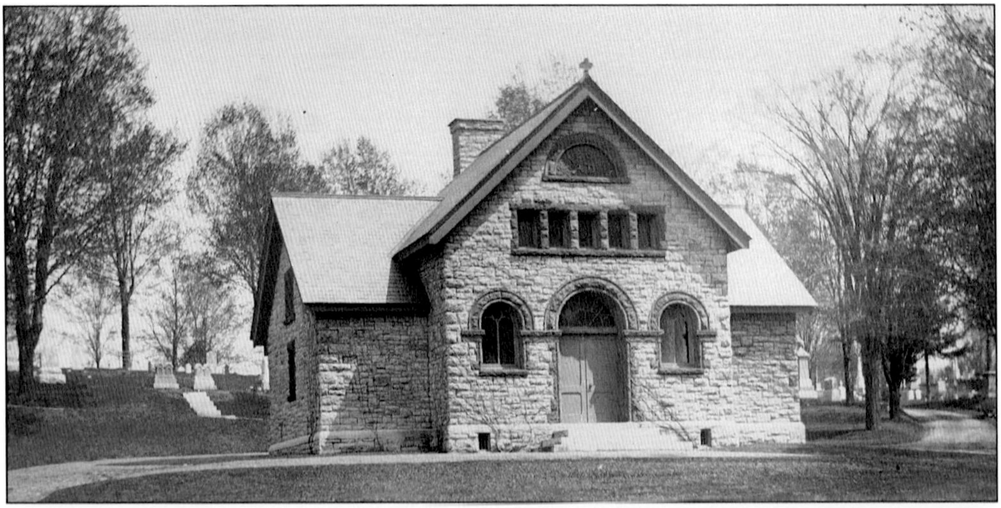

The Sauquoit Valley cemetery was organized by valley residents in February 1851 at a meeting at the Hollister House. The site of Theodore Gilbert's original homestead on present Church Road was chosen for the cemetery. The first interment was held the following day for Eliza Mould, age 22, a sister of former town supervisor William F. Mould. The cemetery has become "a beautiful place of repose" for many of its early pioneers. Henry C. Rogers, the author of *The History of the Town of Paris and the Valley of the Sauquoit*, is buried here.

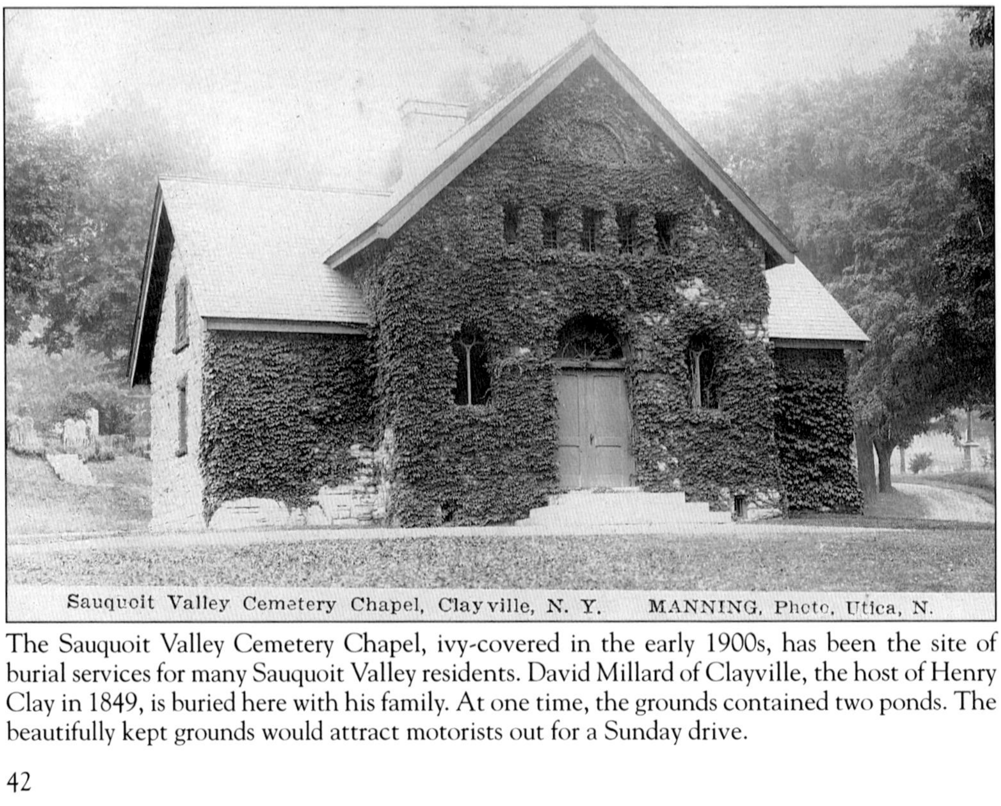

Sauquoit Valley Cemetery Chapel, Clayville, N. Y. MANNING, Photo, Utica, N.

The Sauquoit Valley Cemetery Chapel, ivy-covered in the early 1900s, has been the site of burial services for many Sauquoit Valley residents. David Millard of Clayville, the host of Henry Clay in 1849, is buried here with his family. At one time, the grounds contained two ponds. The beautifully kept grounds would attract motorists out for a Sunday drive.

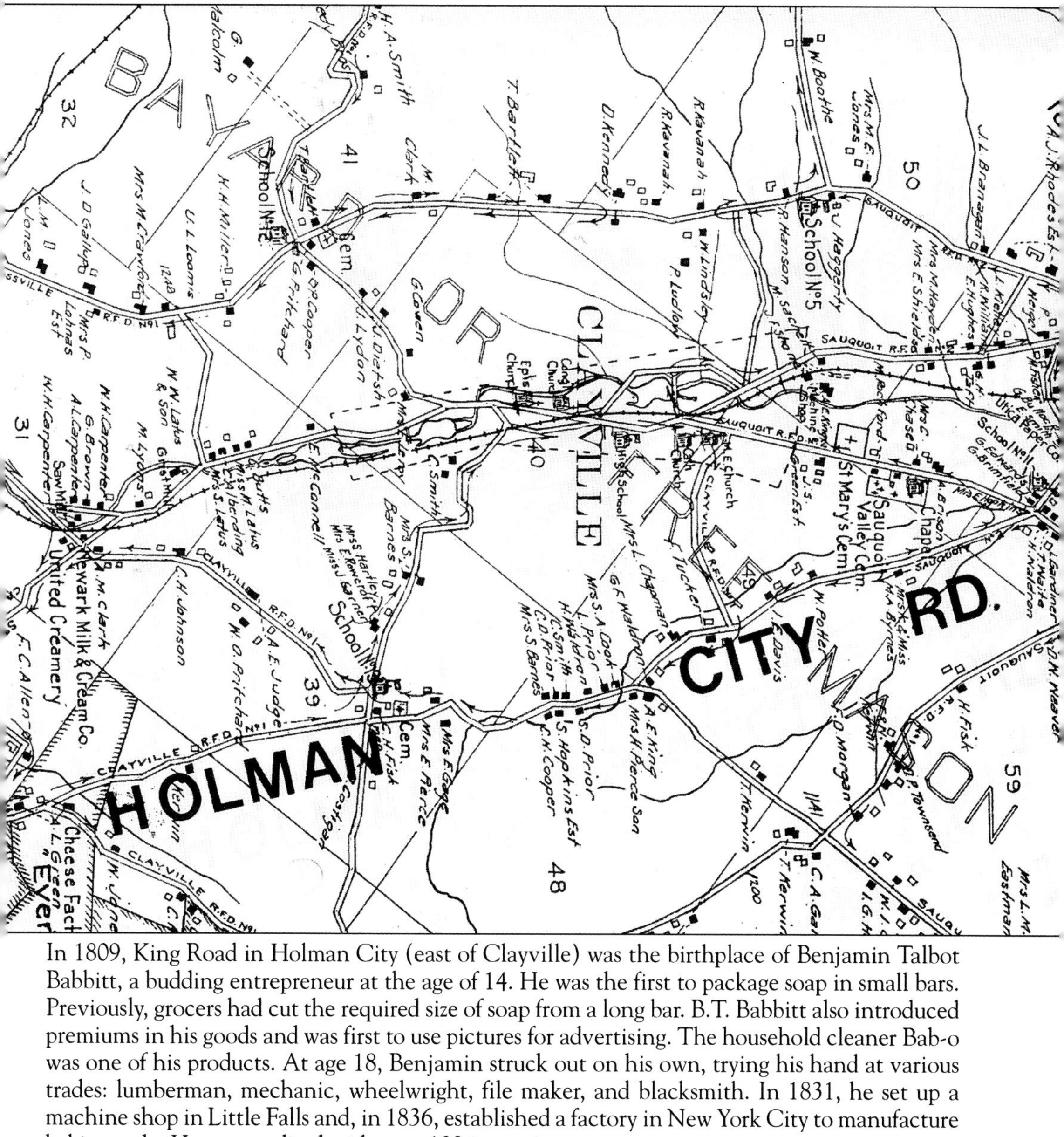

In 1809, King Road in Holman City (east of Clayville) was the birthplace of Benjamin Talbot Babbitt, a budding entrepreneur at the age of 14. He was the first to package soap in small bars. Previously, grocers had cut the required size of soap from a long bar. B.T. Babbitt also introduced premiums in his goods and was first to use pictures for advertising. The household cleaner Bab-o was one of his products. At age 18, Benjamin struck out on his own, trying his hand at various trades: lumberman, mechanic, wheelwright, file maker, and blacksmith. In 1831, he set up a machine shop in Little Falls and, in 1836, established a factory in New York City to manufacture baking soda. He was credited with over 100 inventions.

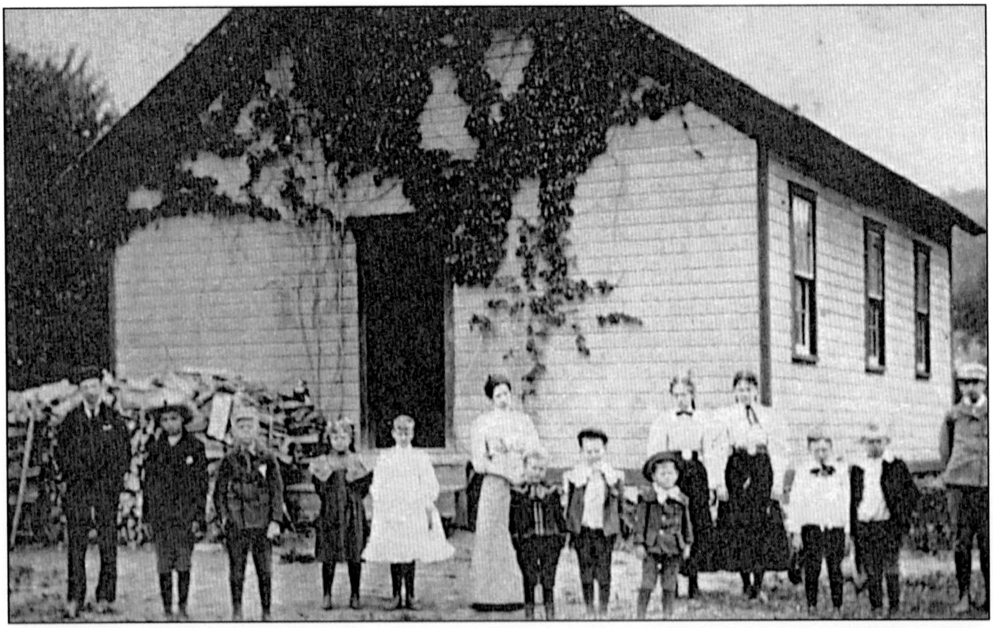

This ivy-covered Holman City one-room schoolhouse was located at the corner of Holman City and Allen Roads at the southern end of Holman City. The woodpile on the left was used to fuel the potbelly stove for warmth in the winter. The children look quite dressed up in comparison to today's school children. (From the collection of Polly Blunk.)

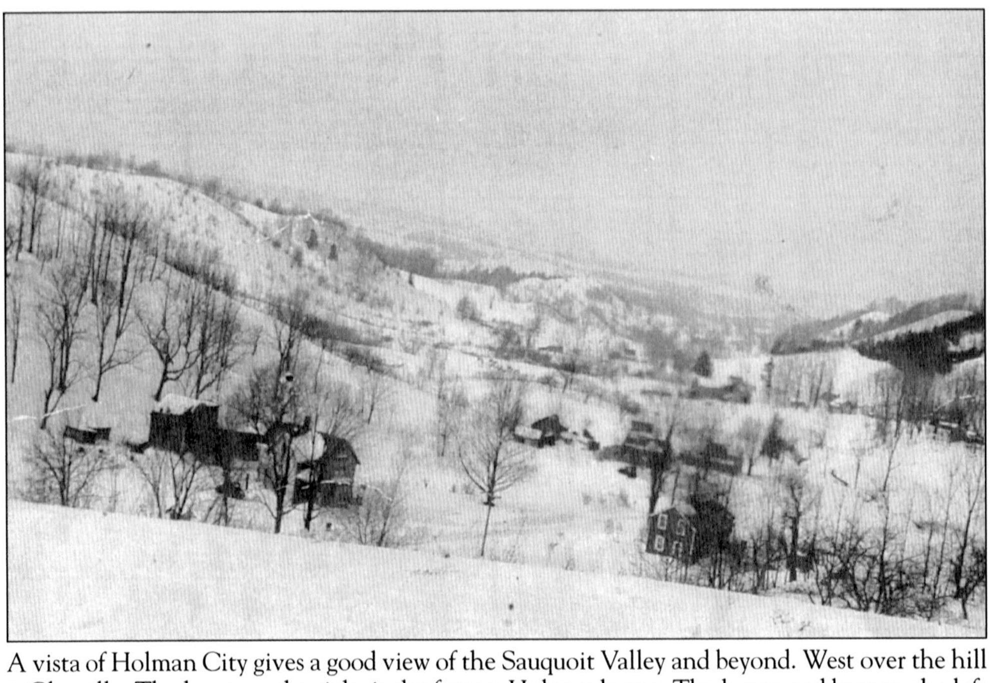

A vista of Holman City gives a good view of the Sauquoit Valley and beyond. West over the hill is Clayville. The house at the right is the former Holman house. The house and barn to the left is the Charles H. and Hattie Smith homestead. This home was the gathering place each Sunday of the numerous children and grandchildren of the Smiths, many of whom lived along Holman City Road. (From the collection of Bernard Smith.)

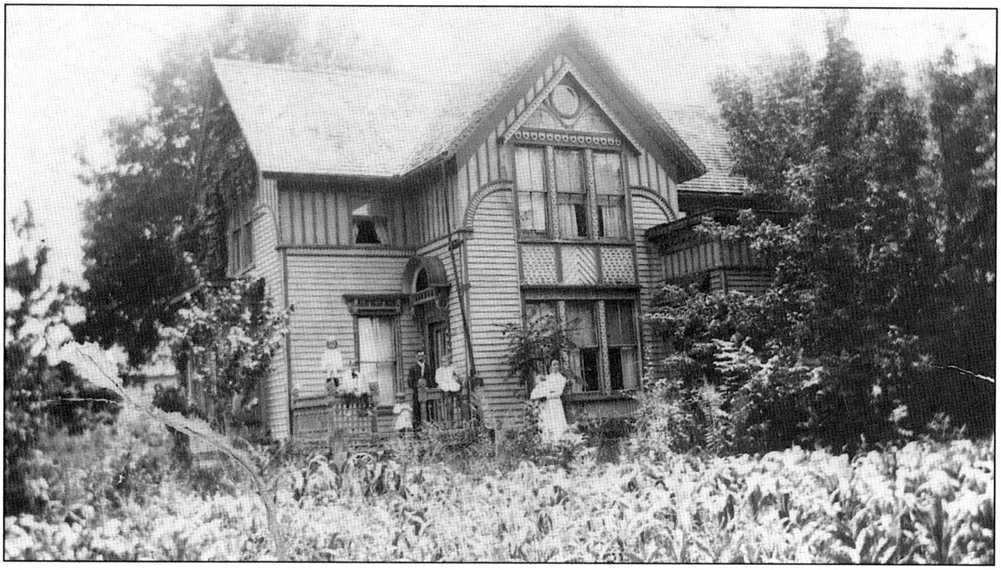

An old Victorian house with ornate woodworking was home to the Charles H. Smith family from the early 1900s until the late 1950s. In this c. 1910 postcard showing a side view of the home are, from left to right, Harry, William Crawford, Leland (Pete), Mr. Smith, Ruth, and Mrs. Smith, who is holding Russell. Joyce Richards Shephard, one of the Smith's grandchildren, was born in this house. The residence was built by a Mr. Cooper, who had a furniture factory across the road. (From the collection of Joyce Shephard.)

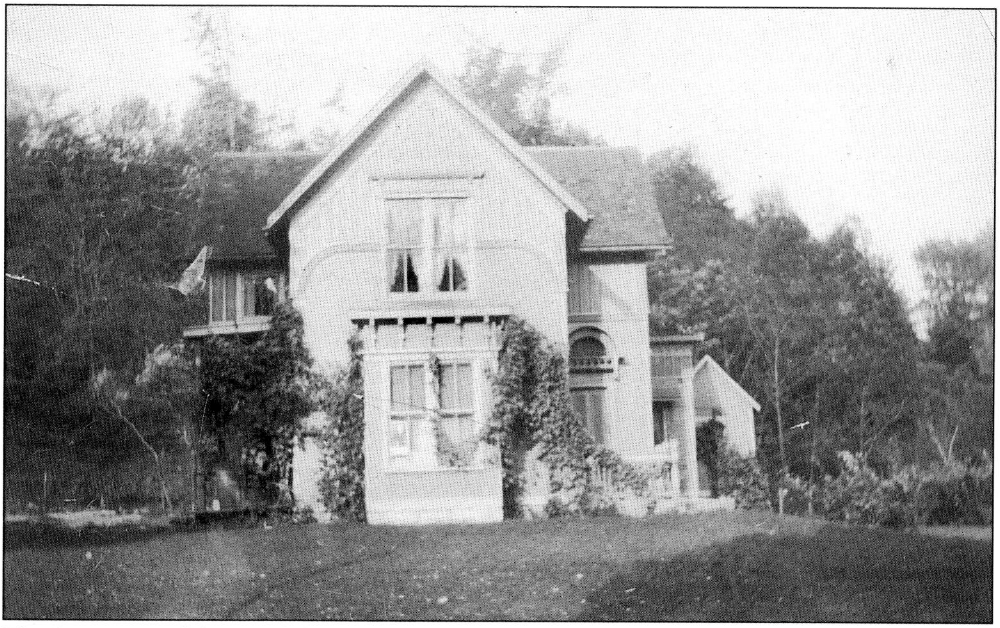

The front view of the Smith homestead is a photograph taken after the demise of the cornfield, replaced by lawn and raspberry bushes. The elaborate outhouse on the right is the same style of architecture as the house. A little stream with spearmint growing along its banks, dammed up to create a little pond, ran through the back of the property. Sadly, this home was destroyed by fire on March 17, 1983. A new home, built here by owners Glenn and Polly Blunk, is also the site of Polly's Landmark Art Studio.

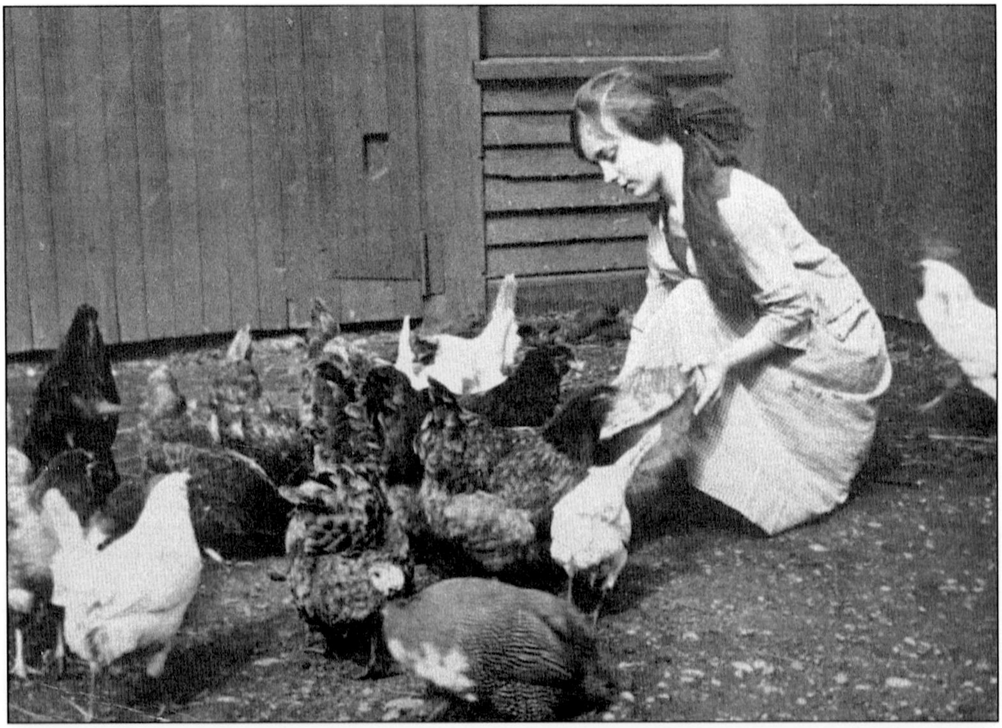

Feeding chickens in front of the barn behind the Charles Smith family home is daughter Ruth (the author's mother) at about age 16. She was the only daughter in the family of ten boys. A few years later, when Ruth had her long hair cut short in the 1920s style, her father voiced his disapproval, as it was considered rather radical at the time (at least by fathers).

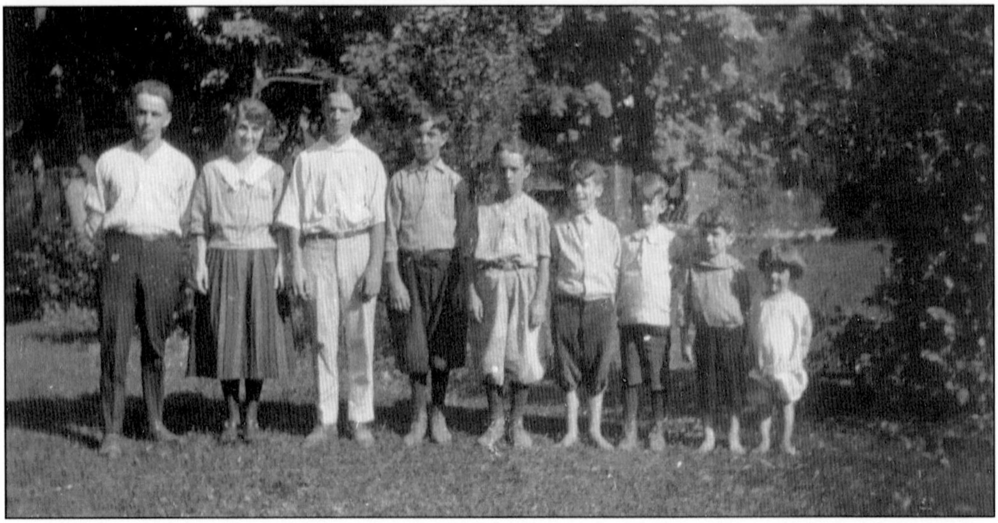

The children of Charles and Hattie Huestis Smith lined up for this photograph in August 1923. Shown chronologically are William Crawford, Ruth, Harry, Leland (Pete), Russell, P. Merwin, Robert, Earl Kenneth, and Harold John. Russell, 90, and Johnny are the sole surviving children. For many years a beekeeper, Crawford's honey stand still graces the roadside in front of his former home. Johnny, who built many of the newer homes along Holman City Road, currently resides in Holman City. (From the collection of Joyce Shephard.)

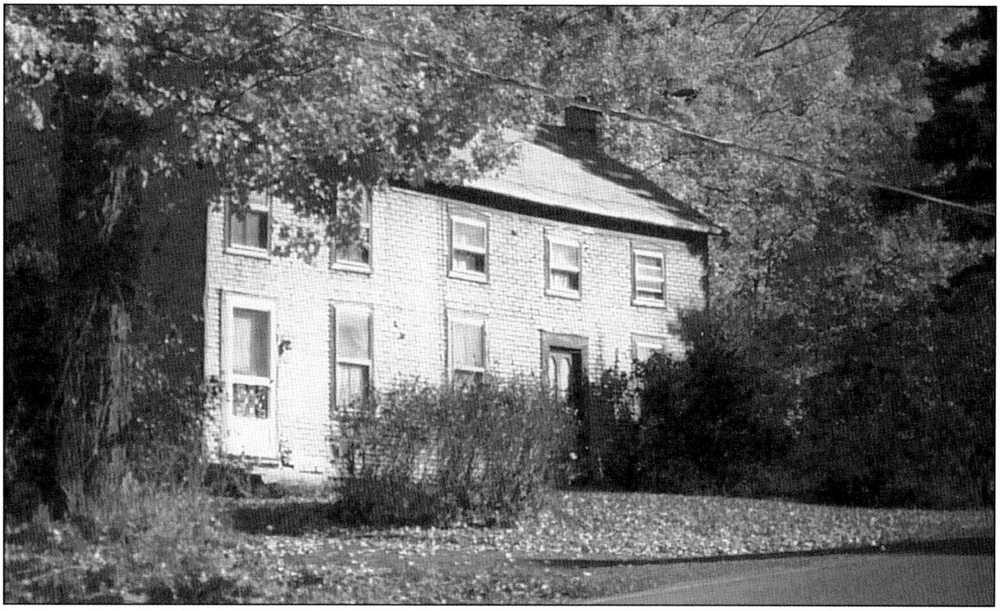

Before 1840, Holman City was called Log City because of the many log homes there. It was changed to Holman City in deference to the numerous Holman residents. Arriving in 1812, David Holman erected a gristmill, a sawmill, and a clover mill. Later, the gristmill site became a factory for the manufacture of agricultural implements. William Holman and David Holman Jr. both had stores in Holman City. The Holman house pictured was at one time a hotel. Later converted to a private residence, it remains so today. (From the collection of Polly Blunk.)

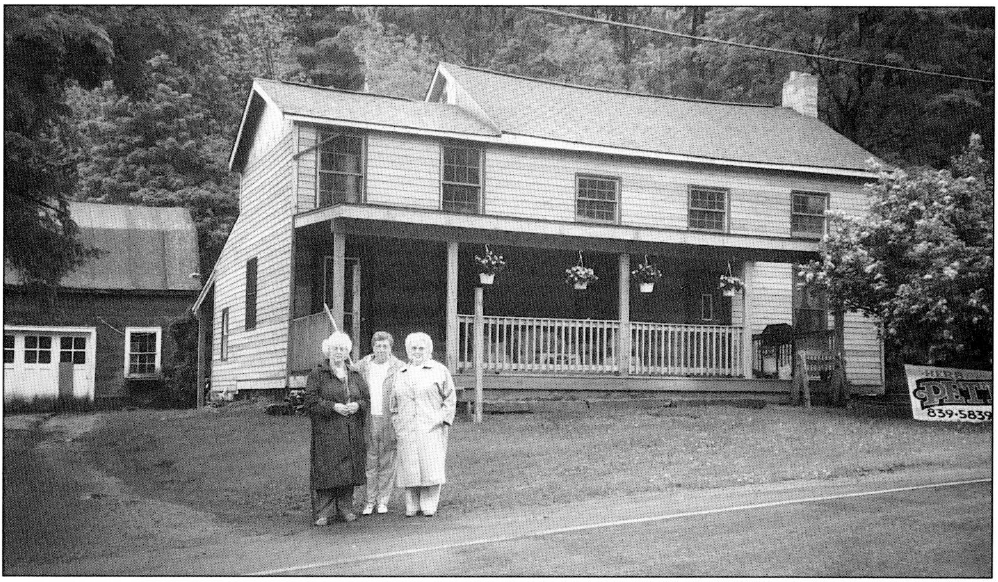

For many years, the Holman home has been in need of some tender loving care. Unpainted and weather-beaten, then sided with shingles, its appearance had deteriorated. Currently undergoing a transformation, it has been covered with natural wood clapboards, and an attractive front porch has been added. Posing in front of the newly improved home are, from left to right, the author, Joyce Shephard, and Marian Jones. Marian was born in this house across from the Smith homestead.

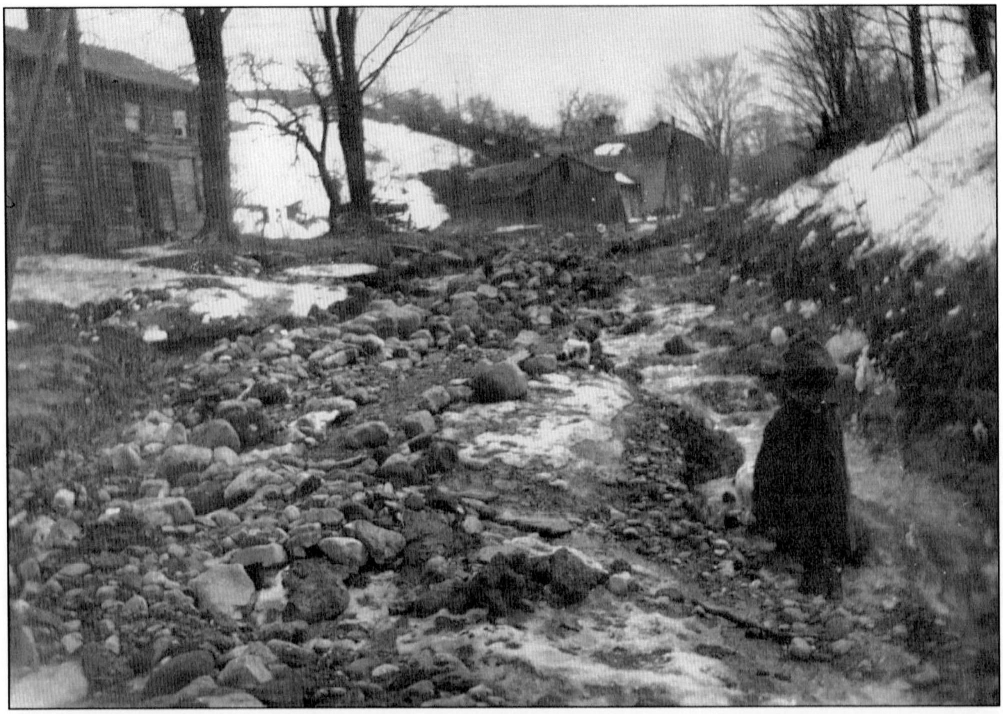

This 1922 photograph was taken just below the Smith homestead. Rapidly melting snow had gouged out the dirt road, leaving cobblestones strewn in its path. (The Holman house is on the left.) Early roads were not conducive to comfortable travel. It was not until after WWI that serious thought was given to road improvement, and rural back roads were not a priority. Scenes such as this and the increasing popularity of the automobile contributed to a demand for paved roads.

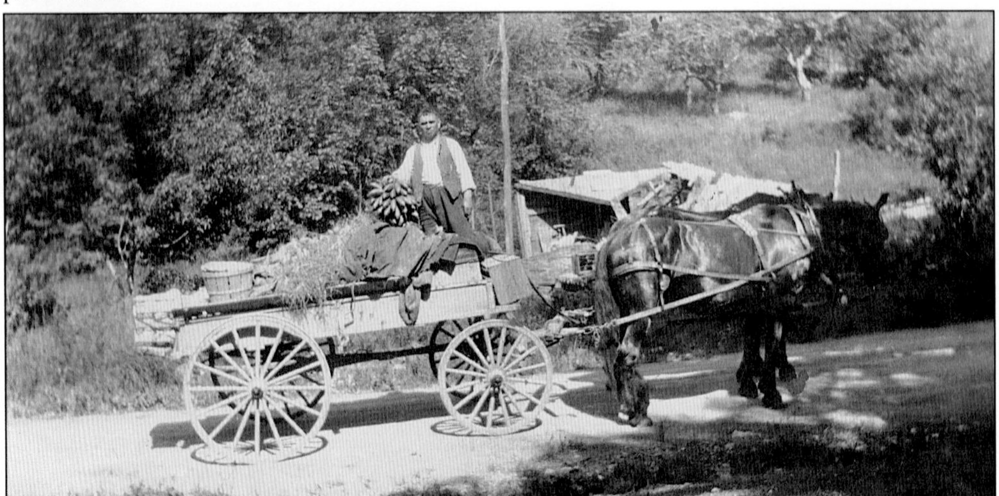

"Yes, we have some bananas." Peddlers like this enterprising vendor, called Jake the Banana Man, were a common sight in rural areas in the 1920s and 1930s. This traveling produce wagon provided fresh fruits and vegetables to homemakers in the days before supermarkets. One of Mrs. Smith's grandchildren recalls purchasing a large stalk of green bananas from Jake to hang in the cellar to ripen. (From the collection of Marian Jones.)

Four

SAUQUOIT

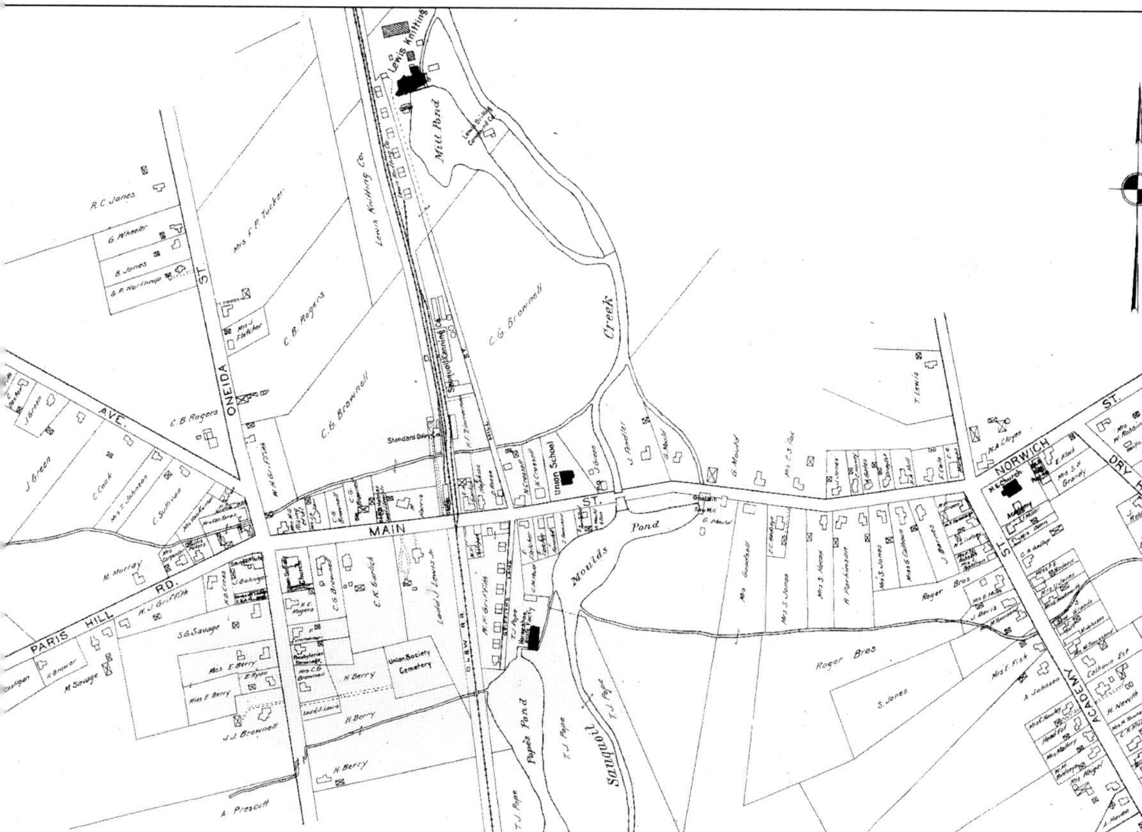

Sauquoit was a village of many names. The Oneida Indians called the creek Saghdaqueda, meaning "smooth round pebbles." The Brothertown and Stockbridge Indians called it Sauquoit, signifying "short and rapid," and early settlers adopted the name for the entire valley. Before 1820, the eastern section of the village was designated East Sauquoit, Bethelville, or Methodist Corners. The western portion was called West Sauquoit or Savage's Corners. When the post office was established in 1820, the entire village was officially named Sauquoit. Main Street and Norwich Street on this 1907 map are now known as Pinnacle Road. Academy Street is now Mohawk Street.

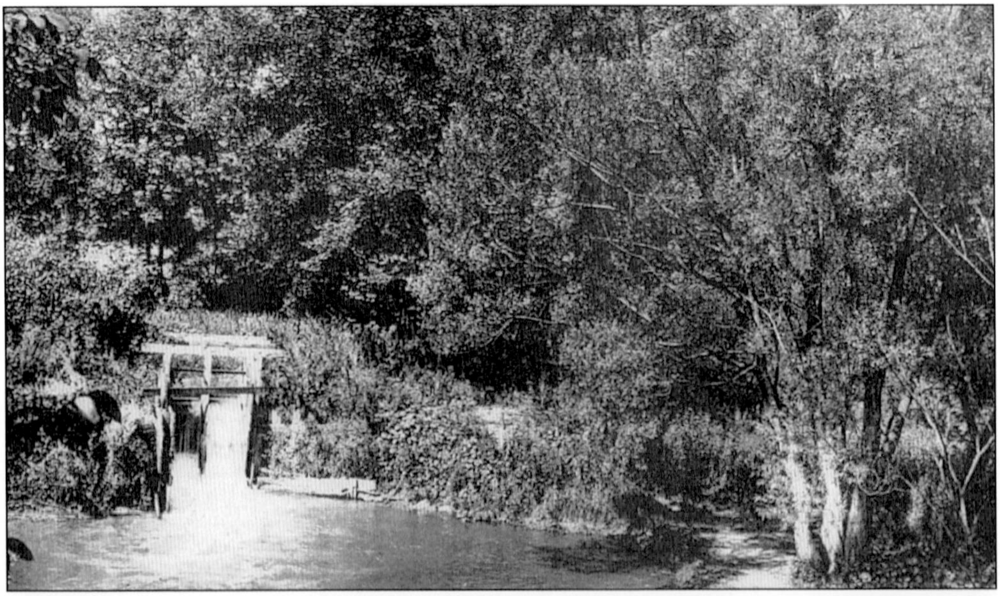

Pictured here is the "Old Swimming Hole," believed to be the one at the corner of Holman City Road and Church Street between Sauquoit and Clayville. It was once open to the public. In the 1930s and early 1940s, it was known as Miller's Pool. At one time, a long row of poplar trees stood between the roadside and the pool. (From the collection of June Rosborough.)

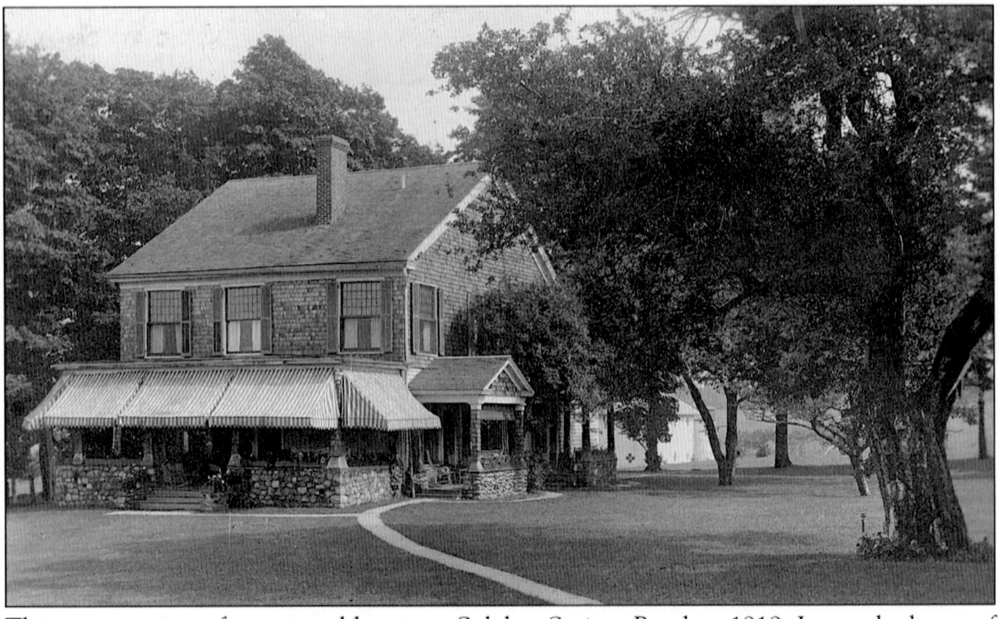

This is a rear view of an unusual home on Sulphur Springs Road, *c.* 1919. It was the home of the wife of a local New York City stockbroker. Because of some irregularities in his transactions, he was sent to Sing Sing Prison and was unable to enjoy his unique cobblestone country home. The barn across the road with the unusual cloverleaf windows still stands.

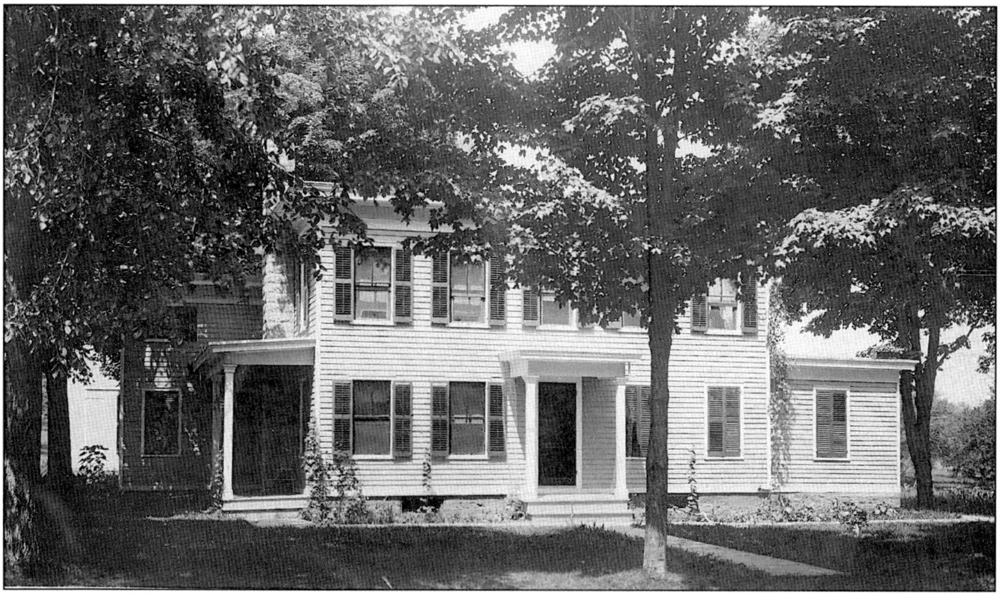

The former E.W. Daniels residence on the west side of Sulphur Springs Road is currently the home of Brian and Diane Benn. This was the area where pioneer Theodore Gilbert made his campsite when he arrived from Connecticut in 1789–90. Rogers relates that the Gilbert father and sons built a log house "opposite where was afterward erected the Burning Spring Hotel." This hotel was near where the Shady Rest Inn was located in the early 1900s (see page 52).

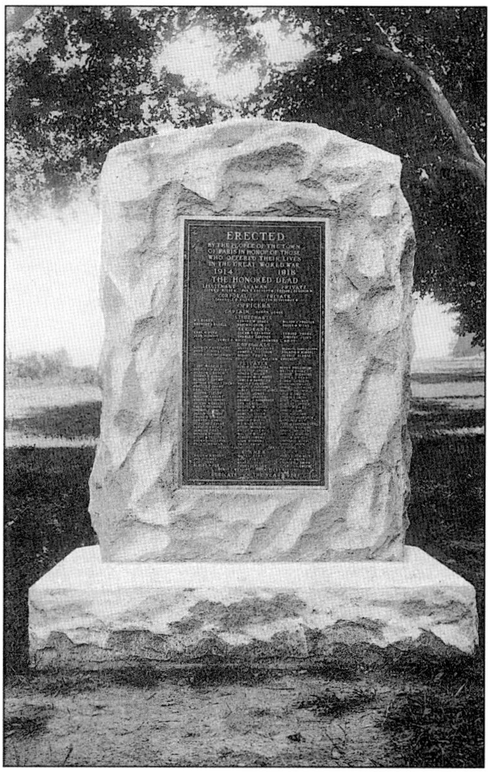

The 1920 veteran's monument now located in the park at the juncture of Sulphur Springs Road and Old Route 8 once stood next to the old Wicks-Staley American Legion Post No. 231 (formerly the McAdam Hose Company) in Clayville. Originally dedicated to WWI veterans, the monument was moved to Sauquoit in 1981, and a plaque was added to "honor [all] those who served and died in war" from the town of Paris.

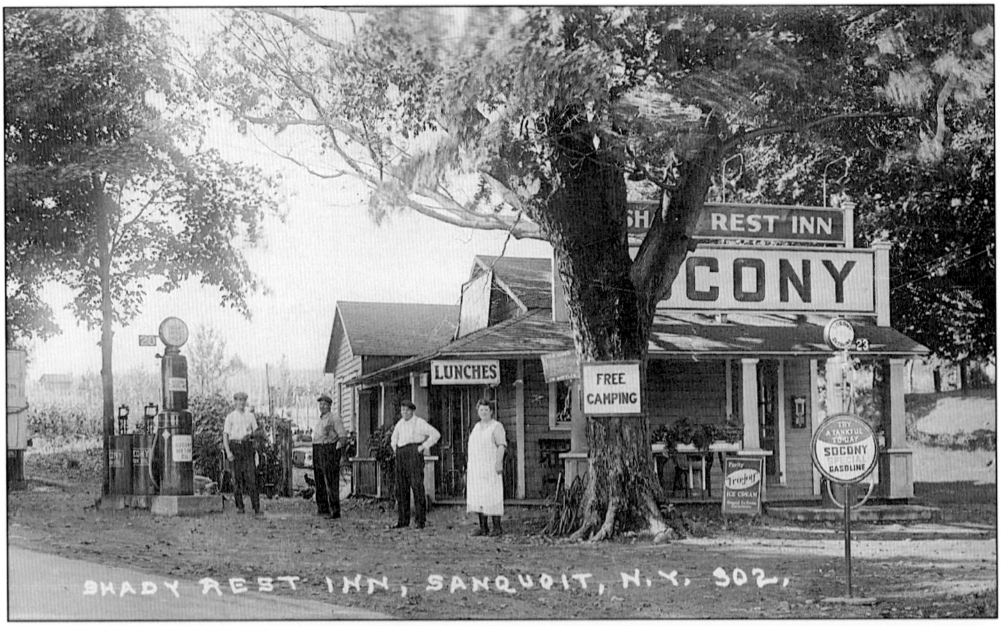

The Shady Rest Inn, a 1930s multi-service stop, provided Socony gas and oil, lunches, Fro-Joy ice cream, and free camping. Tom O'Neill, standing next to the woman in the apron, still has descendants living in the Sauquoit Valley. The woman is Mrs. Niles, whose apron suggests she was the lunch chef. The site today (shown below) is bare of buildings, but has a veteran's monument in its park setting at the juncture of Oneida Street and Sulphur Springs Road.

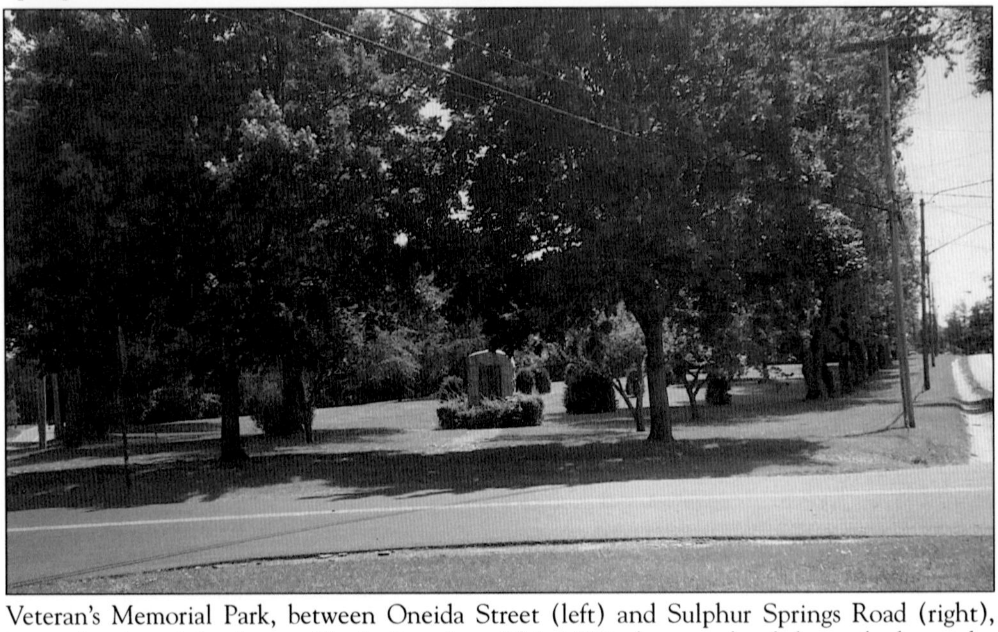

Veteran's Memorial Park, between Oneida Street (left) and Sulphur Springs Road (right), is on the site of the former Shady Rest Inn. This 1996 photograph of the park shows the veteran's monument. A new plaque was added to honor those who served in WWII, Korea, and Vietnam. Donated by friends of John G. Beasman, U.S. Navy, the monument was rededicated on August 24, 1981.

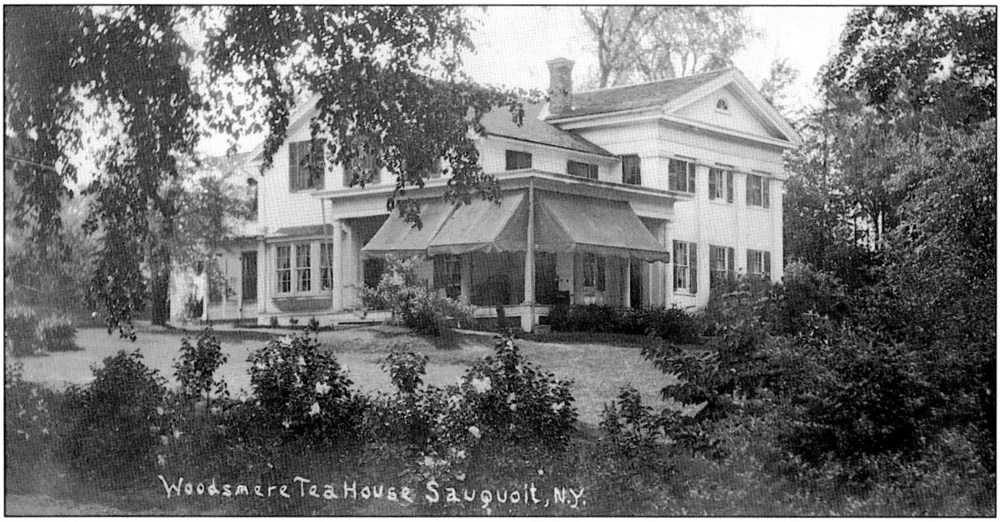

Woodsmere Teahouse, operated by Edith Brownell in her home in the early 1900s, was the residence and office of Dr. Garnet Higgins from 1939 to 1960. The home, located on old Route 8, has been the home of June Rosborough since 1976. Edith Brownell—whose father, John, purchased the home in 1904—inherited the house in 1927, selling it in May 1939 to Daniel and Madeline Doran. They sold it that same year to Dr. Higgins.

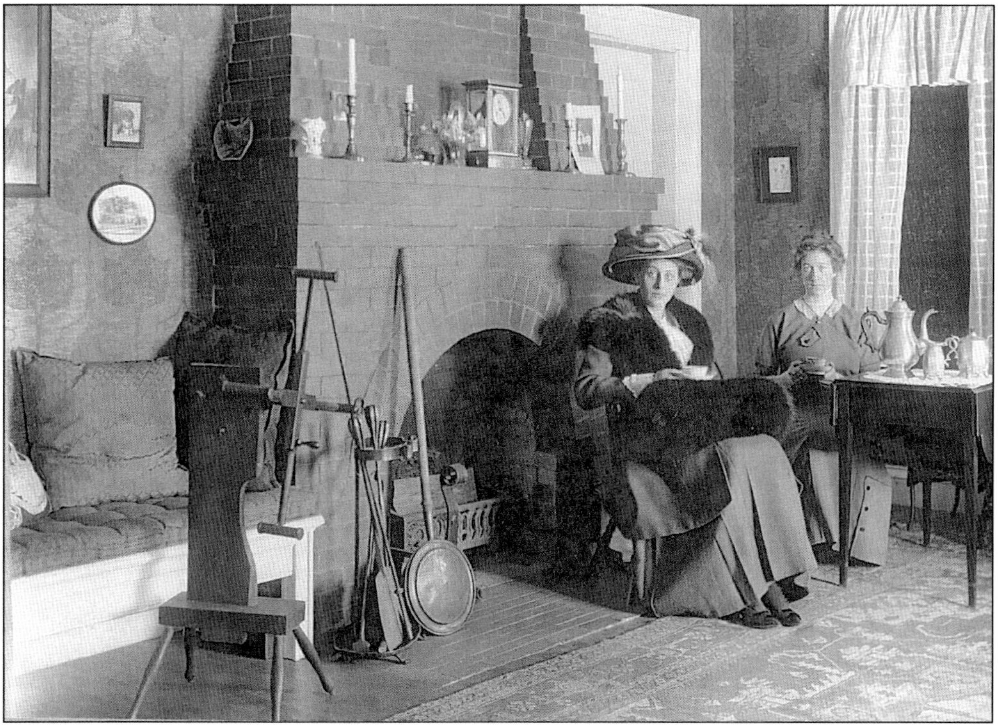

An interior view of the Brownell home shows Edith (right) seated in her teahouse with her friend, Peggy Williams, who is wearing a stylish fur-trimmed coat and hat. A large fur muff completes her ensemble. On the back of the photograph, Edith has written "Peggy and me in the living room of house in Sauquoit."

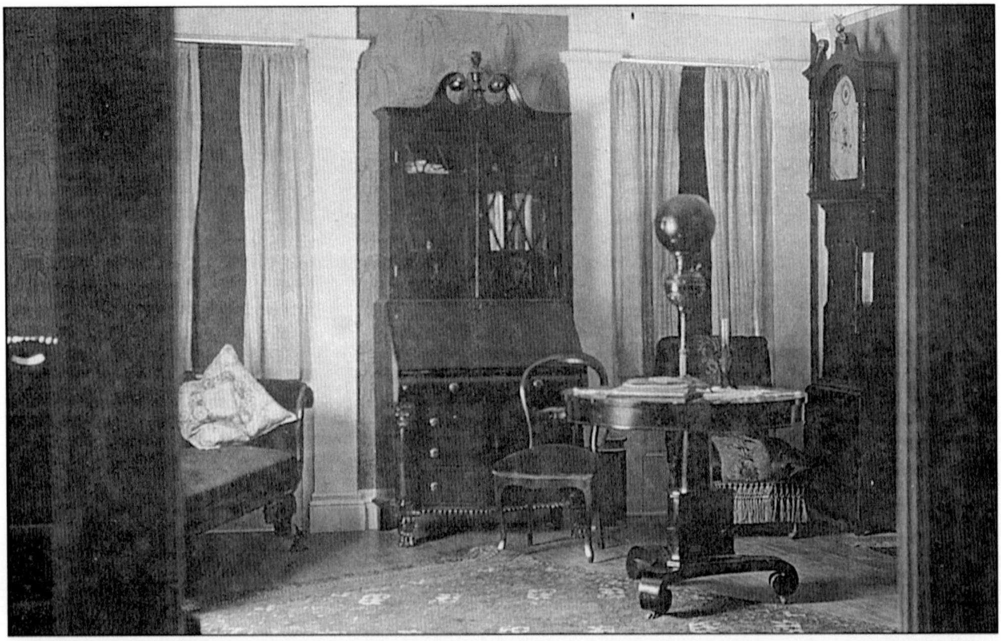

Another interior view of the Brownell home shows a typical Victorian parlor with its large secretary and a very tall grandfather clock. The flowered carpet with fringed ends was also typical of the late 1800s and early 1900s). This room later became Dr. Higgins's waiting room. Edith noted on the back, "Parlor Sauquoit House built by my great Uncle Henry Brownell."

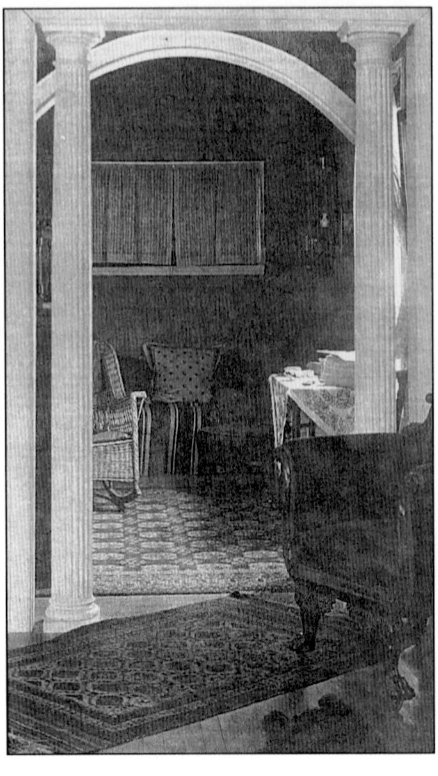

Serving as a den during the Brownell years, this room and the portion that extends further to the left was Dr. Higgins's office from 1939 to 1960. The Greek columns at each side of the doorway are no longer there.

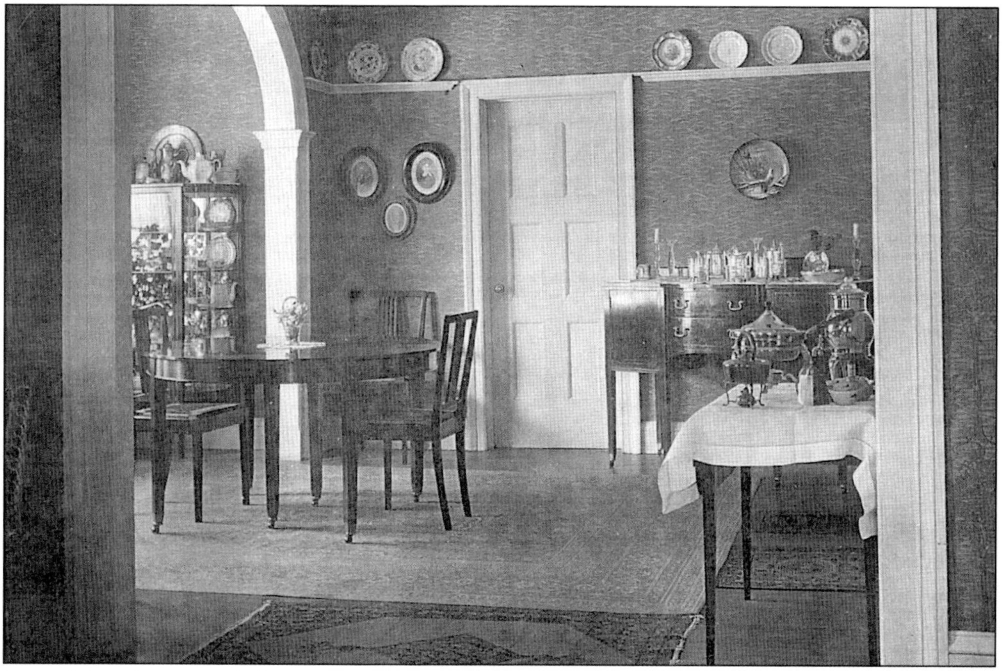

Graceful archways and decorative plate rails were common features in Victorian homes. The china closet displays a marvelous array of dishes and teapots, items that would be cherished by today's antique collectors. On the back of the photograph, Edith Brownell has written, "Dining room of Sauquoit house." (All photographs of the Brownell home's interior are courtesy of June Rosborough.)

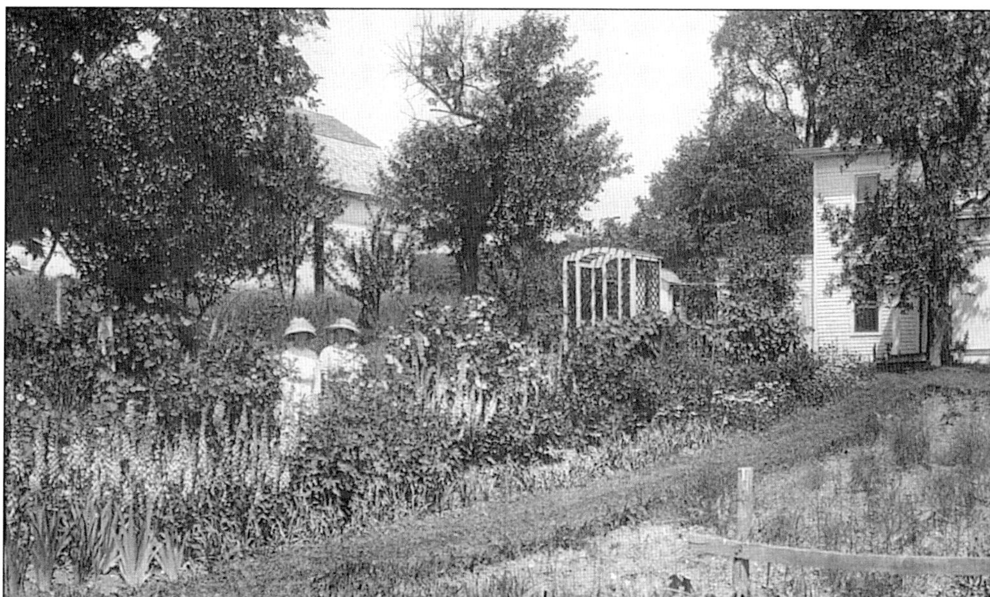

This real photo postcard showing Edith Brownell and her friend, Peggy Williams, was taken in the garden behind Edith's home. She notes on back that her asparagus patch is on the right. When Peggy was in her 90s, she moved to the Harding Nursing Home in Waterville, where she died at the age of 101. (From the collection of June Rosborough.)

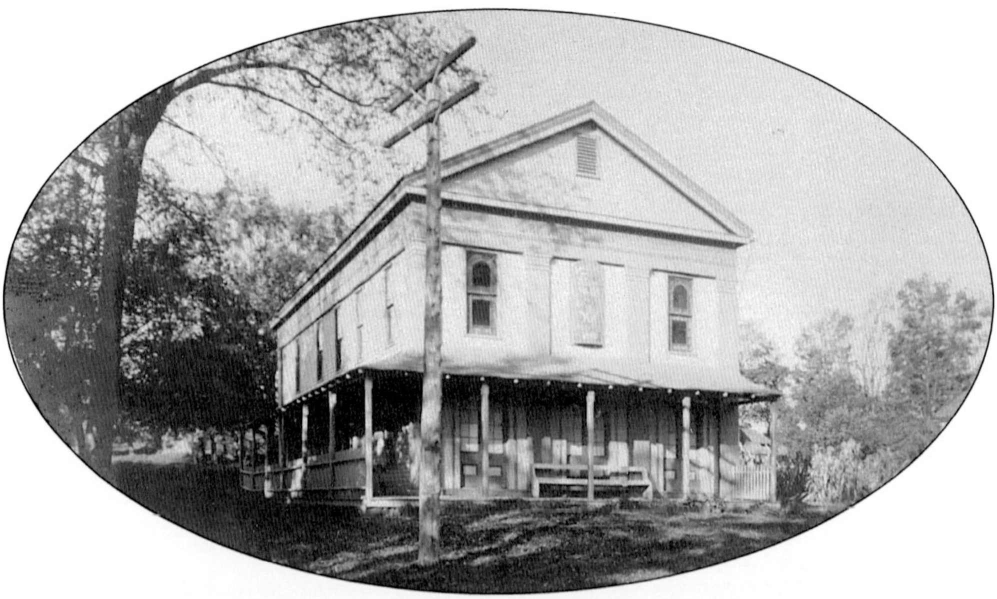

In 1849, the Masonic Hall, located on Oneida Street, was the Union Hall. The Sauquoit Lodge No. 150, Free and Accepted Masons, sublet a room for their meetings until the lodge raised funds to buy the building in 1869 at a cost of $1,750. Earlier plans to erect a new building were abandoned because of the anti-Masonic sentiment of 1826, referred to as the "Morgan excitement." A man named William Morgan was thought to be writing a book disclosing the secrets of Free Masonry. Jailed for debt, he mysteriously disappeared.

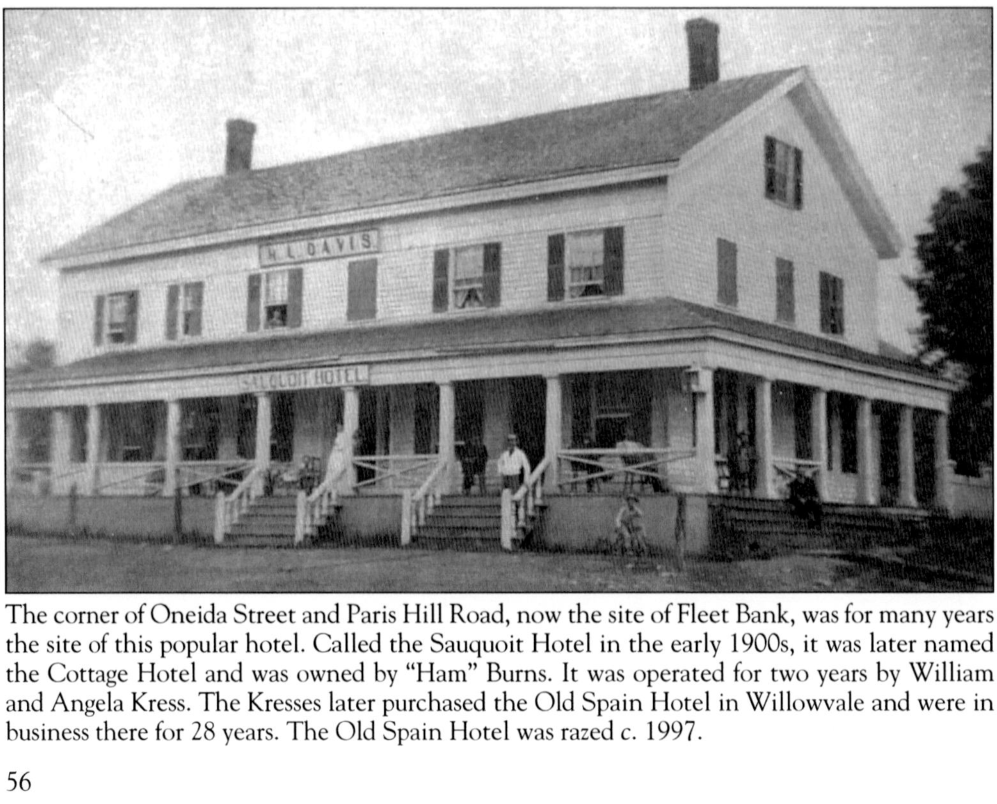

The corner of Oneida Street and Paris Hill Road, now the site of Fleet Bank, was for many years the site of this popular hotel. Called the Sauquoit Hotel in the early 1900s, it was later named the Cottage Hotel and was owned by "Ham" Burns. It was operated for two years by William and Angela Kress. The Kresses later purchased the Old Spain Hotel in Willowvale and were in business there for 28 years. The Old Spain Hotel was razed c. 1997.

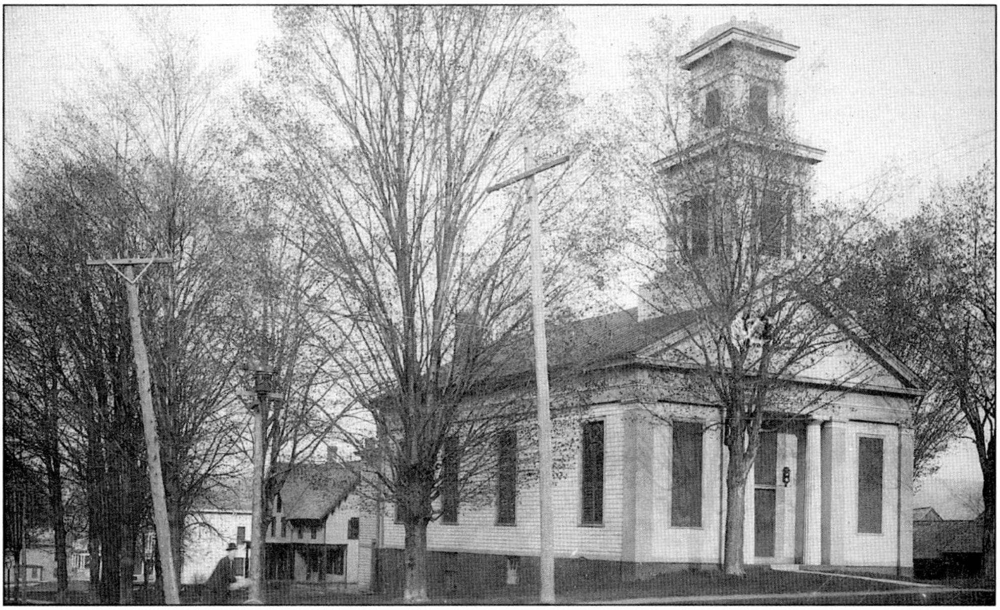

An interesting message sent to a cousin appeared on a 1906 postcard written by Hattie C. Rogers (a local music teacher, church organist, and sister to Henry C. Rogers.) She wrote, "Presbyterian Church, Sauquoit, Oneida County, New York organized in 1810, with 26 members of whom Theodore and Hannah (Chapin) Gilbert were among the original number. —The church was Congregational at first but changed its form to Presbyterian in the year 1832. The present church edifice was built in 1843, near the site of the first one—built in 1822."

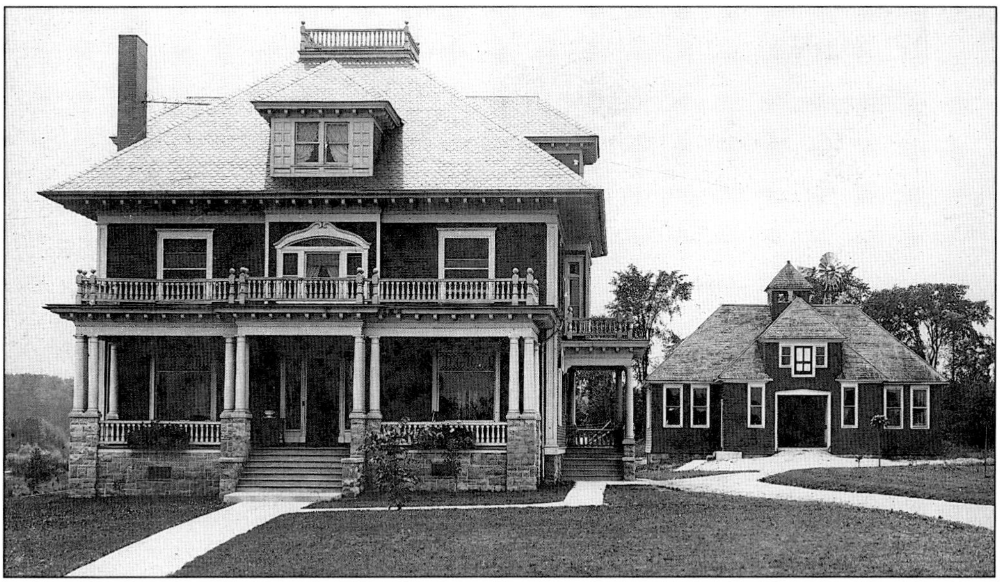

In the early 1900s, Ladd J. Lewis Jr., a prominent Republican, was president of the Republican Club of the town of Paris, and a justice of the peace. He married Frances Campbell, and had three children. In 1906, he was elected a member of the New York State Assembly, and served for several years. His grandson, John Crossley, lives today in nearby Clinton. The building to the right of the house was at one time used as a school. A 1914 postcard identifies this home as the residence of Dr. Burhyte.

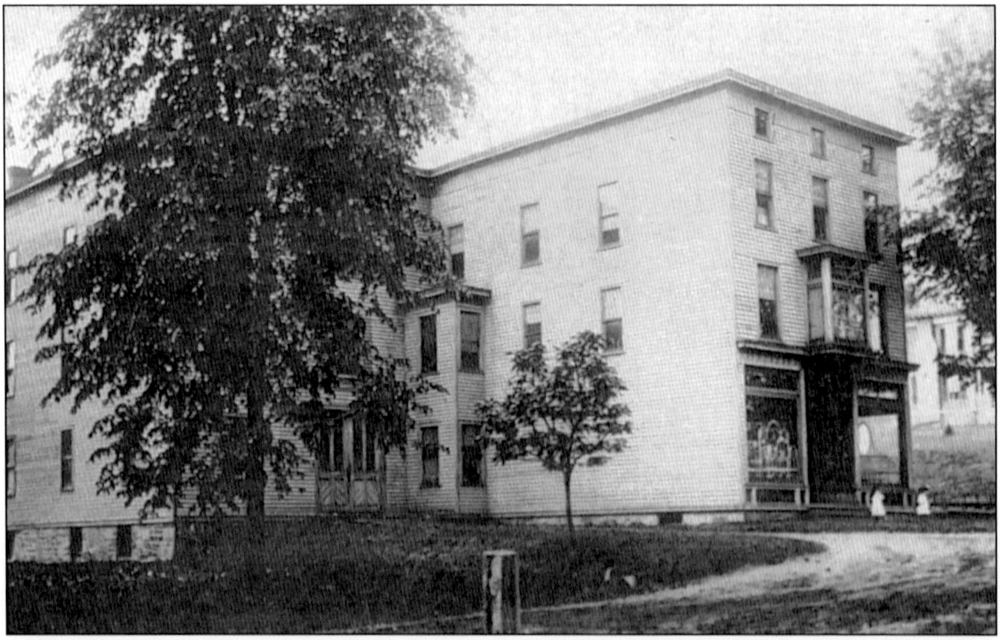

Costigan's Store was located on the south side of Pinnacle Road (then Main Street), below the Ladd J. Lewis residence and across the railroad tracks. Briggs Insurance Agency is located there today. This building has been a furniture store, an undertaker's parlor, and a school. The railroad ran along the west side of the building and the depot was just across Pinnacle Road. In later years, the top two stories of the building were removed. (From the collection of June Rosborough.)

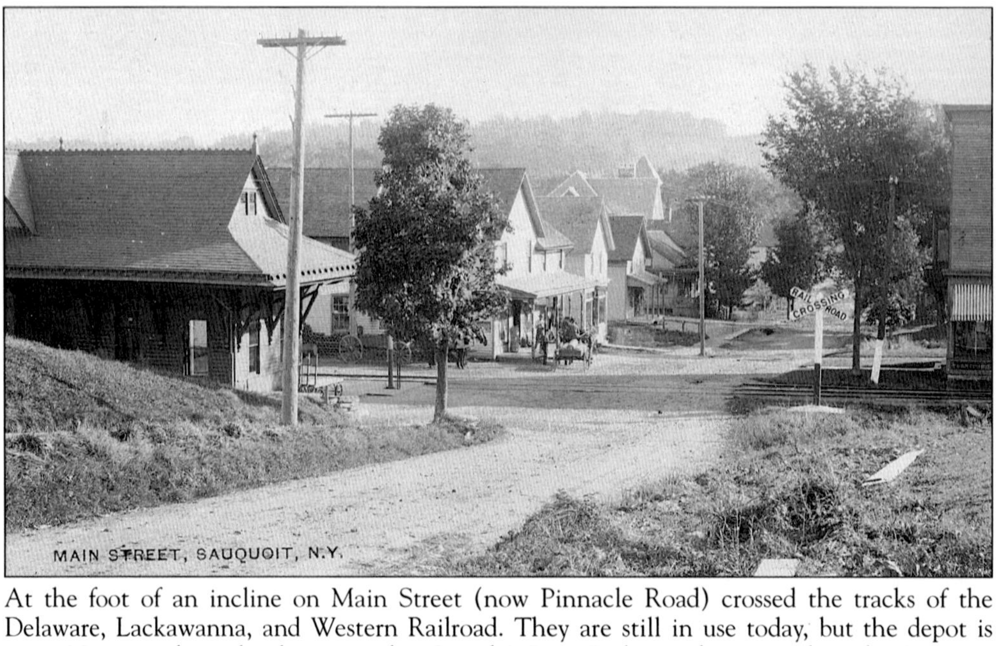

At the foot of an incline on Main Street (now Pinnacle Road) crossed the tracks of the Delaware, Lackawanna, and Western Railroad. They are still in use today, but the depot is gone. Next to where the depot stood is Grande's Pizza Parlor, and next to that, the Sauquoit Fire Department. Narrow, unpaved dirt roads such as these were common for motorists in the early 1900s.

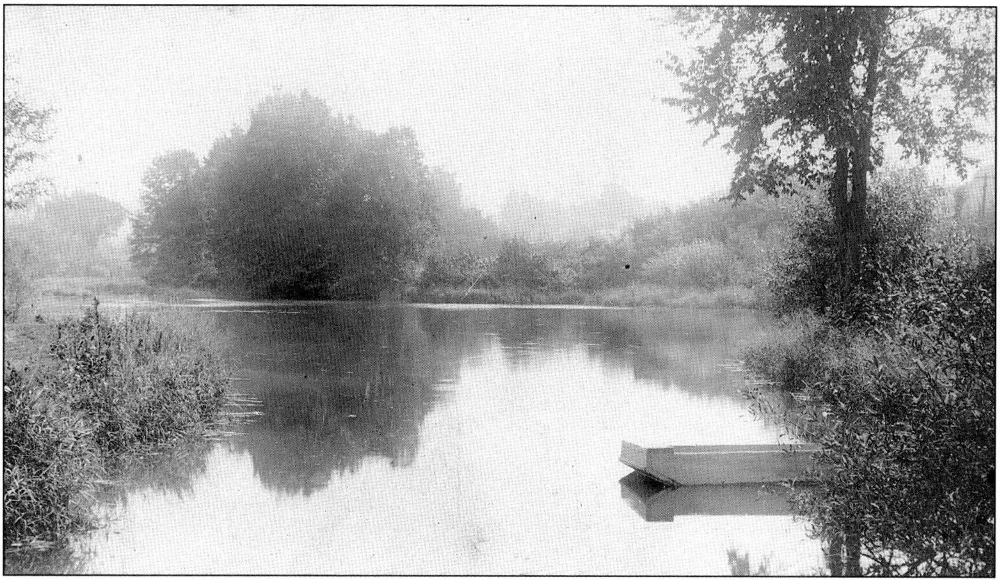

Griffith Place, the street that led to Pope's Pond south of Pinnacle Road, appears on an 1874 map with tenement houses lining its western side. A few houses remain, but the pond has been filled in, and the factories have disappeared. At one time, Brownell & Company had a cotton factory that was acquired in 1825 on Pope's Pond. In 1907, the Horseshoe Knife Factory was located on the site.

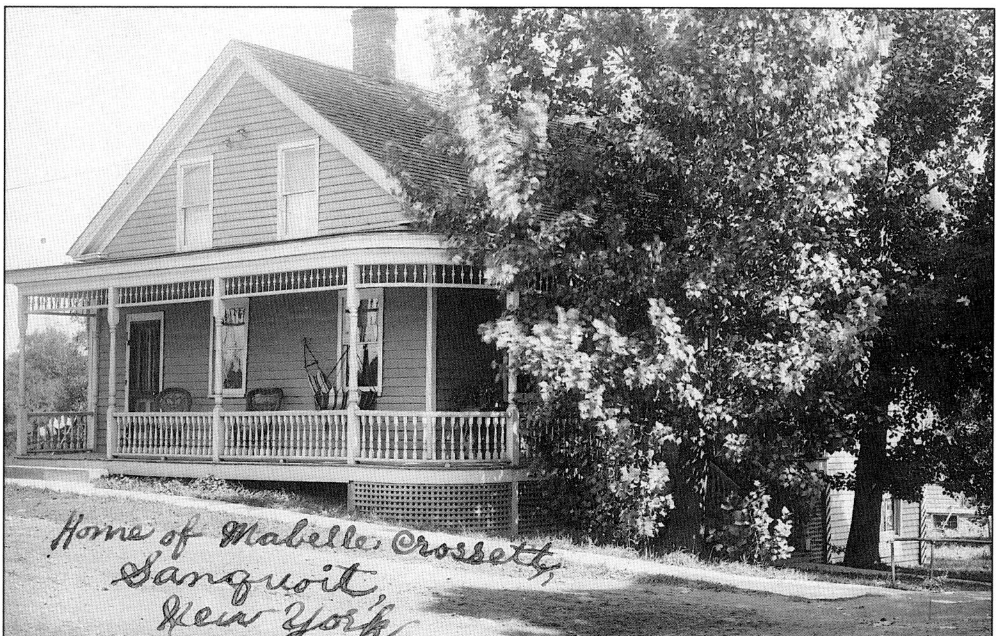

Mabel Crossett's house was located below the depot on the corner of Mill Street and Pinnacle Road. Only a fragment of the old ornamental porch remains. Behind this residence on Mill Street is another building that was once known as Crossett's Hotel, presumably operated by the same family. This is now a private residence.

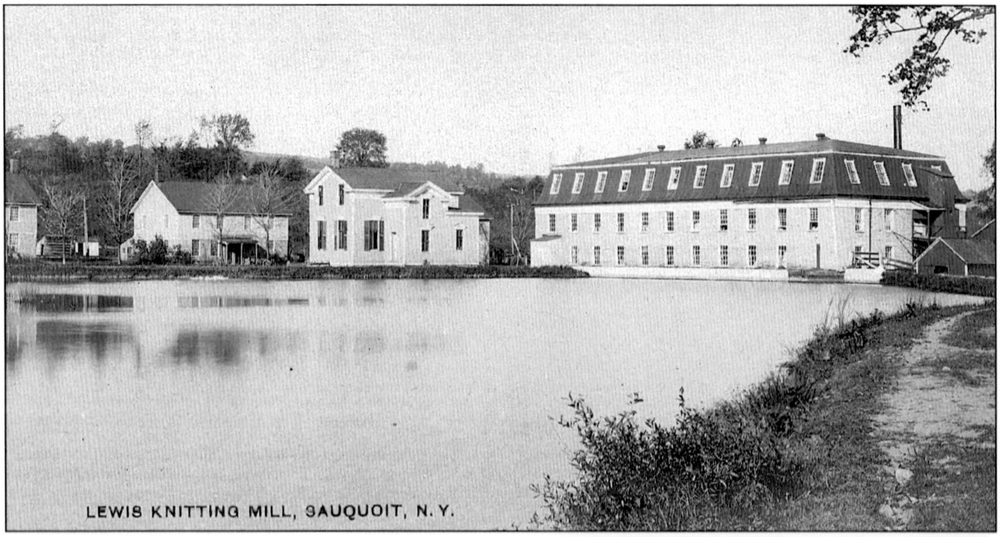

Ladd J. Lewis Jr. operated the Lewis Knitting Mill in 1900. The 1886 graduate of New Hartford High School began his career at age 21. In the 1890s, he moved to Sauquoit and started the factory on Mill Street north of Pinnacle Road. The large residence in the center, still on the site, has been partially razed. On the left are two of the unusual tenement homes, their bottom stories built of limestone. Several of these residences are extant. The millpond has been filled in. Nearby is a Little League baseball field.

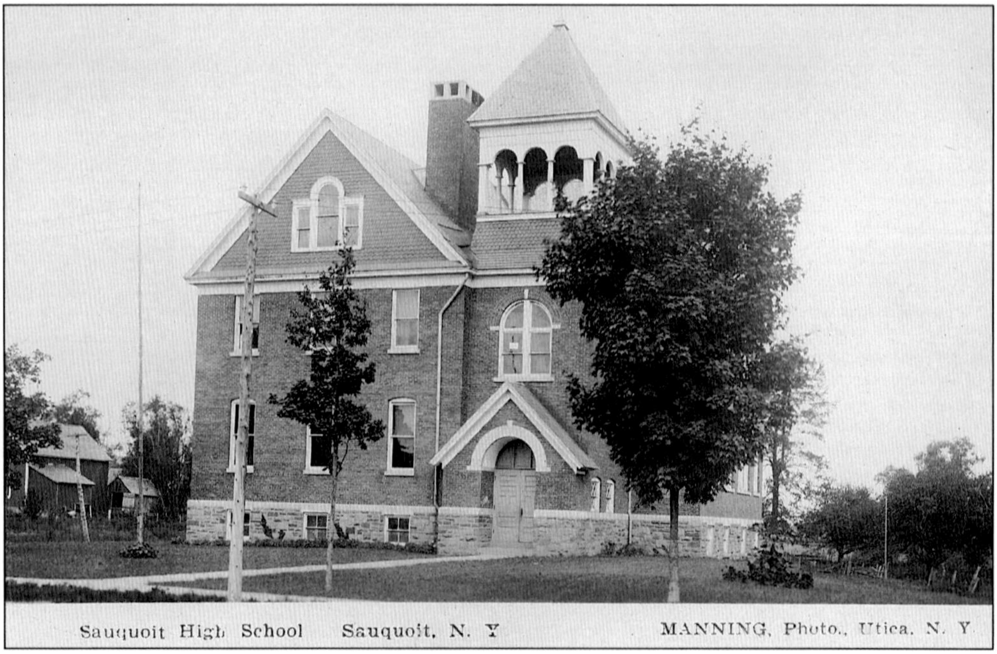

Sauquoit High School, shown here in 1909, no longer stands on Pinnacle Road—a victim of the construction of the Sauquoit Valley Route 8 Arterial in 1968–69. The new central school, completed in 1932 on old Route 8 (now Oneida Street), has expanded its campus along Sulphur Springs Road; it now includes students displaced by the closing of Chadwicks High School, as well as children from Cassville, Clayville and Sauquoit. Now occupying the old school grounds is Reilly's Dairy Store and a Subway shop.

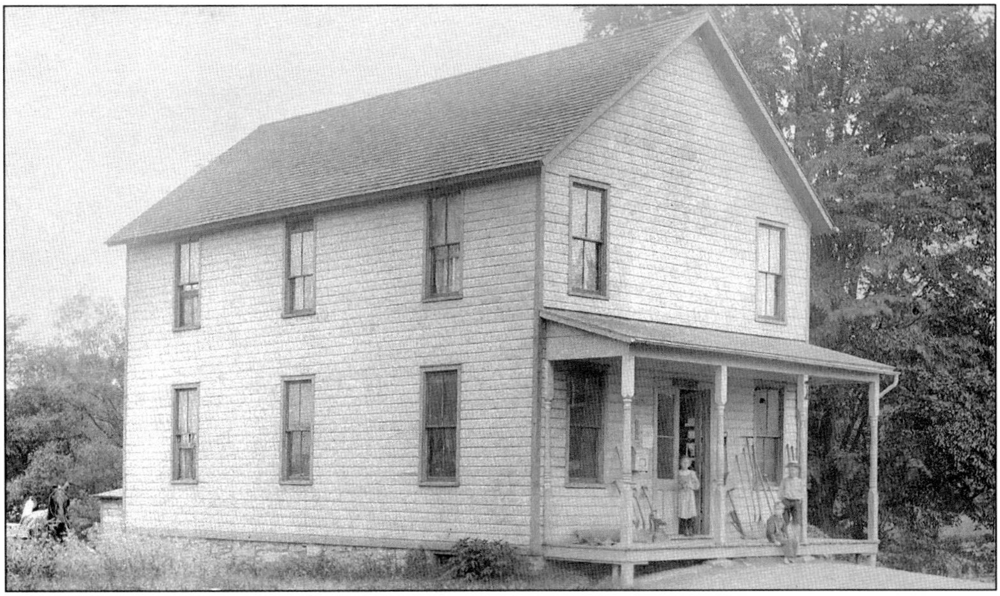

An early postcard (dating to before 1907) is of the Sauquoit Post Office. A multi-purpose building as many early post offices were, a general store was on the first floor, operated by Hobart Graves, the first postmaster. A private residence occupied the second story. This building, too, was torn down in 1968–69 to make room for the Sauquoit Valley Arterial that crosses Pinnacle Road nearby. At one time, it was the home of Mr. and Mrs. Jerry Schafer.

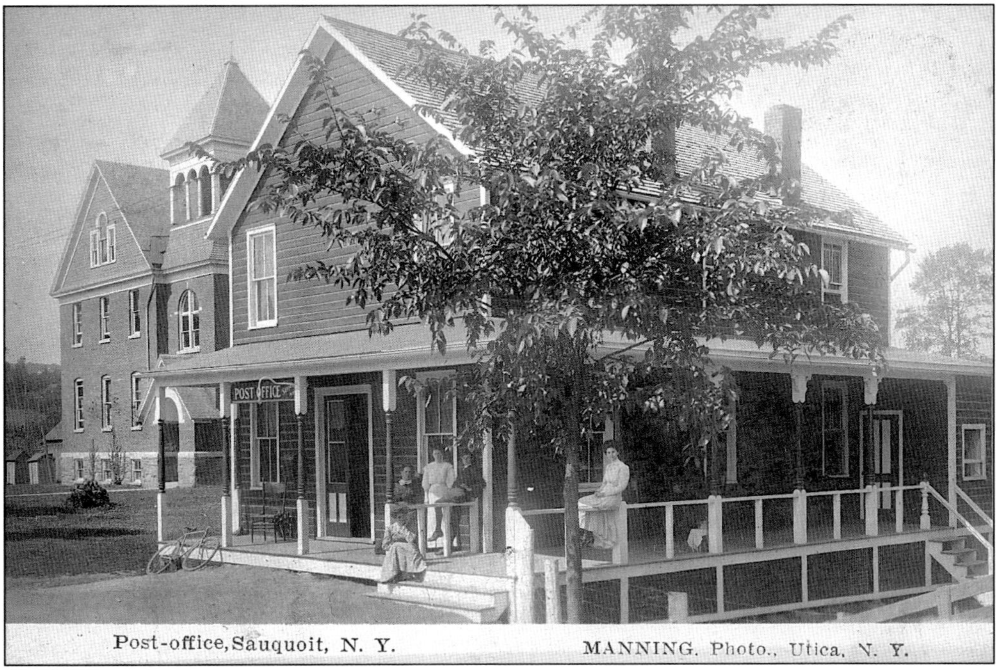

By 1909, this building (also shown in the previous postcard) had a large porch. It was still a post office, but the store was no longer there. The high school can be seen on the left.

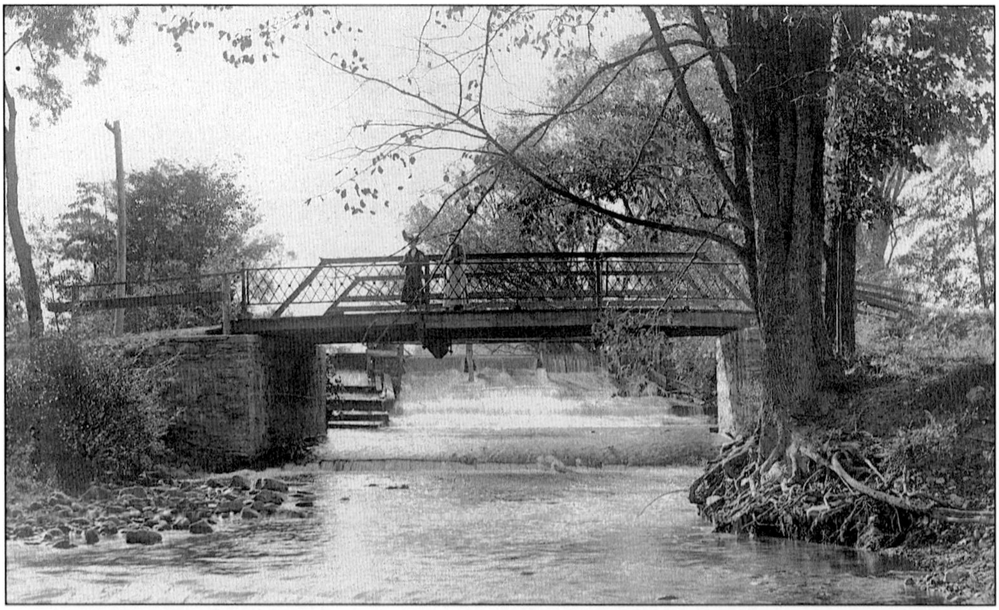

A concrete bridge now spans the Sauquoit Creek where this iron bridge once crossed. The falls under the bridge are no longer there. Over the years, the creek has been a victim of pollution from the various mills, sewage, and agricultural runoff. A 1998 *Observer Dispatch* article by John Pitarresi warned that PCBs had been noted in some of its fish. This problem still exists. Sauquoit Valley residents can fish the creek, but are advised not to eat their catch.

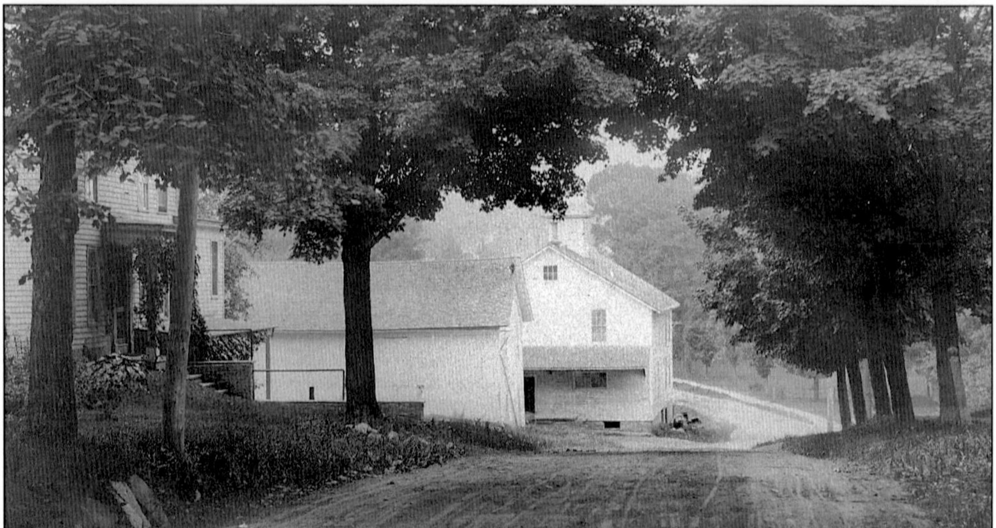

East Main St. Sauquoit, N. Y.
MANNING, Photo., Utica.

Located on East Main Street (present Pinnacle Road) the gristmill and sawmill was operated by the Mould Brothers. On an 1874 map, there is a Mould sawmill across the road from the gristmill, and three Mould residences nearby, just east of the Sauquoit Creek. Two of these residences on the north side of the road are extant, just past the new arterial. Built in 1796, the mills were purchased in 1852 by William L. Mould and his three sons, William, George, and Washington.

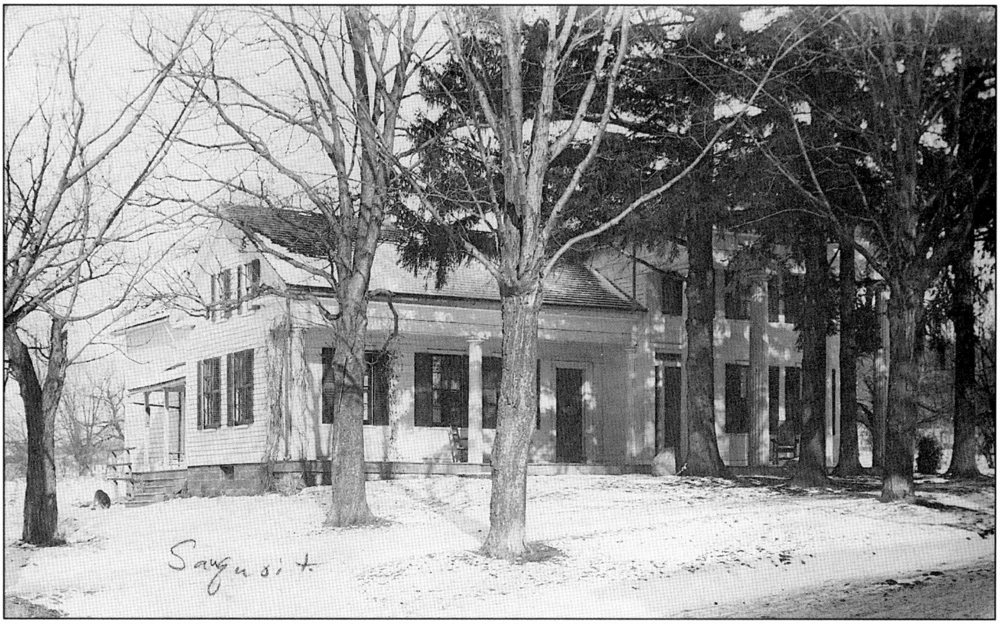

Shown is a Mould family home that still exists on Pinnacle Road. One of the Mould sons, Fred L., who operated a feed and grain business, married a daughter of the town of Litchfield residents Dolphus and Caroline Hadley Marshall. Dolphus Marshall was a Civil War veteran who served with the 121st New York Infantry. Most of this regiment was made up of Herkimer County residents.

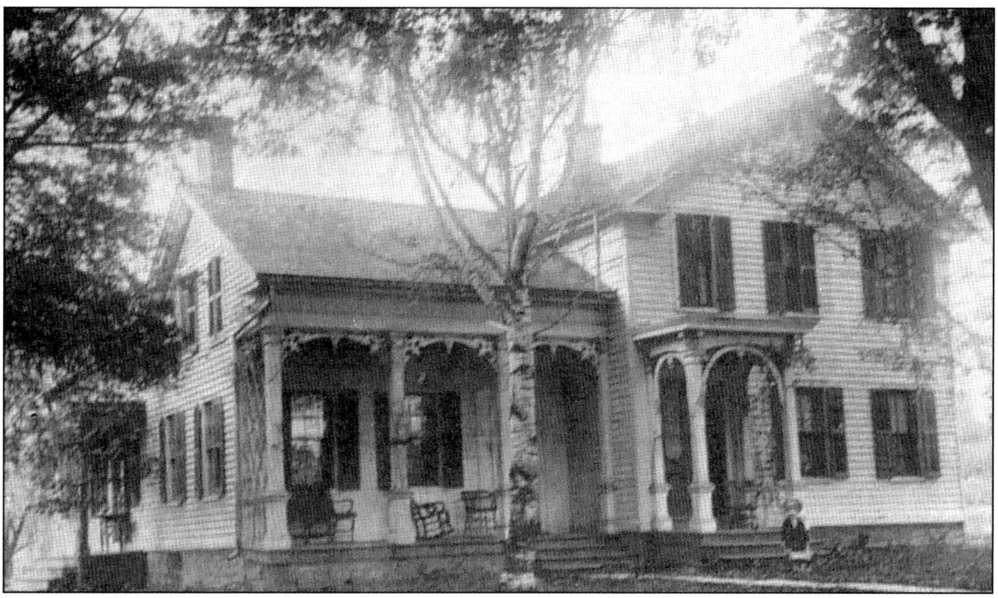

Pictured is another existing Mould family home on Pinnacle Road. Francis Carren, who served in the same Civil War regiment as Dolphus Marshall, Fred Mould's father-in-law, in letters home relates, "the boys from Cedar Lake were disposing of a box…that Doll [Dolphus Marshall] received yesterday." Mr. Marshall later operated a farm in Cedar Lake that was, in 1979 and earlier, the Lewis H. and Olive Smith Farm. Mr. Marshall owned a shoe store in West Winfield for many years.

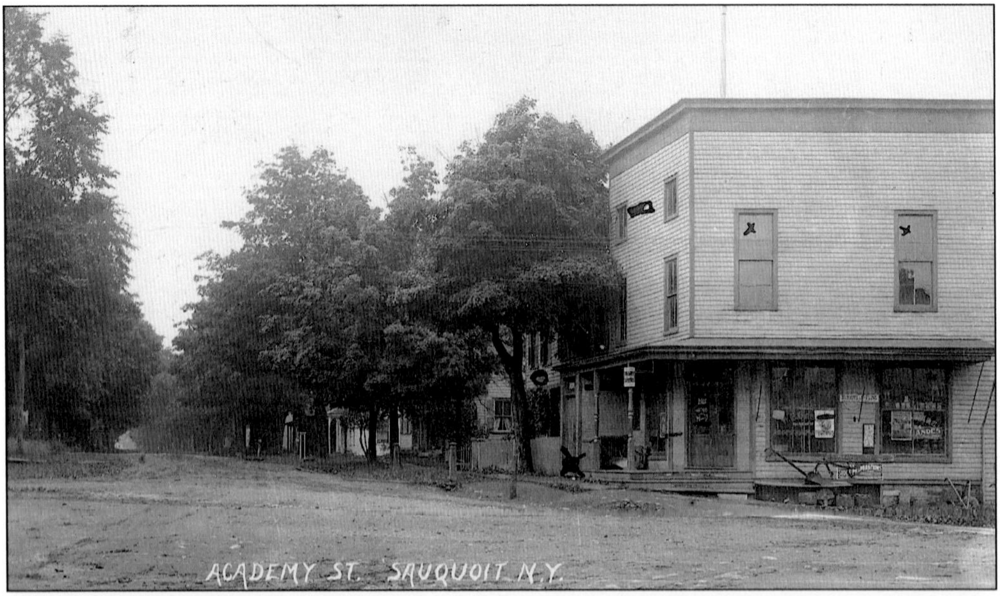

Now called Mohawk Street, this north-south road was called Academy Street in 1911. The writer of the card identifies for her mother the attic (indicated by a rectangle), the hall and opera house (indicated by small X's on the windows), the door going up to the hall (indicated by a large X), the pool parlor (indicated by a dash), and their bedroom windows (indicated by an O). The building at the northwest corner of Mohawk and Pinnacle Roads no longer has a flat roof.

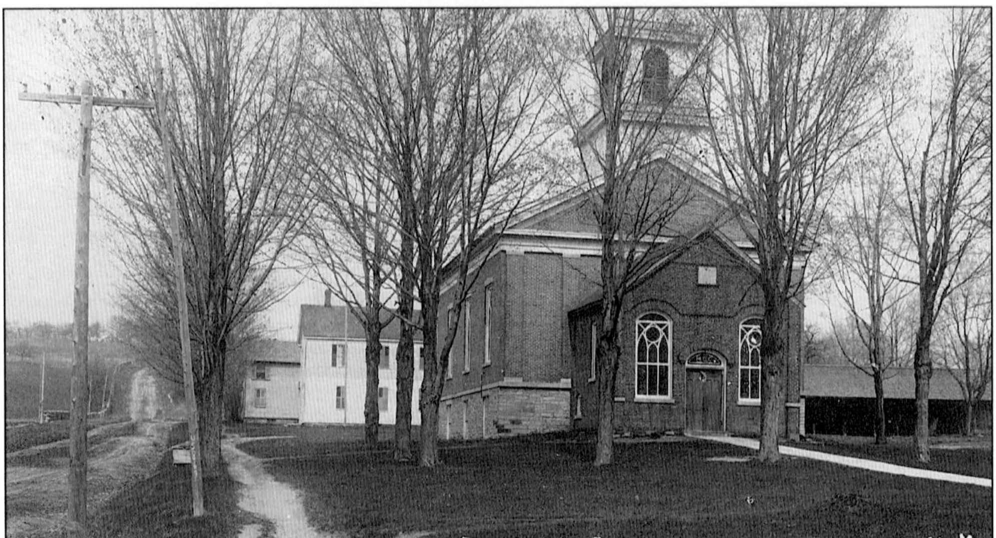

In 1801, a deed conveyed one acre to the Methodist Episcopal Church, and the church was built at a cost of $950. The present brick church, which includes the cornerstone from the old church, replaced the original wood frame one in 1842. A burying ground originally occupied the churchyard, but was moved about one-half mile eastward. Some chose not to disturb their ancestors' graves, and the church was built over the grave sites. Others were later re-interred in the Sauquoit Valley Cemetery. The old church was moved next door and used as the Sauquoit Academy.

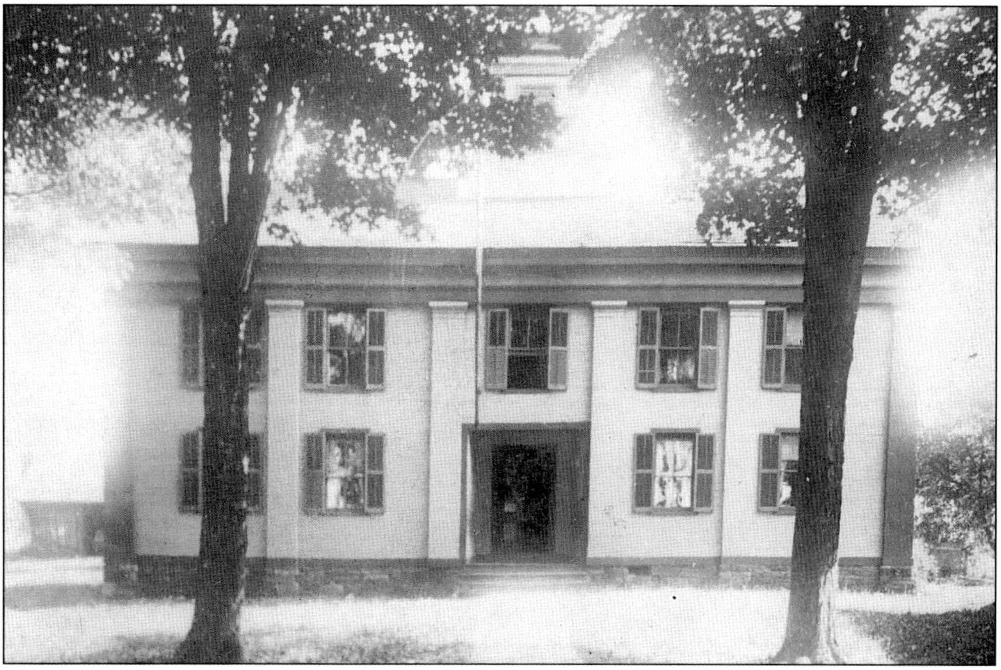

The first Methodist Episcopal Church building was donated for use as the Sauquoit Academy. In 1841 and 1842, a subscription drive was held to raise money for renovating the edifice for a school, resulting in a total of $1,044. Prominent citizens, such as William F. Mould and Henry C. Rogers, were trustees of the school. In the winter session of 1845–46, there were 200 students enrolled in the academy. The school merged with the Sauquoit Union School in March 1895.

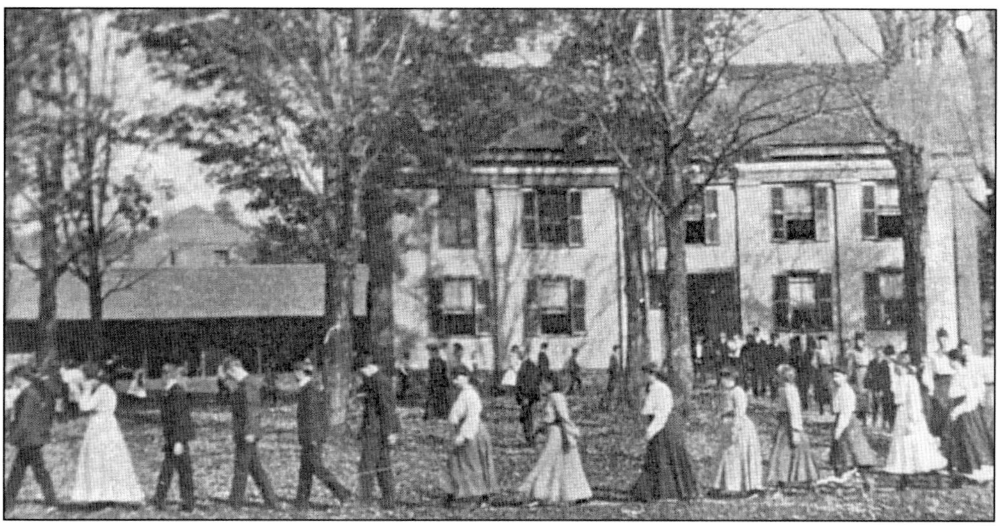

Located in a parklike setting next to the Methodist Church, the academy was a co-educational institution. Susie B. Charles of Cassville attended school here in 1887–88. On display at the Town of Paris Historical Society are some of her report cards. Shown here in the early 1900s, the students are participating in a fire drill. A 1925 *Observer Dispatch* article written by Edith M. Jones states the academy was torn down in 1906, and the timbers were used in building apartment houses in Utica.

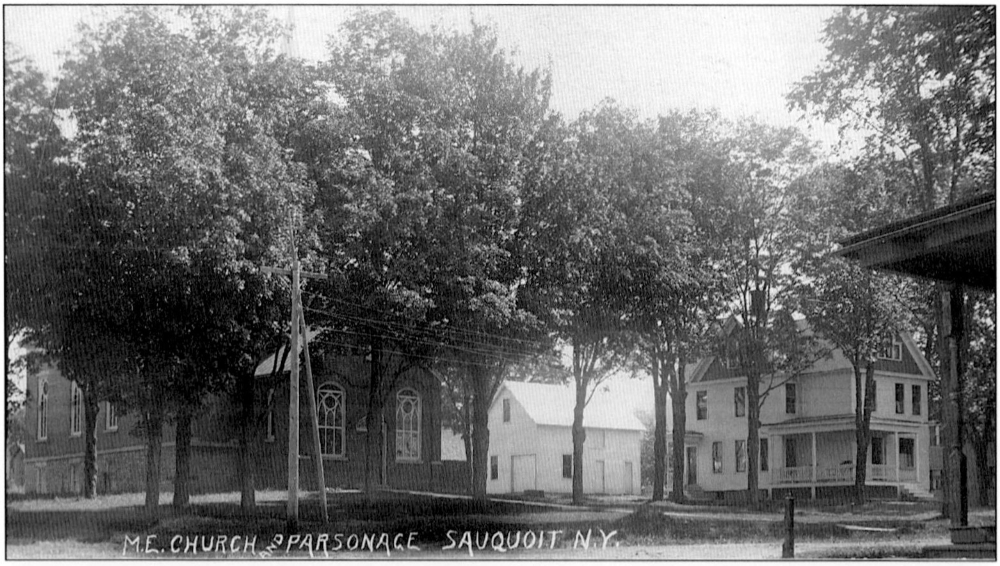

On an 1874 map, the Methodist Episcopal Church parsonage is on the west side of Academy Street, across from the church and the academy. The old red horse shed seen in the previous picture has been removed, and a new parsonage, built in 1910, stands next to the church. In recent years, a new parsonage was purchased on Oneida Street, and the former one is now rented. Stained glass windows were installed in 1885 and a pipe organ in 1888. The Church was renamed the Sauquoit Valley United Methodist Church when they merged with the Willowvale United Methodist Church in 1995.

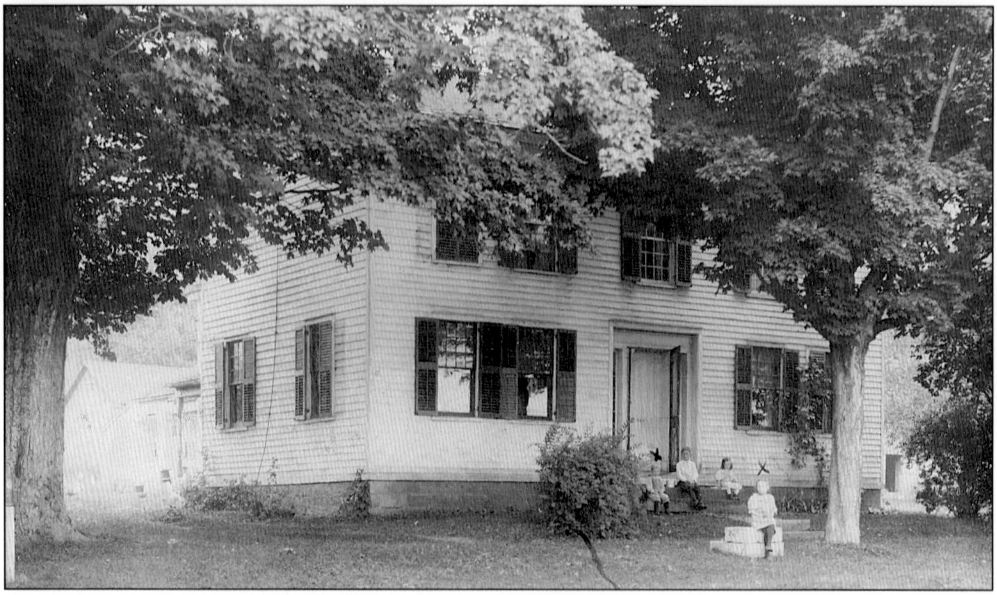

The site of the Asa Gray homestead on Pinnacle Road about one-quarter mile east of Mohawk Street is identified by a state marker. Born in Sauquoit, Asa Gray (1810–1888) was a world famous botanist. Although displaying an interest for flora at a young age, he was educated as a physician. Finding this field not to his liking, he became a botanist. A founder of the American National Academy of Sciences and author of the *Manual of Botany*, a standard reference on eastern flora, Asa Gray was also a professor of Natural History at Harvard.

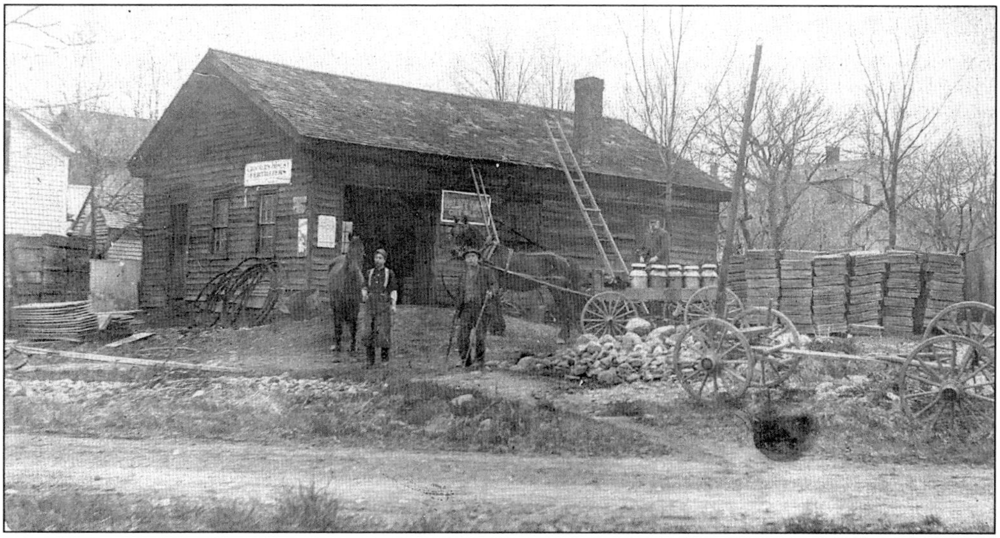

The writer of this 1906 postcard identified the building as Griffith Blacksmith Shop, and has written "Arthur" under the man on the left, "W. Griffith" at center, and "Father" under the gentleman on the wagon. The shop was located on the southwest corner of Butler Road and Oneida Street, now an empty lot. The present law office of Stephen W. Johnson, facing Oneida Street, was the blacksmith's residence. The piles of lumber and extra wagon wheels propped against the shop indicate wagon repairs were also provided.

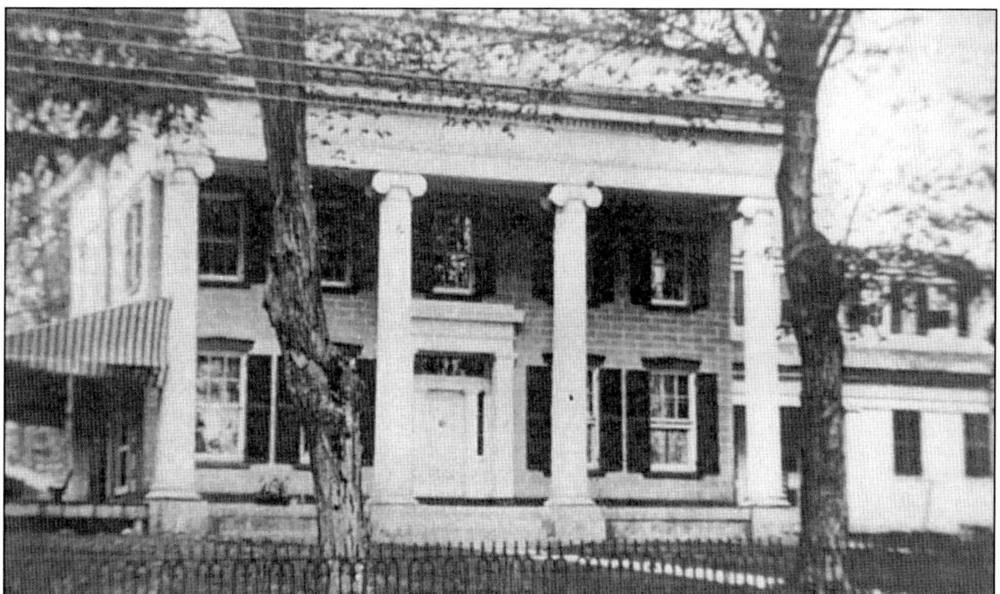

Orchard Hall was once the site of the home of the early settler Capt. Abner Bacon. For his service in the Revolutionary War, he was given a grant of 410 acres from Gen. George Washington. The first floor of the two-story frame house was used as a tavern. In 1840, Chauncey Butler, the son of John Butler, moved the house off the site and built a spacious mansion that included servants quarters and seven massive fireplaces. From 1850 to 1858, Chauncey served as a state senator and was a cavalry officer in the Civil War.

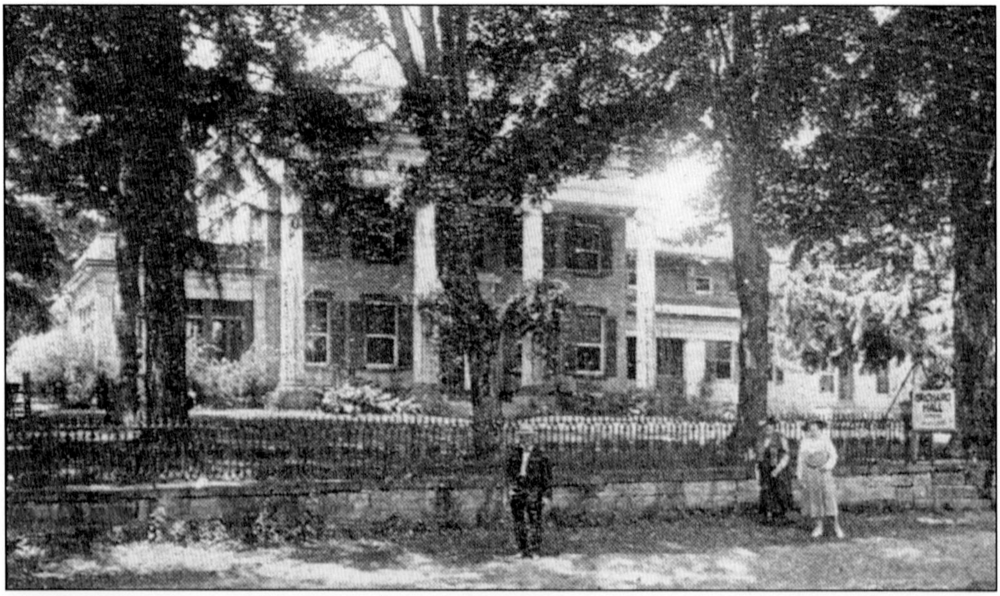

The Butler family owned Butler Hall until 1920, when it was purchased by John Whipple from Old Orchard, Maine, who renamed it Orchard Hall. Mr. Whipple was the proprietor from 1920 to 1925. He sold it in 1925 to Dr. George Armstrong who ran it as a speakeasy until 1932. It was then converted into a private residence by the Borden family.

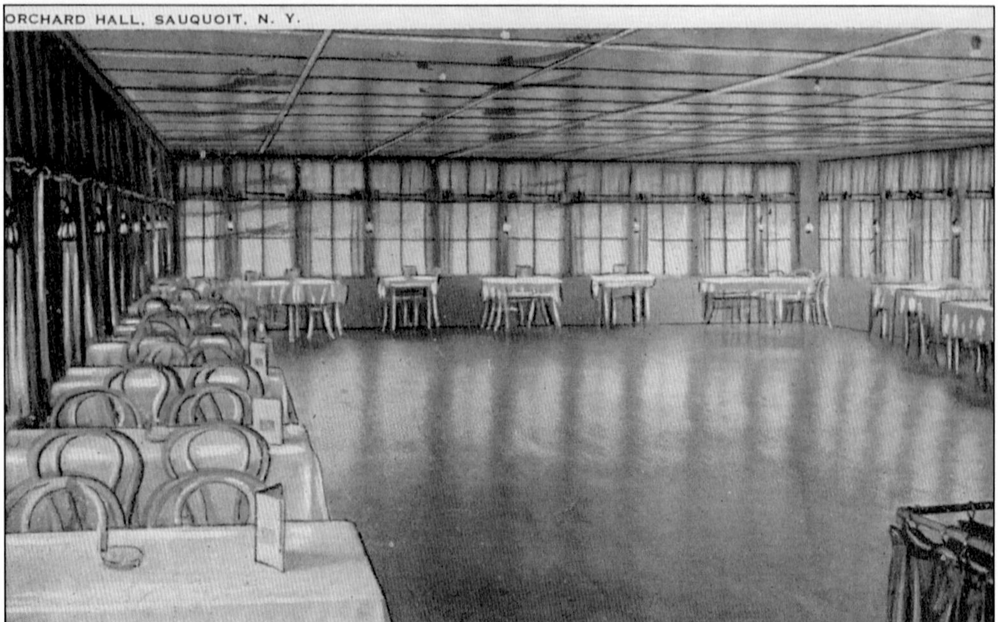

Before WWII, Perry Gillette became the owner of Orchard Hall and re-opened it as a restaurant, adding a bowling alley in 1957. In 1960, he sold it to John and Betty Aubeuf. In 1980, it was purchased, renovated, and landscaped by Bill and Gert Jenkins. In 1992, Gary and Sharon Puleo bought it and continue to operate the restaurant and bowling alley. The postcard shows the dining room, *c.* 1927. Rumors of a ghost on the premises add to the restaurant's ambiance.

Five

CHADWICKS

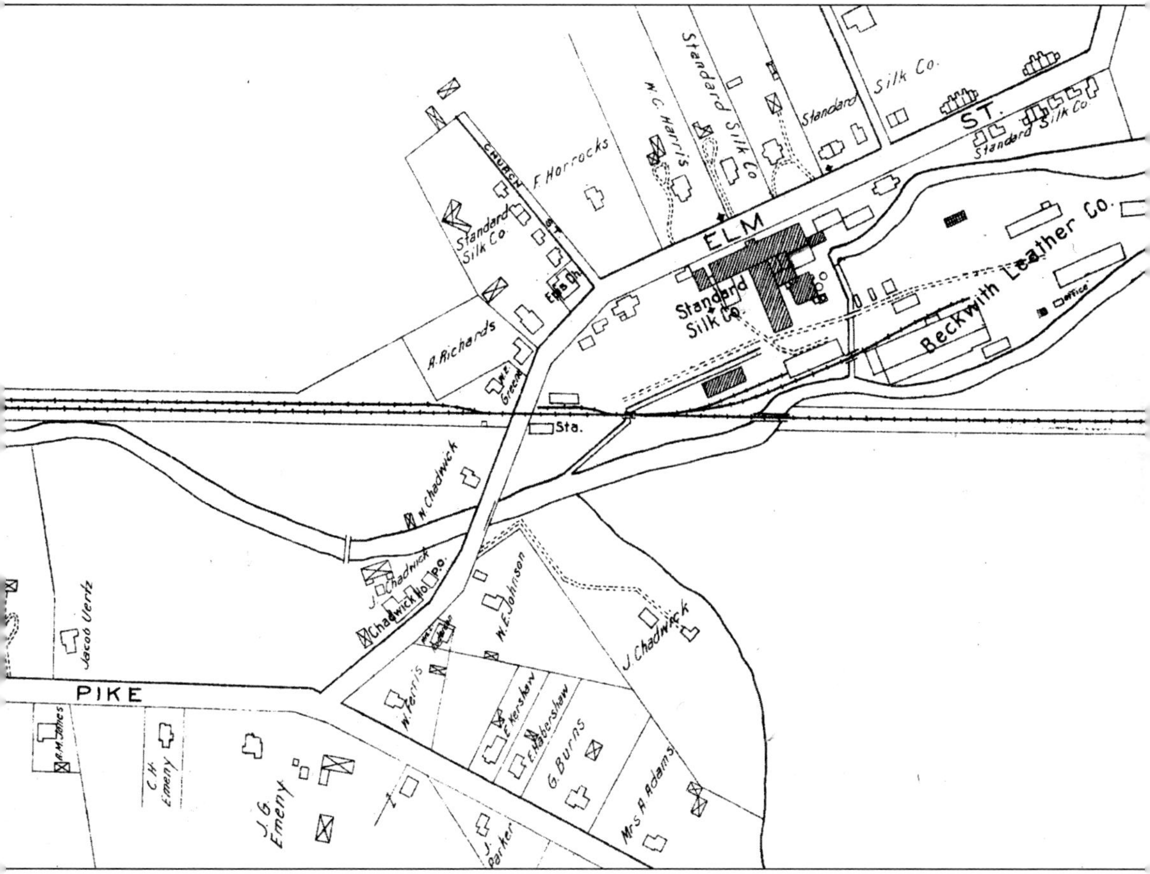

The Pike, or Bridgewater Turnpike, ran south from Utica, crossing Route 20 in Bridgewater. Later designated Route 8, it was the main north-south road through the Sauquoit Valley (north is to the left in this map). The Standard Silk Company complex is visible just to the right of the center. Several properties and businesses of the Chadwick family appear in the village, as well as various mill-owned homes. Elm Street leaves the main road and continues eastward. Chadwicks High School and St. Anthony's Roman Catholic Church were later built on the vacant land northeast of Elm Street along the Bridgewater Turnpike, seen on this 1907 map.

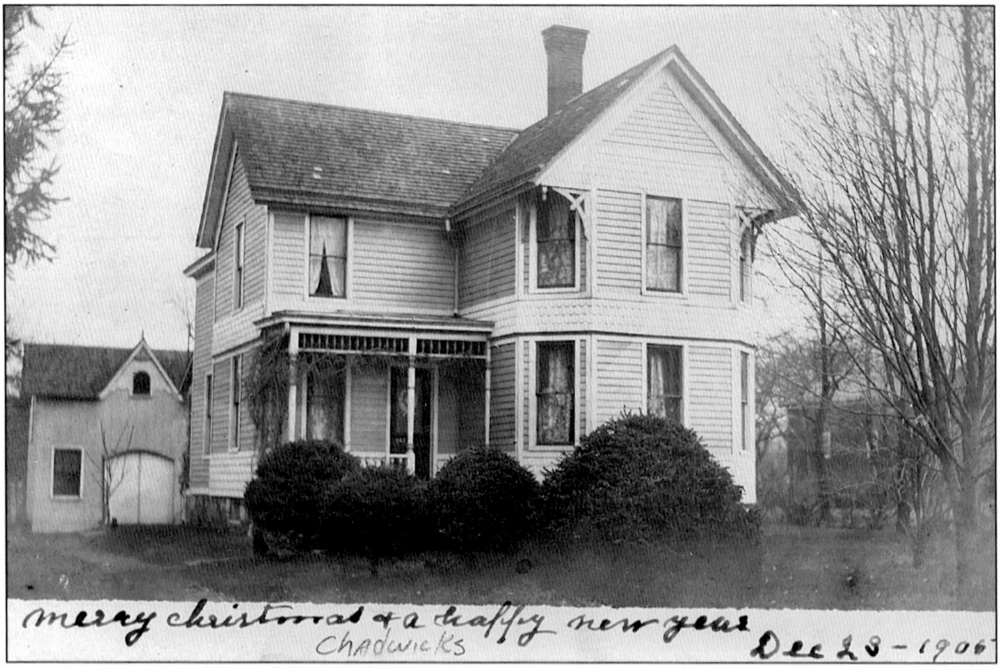

This home with aspects of the Victorian style of architecture looks today very much as it did on this 1906 real photo postcard. The large porch and brackets under the eaves were popular features of houses of this period. The barn in the back now has a different garage door. The distinctive arched window at the front peak remains intact. This home is located on the east side of Oneida Street just south of the Elm Street intersection.

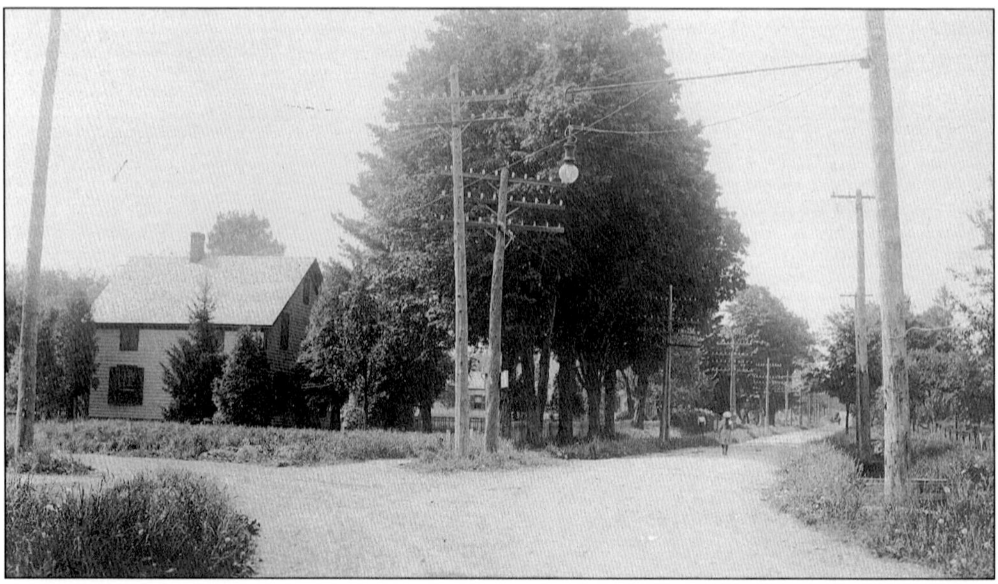
At the intersection of Elm and Main Street was the home of Lena Goff. Next door lived her daughter, Jennie L. Roberts. Jennie's house, built in 1929, is now the home of her daughter-in-law, Betty. It was one of the first pre-fabricated homes in the area, manufactured by Sears and Roebuck Company. Jennie occasionally wrote local history columns for the Utica newspaper.

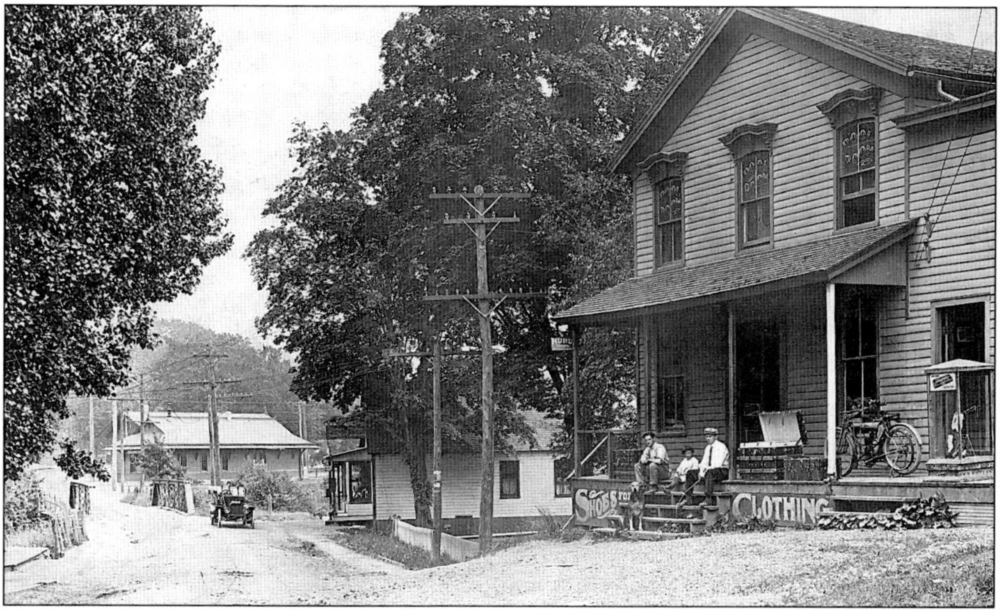

This clothing and shoe store shown in 1917 featured a pool hall upstairs. Located on Elm Street, it was just west of Johnson's Busy Store and the Chadwicks Post Office. In the background is the Delaware, Lackawanna, and Western Railroad station, built in 1905. The buildings that housed the clothing store and post office no longer exist. To the right of the post office, a later building was erected where the Sfeir family operated a meat market. It is now unoccupied.

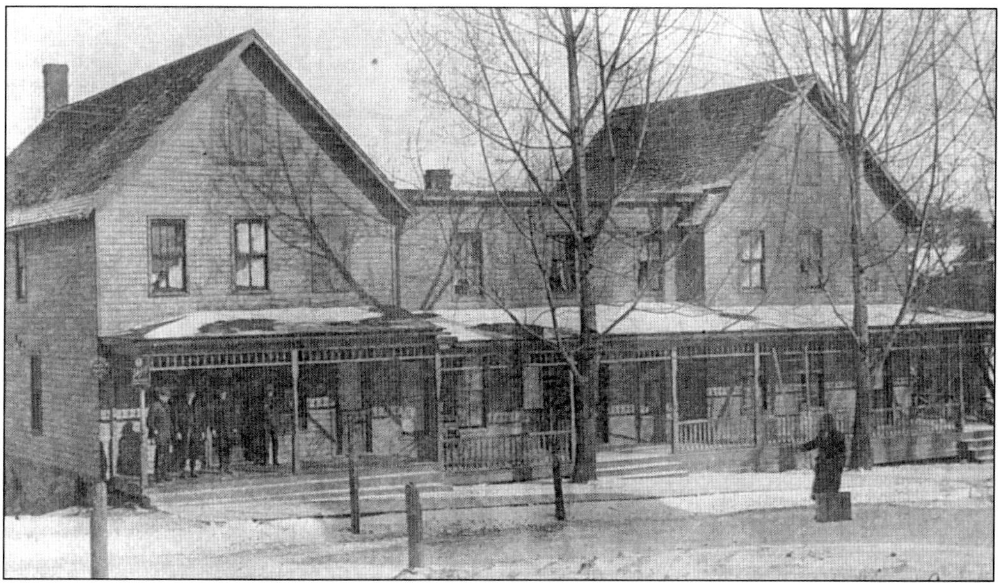

Established in the latter part of the 1800s, the Chadwicks Hotel was another enterprise of the illustrious Chadwick family. In a hotel advertisement, the Chadwick House was listed with John Chadwick as the proprietor. Room rates were $1.50 per day. John and his wife, Margaret, operated it for 19 years, retiring in 1913. Later purchased by the Rosky family, it was continued as a hotel and residence. Rosky's had previously operated a tavern on the eastern end of Elm Street. (From the collection of Tom Schafer.)

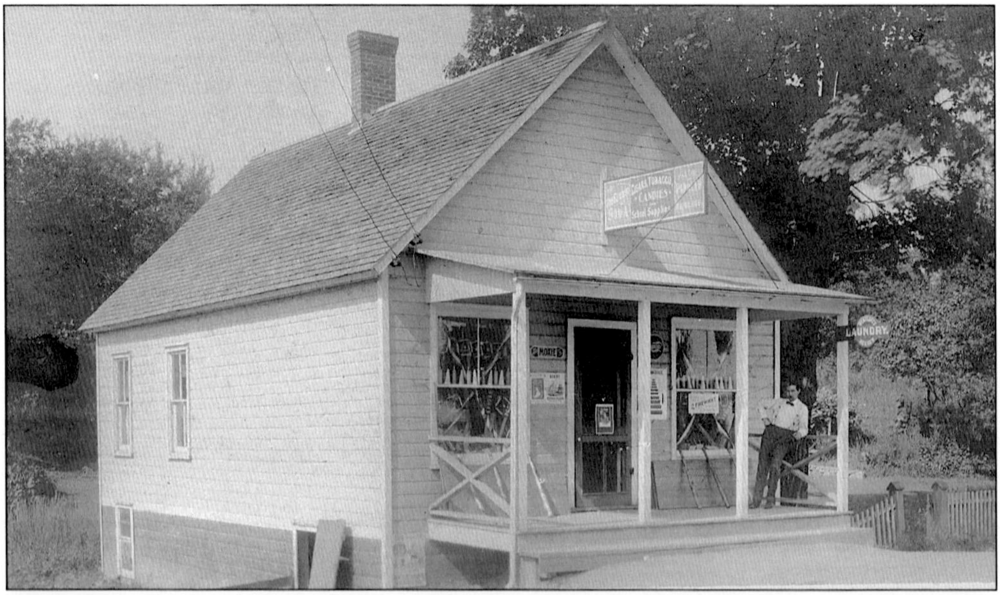

Before the addition of the post office, the sole occupant of this building was Johnson's Busy Store. Among its diverse offerings were cigars, tobacco, ice-cream sodas, school supplies, candy, and all the popular magazines. No one today recalls if the gentleman leaning against the railing is Mr. Johnson. In the right window, a sign advertises fireworks. To the left of the door is a sign for Moxie, a popular soft drink of the time.

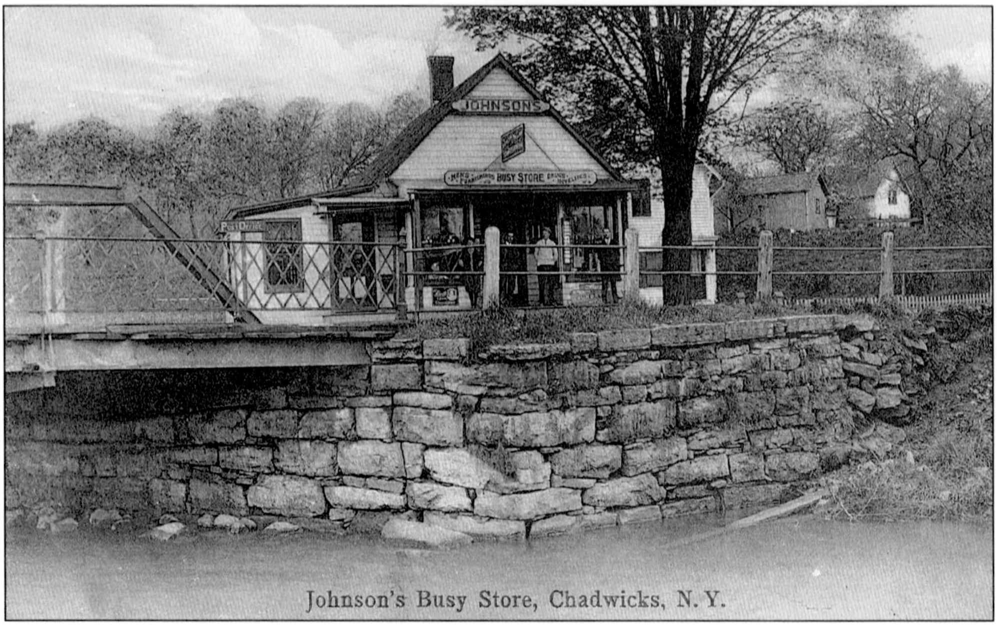

Johnson's Busy Store, built in early 1900 by Mr. Johnson, was a variety store that offered tobacco products+ and drugs, as well as novelties and an ice-cream fountain. By 1914, the post office had been added. The store passed from Johnson to James Reagan, who was also the postmaster, then to Maurice and Anna Kelly. In 1946, the store was purchased and operated by Adelbert Stauring. Later owners sold the building to Williams Tool Company, who razed it for a parking area.

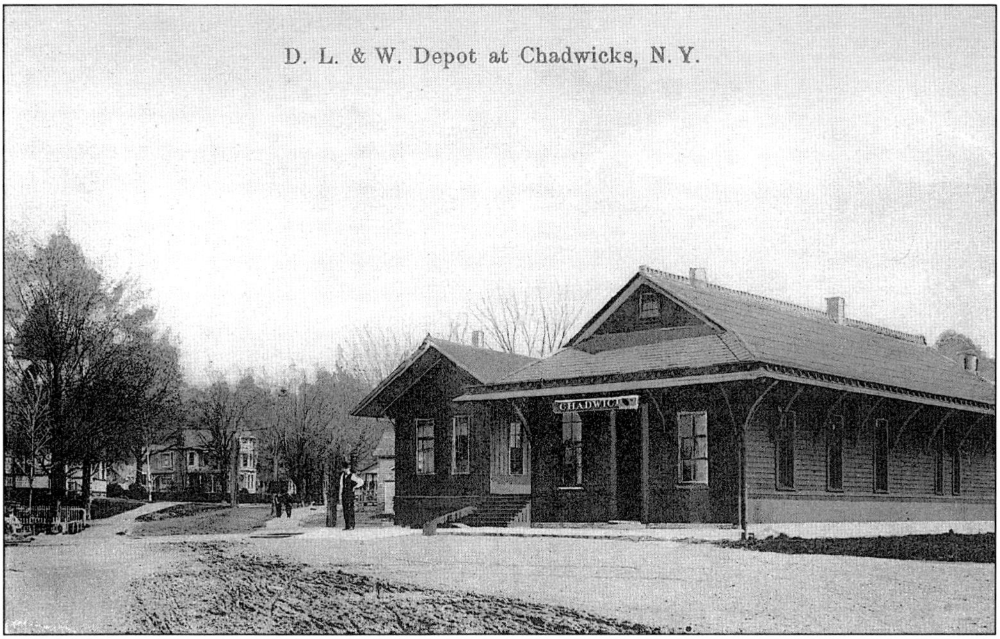

In the early 1900s, a freight house stood next to the Delaware, Lackawanna, and Western Railroad depot in Chadwicks, but had deteriorated and was torn down in the mid-1900s. A station on the Utica to Binghamton division of the DL&W, the line was constructed in the late 1850s. Limited rail activity continues today.

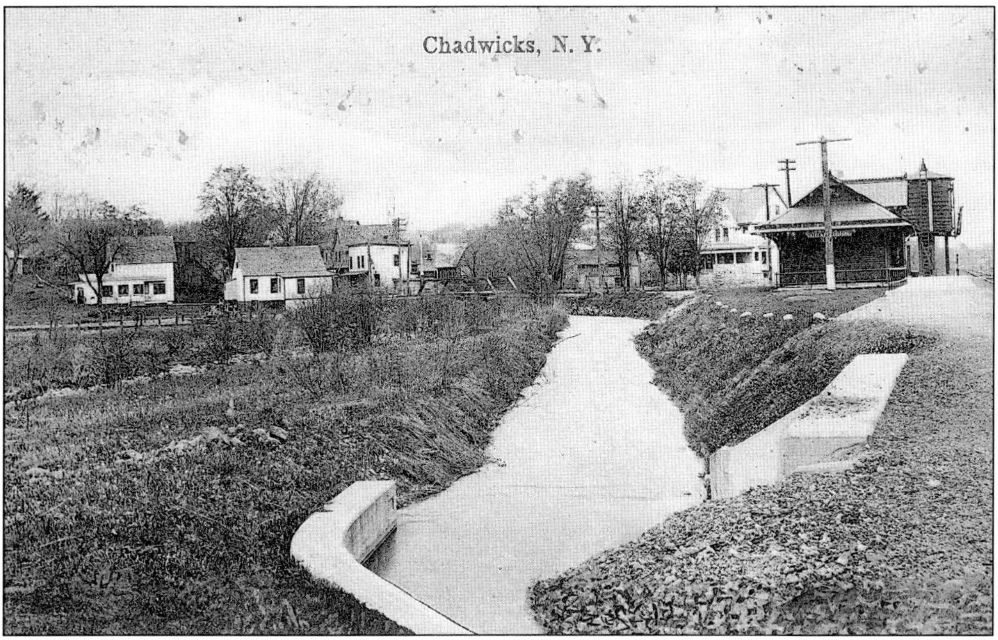

Looking north along the Sauquoit Creek, the railroad depot is on the right. To the left of it is a Chadwick family home; in later years, this was home to the Cieri family. The building to the left of the center was at one time a barbershop and a grocery store. An apartment occupied the second floor. The second structure from the left is the post office and Johnson's Busy Store. On the hill behind the post office (not visible in the picture) was another Chadwick family home.

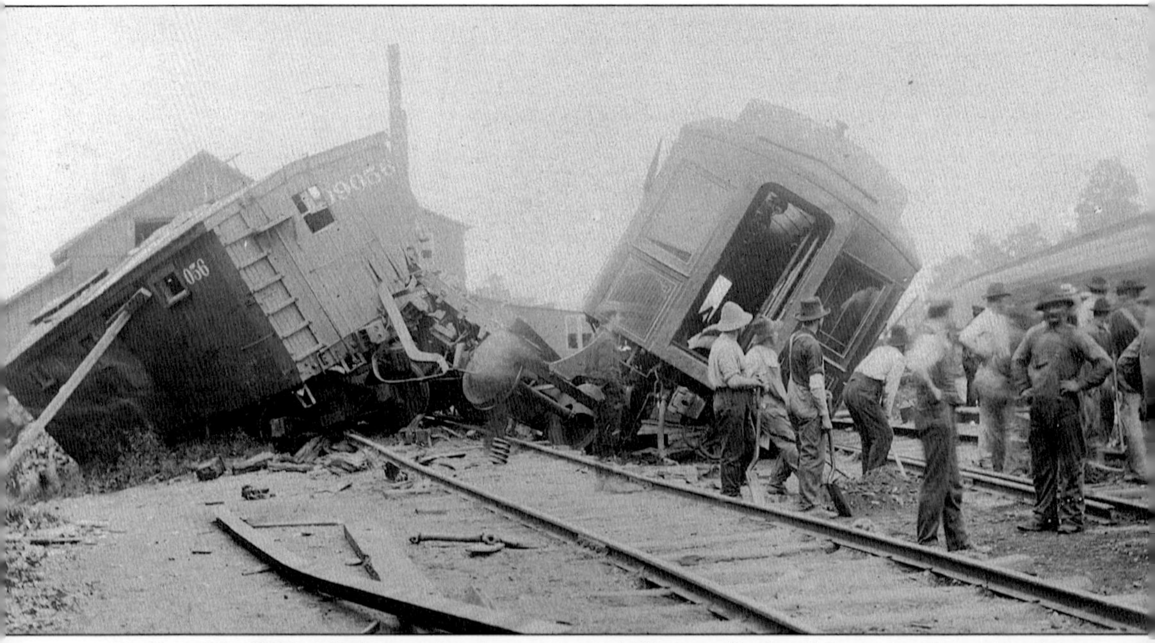

On June 30, 1906, a Delaware, Lackawanna, and Western Railroad train wreck occurred near the Standard Silk Mill and the Chadwick Railroad Depot. It was believed that men working on a new bridge about 100 feet from the station had removed a pin that connected parts of the switch to facilitate their work. It was not replaced, resulting in the mishap. The smoking car shot across the stream and hit the baggage and express cars, which went over the bridge with the engine. Miraculously, no passengers were fatally injured.

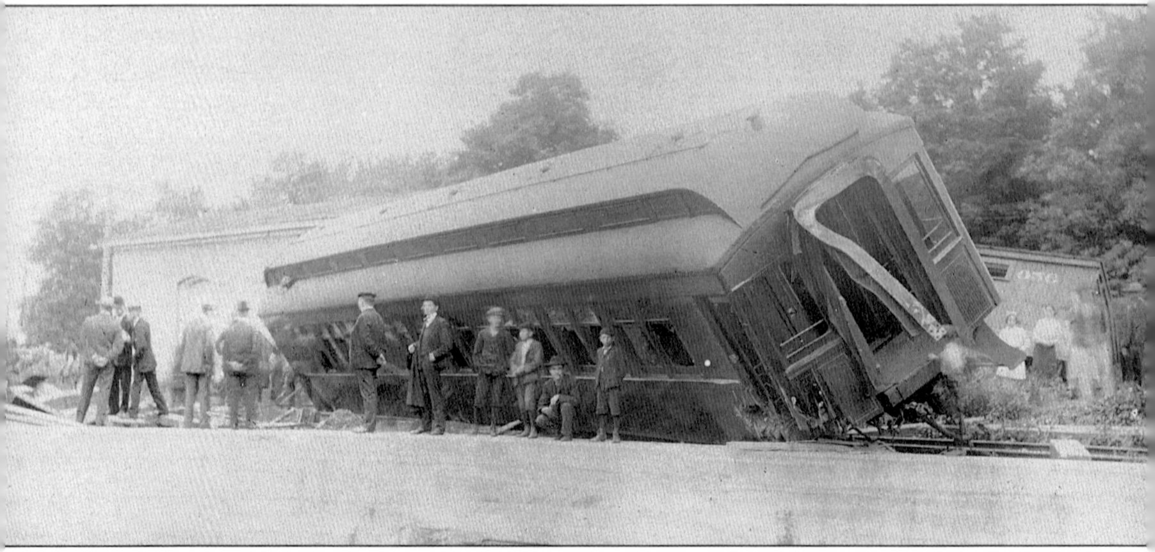

A conductor for 40 years, Daniel H. Hall, a Binghamton resident, stated he had been sitting in the smoking car after collecting tickets when he felt the car swerve and realized there would be an accident. It flashed through his mind that "we would be crushed like an eggshell." He was aroused by someone chopping him out of the wreckage. Although badly injured, Mr. Hall insisted the doctors care for the passengers first. It was estimated the loss to the railroad company for the damages would be $30,000.

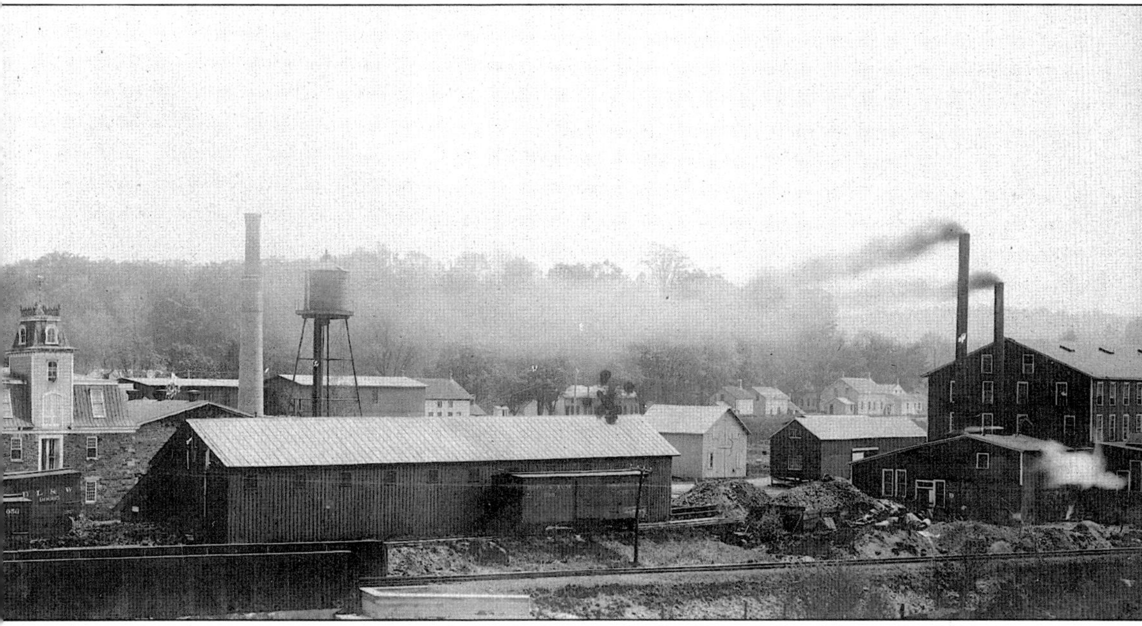

The Beckwith Leather Company was behind the Standard Silk Mill (visible on the left) along the railroad tracks. The *New Century Atlas* of 1907 states that E.D. Beckwith, a resident of Utica, organized the Chadwicks Tannery but disposed of his interest after the organization was completed. Mr. Beckwith owned Meadowview Farm one-half mile south of Washington Mills (on Roberts Road), where he raised an Ayershire herd and chickens. The Beckwith Leather Company burned to the ground *c.* 1920.

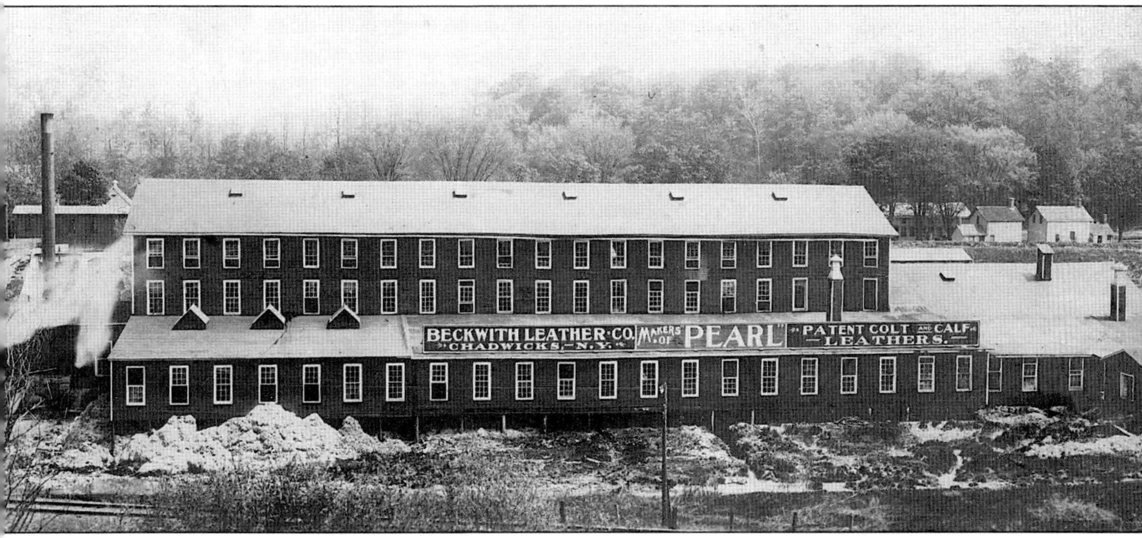

George W. Chadwick Jr., the secretary of the old New Hartford Leather Company and one of its organizers, may have been affiliated with the Beckwith Company next door to the Chadwick-owned cotton mill. The village was named Eagle Mills after the Eagle Cotton Mills. To honor John Chadwick, who was the mill's founder, the name was changed to Chadwick's Mills, later shortened to Chadwick. Over the years, through common usage, it became Chadwicks, much to the annoyance of the Chadwick family who persisted in writing it without the letter S.

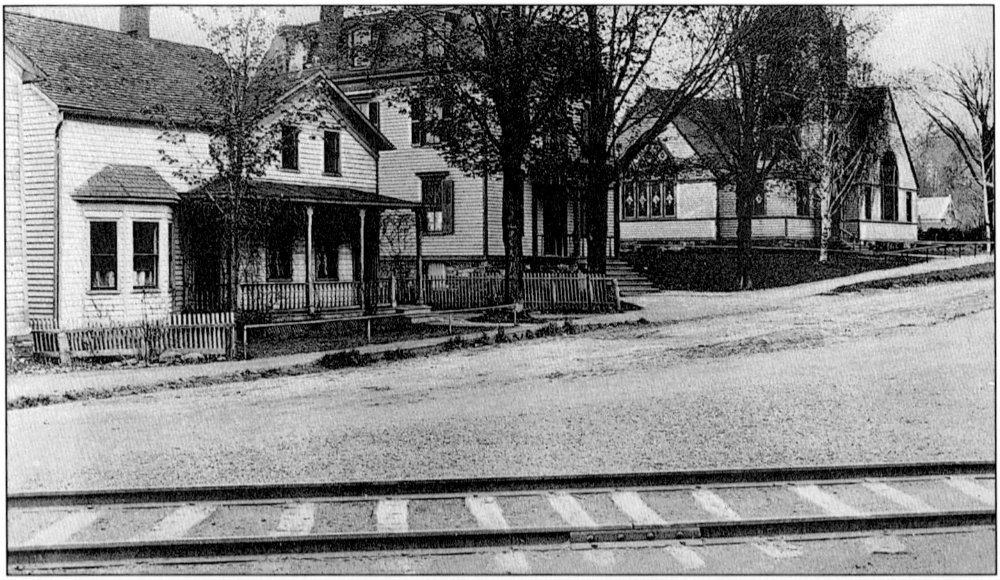

This c. 1911 view of Elm Street shows where the Zambon family lived (on the left) from the 1930s through the 1950s. The apartment house next to it was once home to the Scott, Ryan, and Nicholas families. To the right is St. George's Episcopal Church. The apartment house has been replaced by a road leading to Brookside School. Built by the Chadwicks school system in the 1970s, it is now a junior-senior high school with an Alternative Education Program.

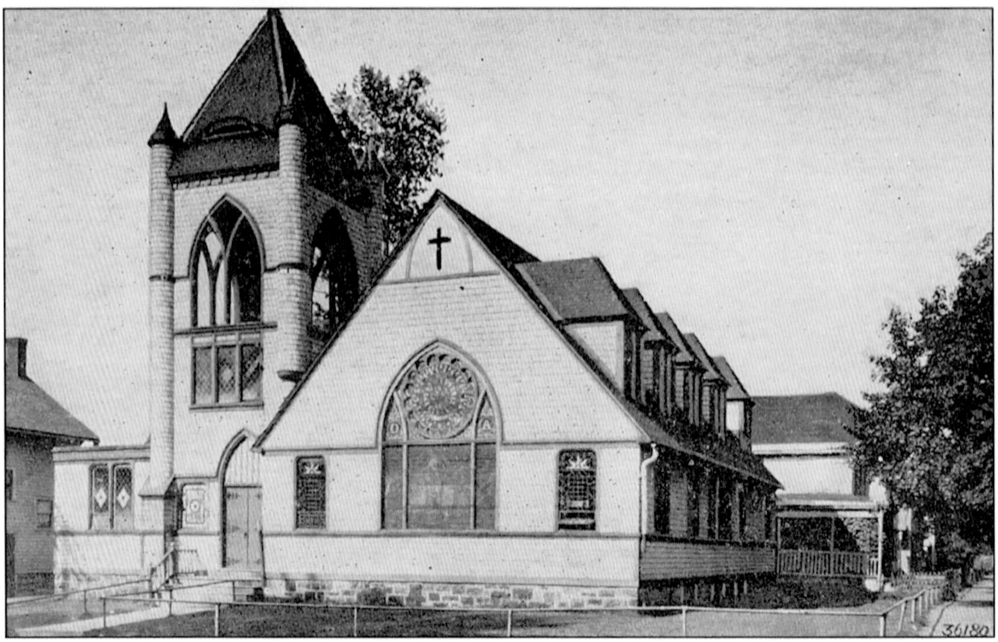

St. George's Episcopal Church, with its Gothic-style edifice and beautiful stained glass windows, was the first church built in the Chadwicks and Willowvale area. Built in 1890, it was erected through the generosity of Mary Ann Wrigley Chadwick in memory of her husband, George W. Chadwick Sr. The congregation of the Church, although small, continues to worship there today.

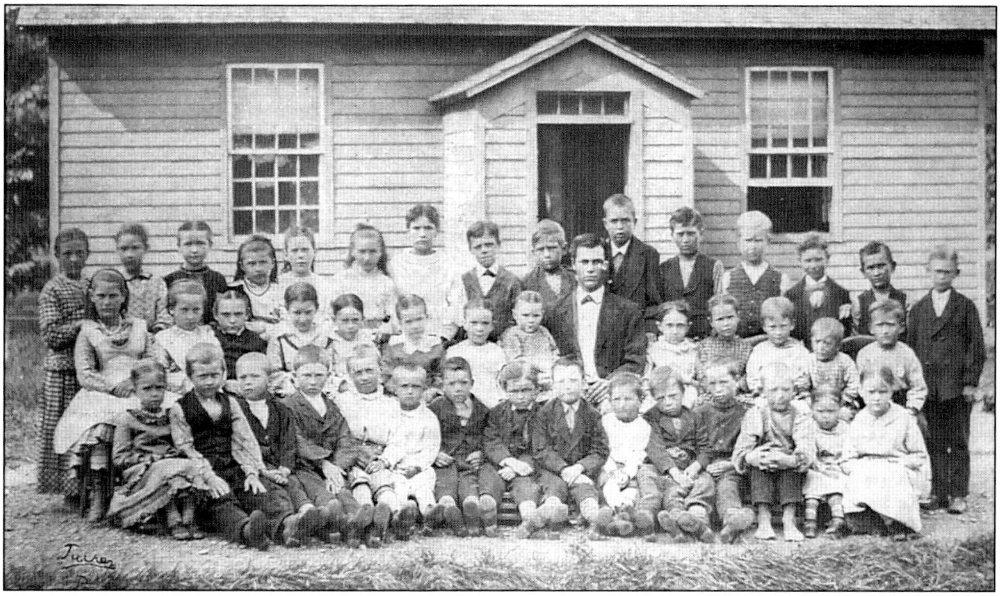

According to Rogers's *History of the Town of Paris* (1881), "the old schoolhouse, located at the forks of the main road, was destroyed by fire" 30 years earlier. The school shown in the photograph was built on mill property to replace it. It was located on Elm Street between the railroad depot and the silk mill. The attire of the pupils and teacher appears to be from the late 1800s. This building was no longer used as a school after a new one was built on School Street. In the 1930s and through the 1940s, the building was the barbershop of Gus DiSavino and Al Caruso. (From the collection of Tom Schafer.)

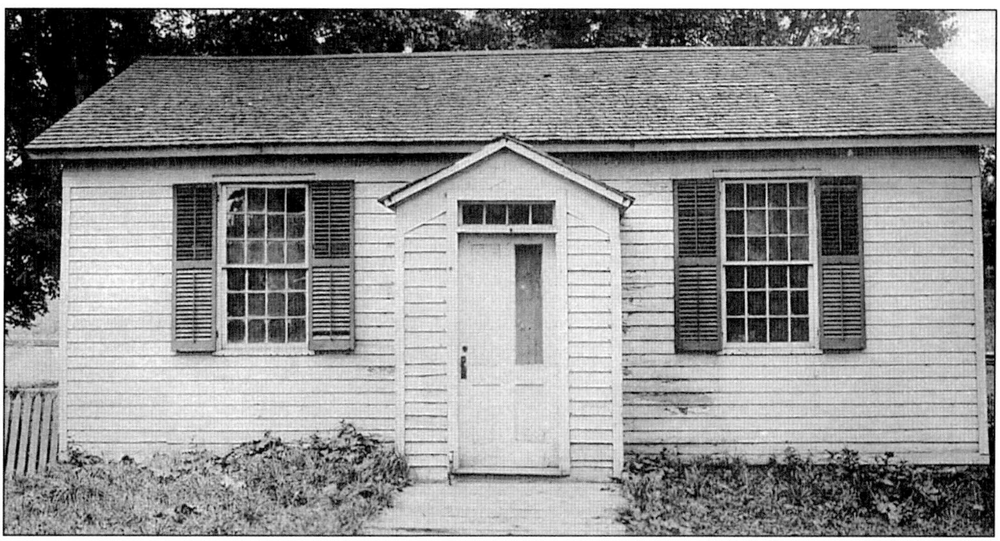

By the early 1950s, the Standard Silk Mill of A.D. Juilliard was preparing to close. The management made an agreement with Martin Shephard to tear down the old school building located on their property. In exchange for this chore, Shephard could salvage the wood and whatever else was usable. The old schoolhouse lives on, built into the rafters of the Shephard's garage on Kellogg Road in Washington Mills. An old cupboard, likely used for school supplies, provides storage in the basement for Joyce Shephard's home-canned preserves. (From the collection of Bob Dicker.)

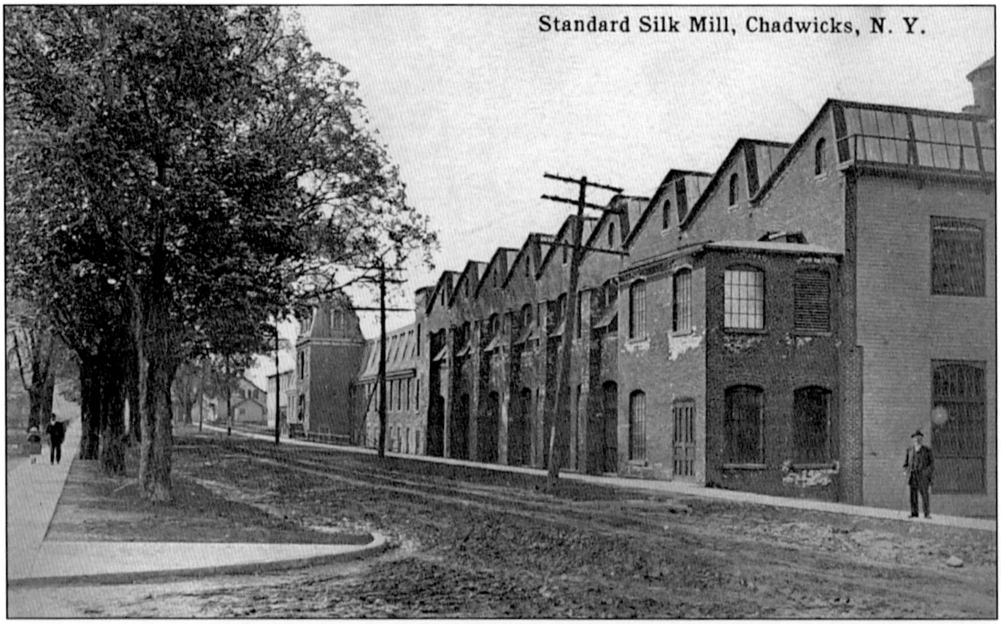

John Chadwick and two other gentlemen formed a partnership in 1813 to establish a cotton goods factory called Eagle Mills. The partnership dissolved and Mr. Chadwick became the sole proprietor. In 1844, the mill burned after being struck by lightning, but was rebuilt. When John Chadwick died in 1858, George W. Chadwick Sr. succeeded his father as proprietor. In 1904, George Sr.'s widow sold the firm to A.D. Juilliard, and it ceased operations in 1953. In 1963, residents petitioned the town of New Hartford to have it razed, stating it was unsafe and a hazard. The Donovan town park now occupies the site.

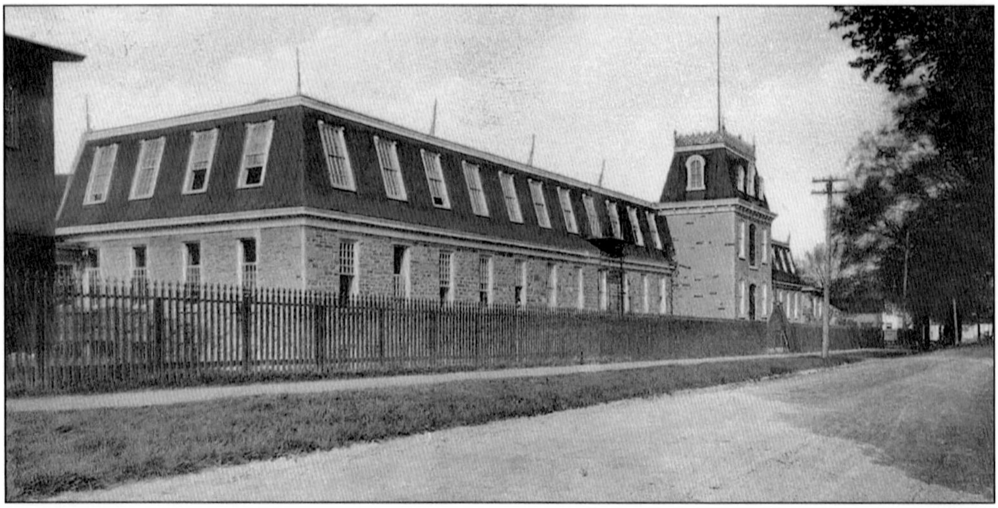

The Standard Silk Company buildings were a place for community activities as well as employment. The maintenance staff of the mill built benches and installed a large screen from ceiling to floor on the second floor to accommodate movie viewers. Adelbert Stauring, a longtime Chadwicks resident, remembers playing the piano for silent movies there, *c.* 1923. At the elaborate "Community Christmas Entertainment", which was held in the "New Building of the Standard Silk Mill" on December 23, 1915, Del Stauring gave a recitation of "Christmas Cheer".

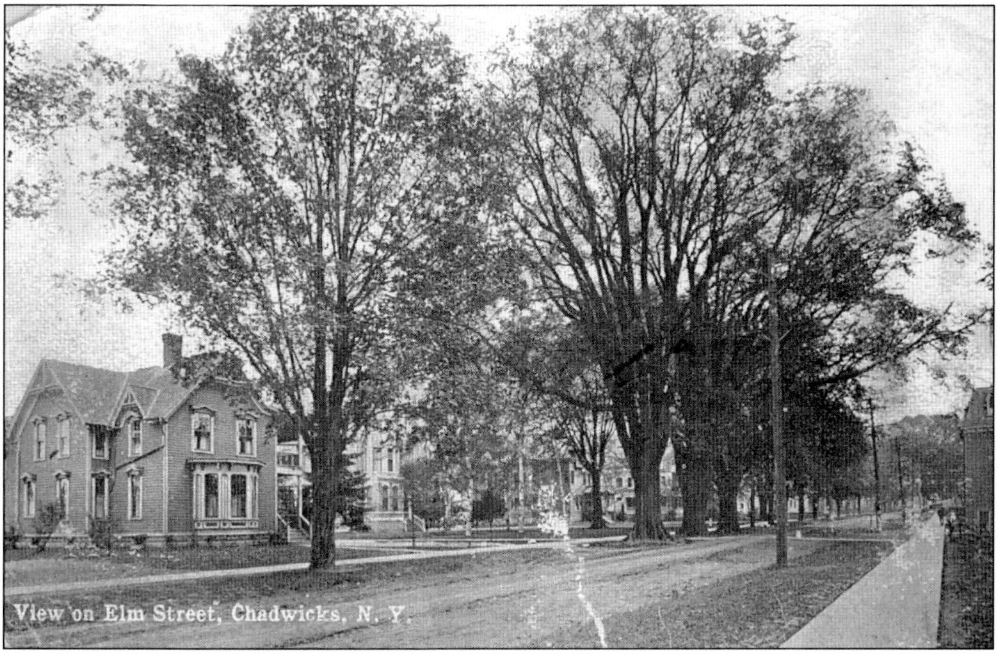

On the south side of Elm Street, on the right of this picture, the stone tower of the Standard Silk Mill is visible. A bell in the tower rang curfew at 9 p.m., signaling children to head for home. The homes on the left have been occupied by the Bast family (who lost two sons in WWII), the Chadwick family, the Donovan family, and the Confer family. The Chadwick family mansion burned in 1962.

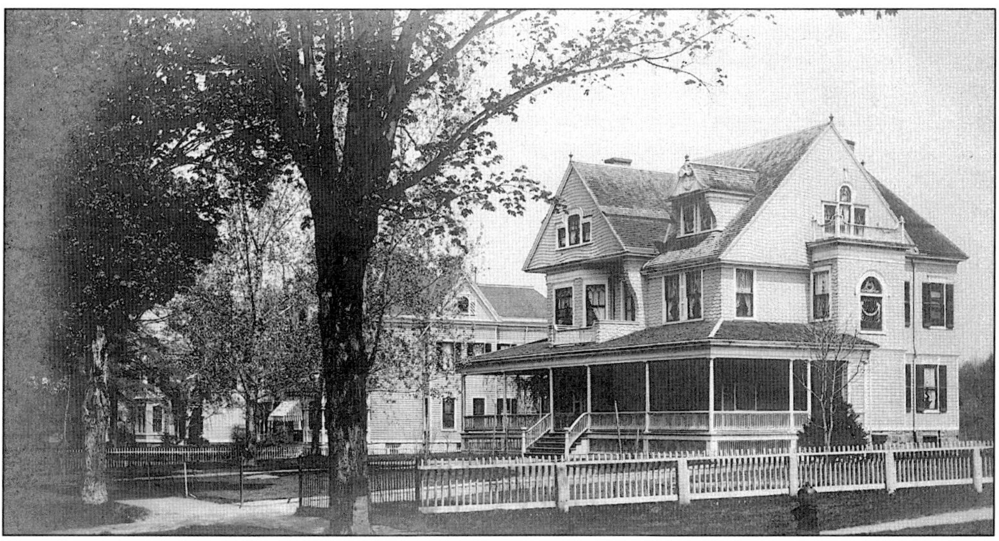

Located across Elm Street from the mill, these homes have been occupied in recent years by the Donald Confer family, Senator James, and Esther Donovan. James Donovan was a popular and respected New York State senator from 1966 until his death in 1990, leaving behind an outstanding record of service. The former Confer home suffered damage to the right section of the porch from a fallen tree during a severe windstorm on Labor Day, 1998.

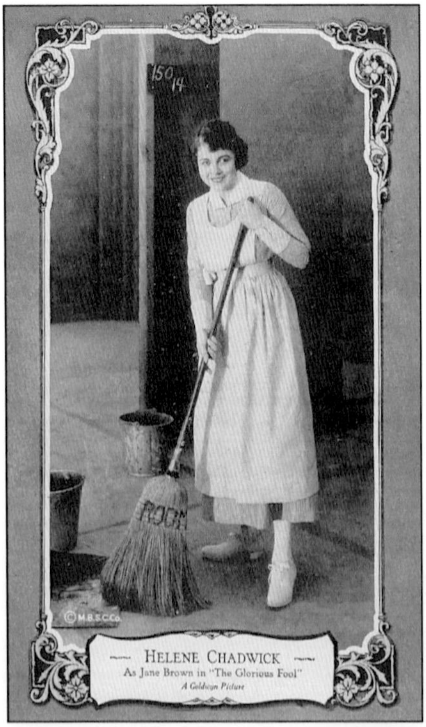

Helene Chadwick, an artist's model who became a silent screen actress, began her movie career in 1917. She was the daughter of George W. Chadwick Jr. and Marie Louise Norton Chadwick. It was reported in a September 1940 *Utica Observer Dispatch* article that Helene Chadwick had died at age 41 as a result of injuries from a fall in her Hollywood home. Considered one of the beauties of the silent screen, she earned $2,000 per week at the peak of her career.

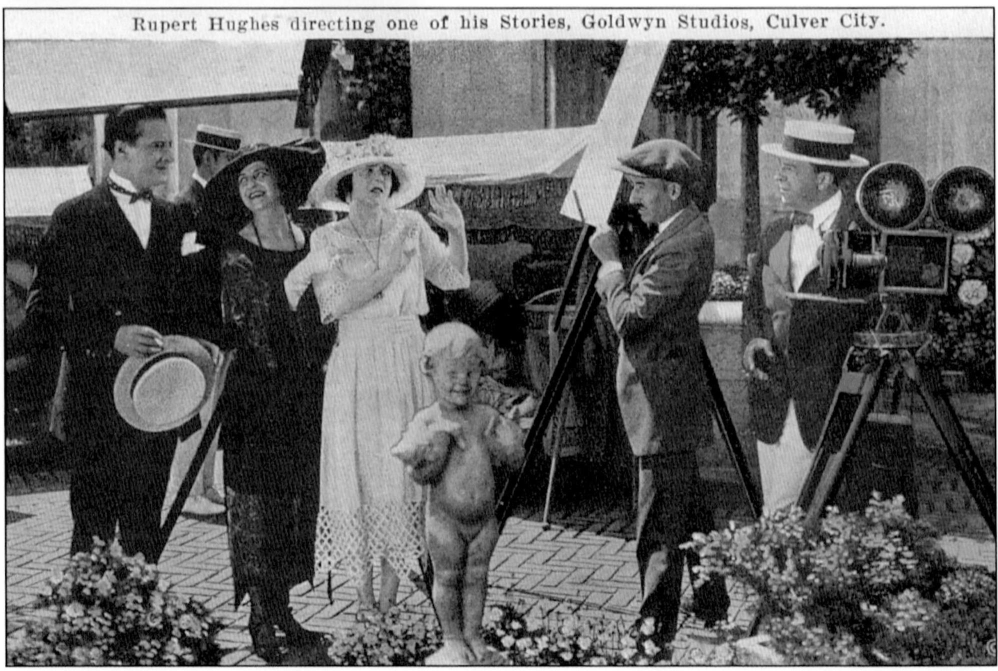

The back of this postcard identifies the people in the scene as, from left to right, Gaston Glass, Mrs. Rupert Hughes, Helene Chadwick, John Mescall (cameraman), and Rupert Hughes, author and director. The scene was from a silent film called *Gimme*. With the advent of talking motion pictures, Helene, like many other actors and actresses who were deemed vocally inadequate, was out of work. She was divorced from director William Wellman in 1923.

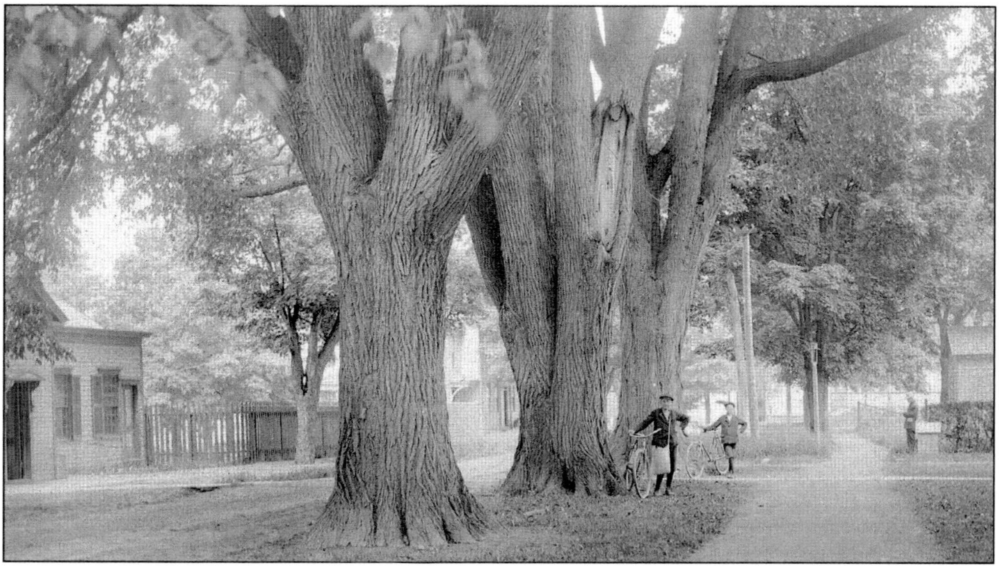

Like many small towns in the early 1900s, Chadwicks had an Elm Street named for the large majestic elm trees gracing its borders. The boys and their bicycles are dwarfed by the giant elms. Some of the trees, planted as early as the 1700s, were victims of the fungus blight of the 1950s that destroyed numerous old elms. Trees of up to 15 feet in circumference were lost, much to the dismay of villagers. This postcard is *c.* 1907.

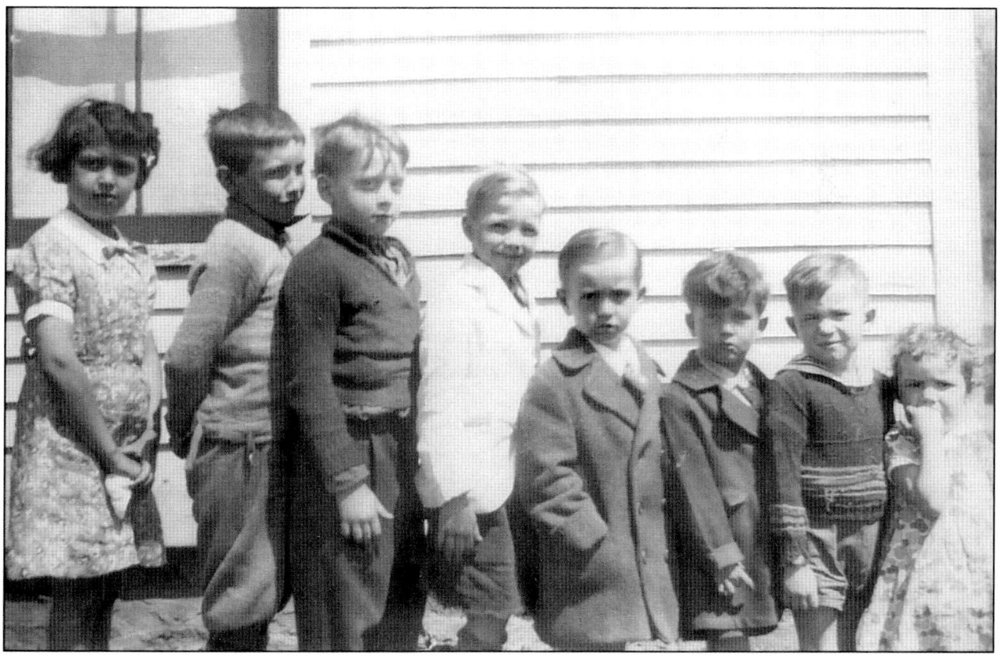

This photograph of Elm Street's version of "Our Gang" was taken *c.* 1937, but the occasion has been forgotten. Shown are, from left to right, Eleanor Gottuso Allen, Robert Jury, Melville Edwards, James Brodt, James Mykytyn, Peter Gottuso, Everett Perkins, and his little sister, Betty Perkins Simmons.

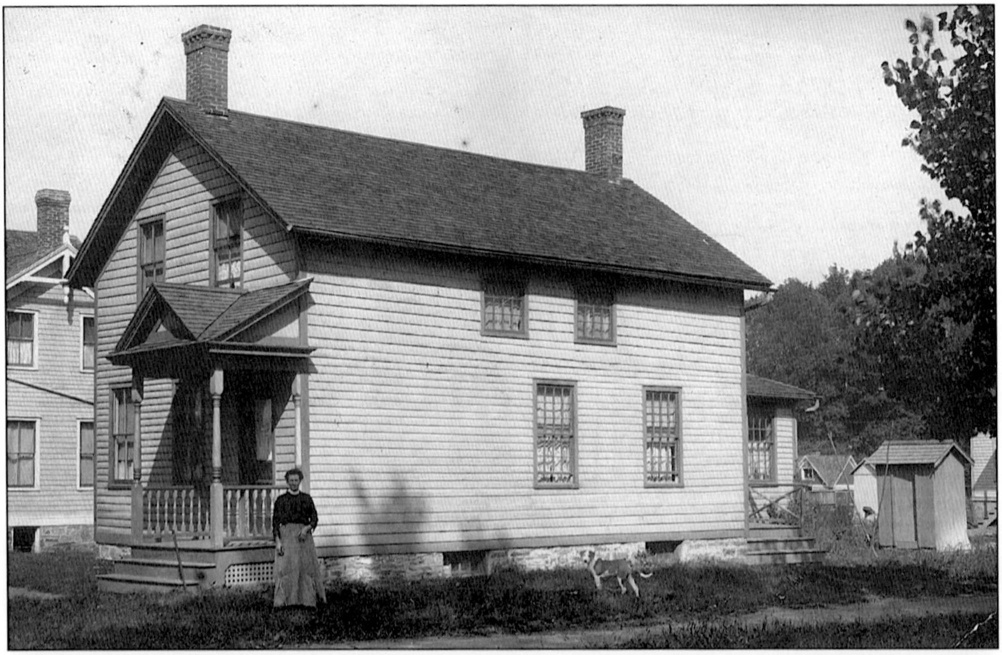

At the corner of Elm and School Street is the home of Michael Belowich, a Chadwicks resident from the age of one. Gone is the outhouse of 1909 that Mike recalls as being the source of a bit of mischief many years ago. A group of neighborhood boys decided to tip over the privy, which was owned at the time by the Camp family. Unfortunately, the lady of the house was occupying it at the time. This trick was apparently a tradition, as another Chadwicks lad 15 years younger than Mike tells a similar story.

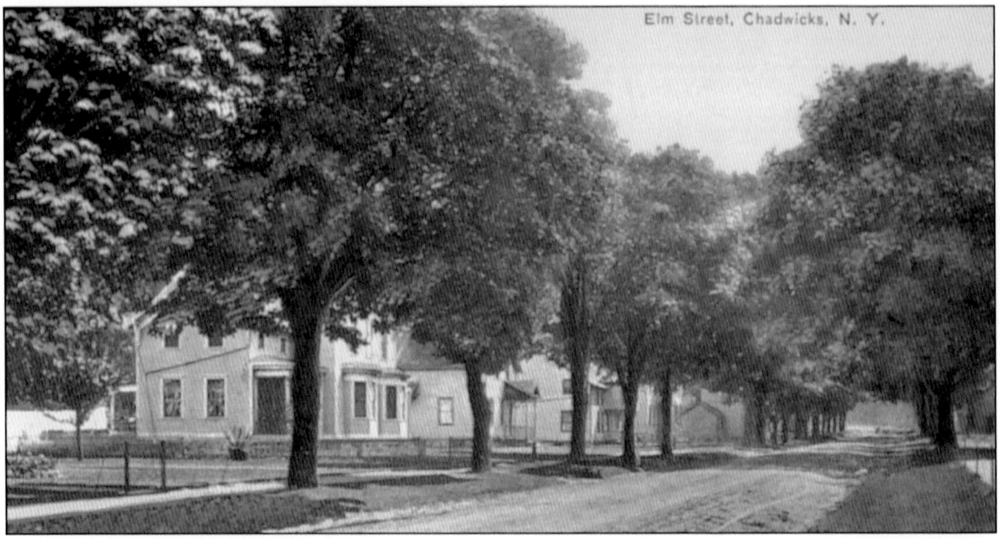

In the 1920s and 1930s, four generations of the Edwards family resided in the duplex house (the third one from the left) of William and Florence Goodier Edwards. In the upper story lived Florence's mother, Adeline Tanner Goodier, who died in 1934 at age 93, and William and Florence's daughter, Luetta, with her daughter Marion. William and Florence's son Alonzo, his wife Lena, and their son Melville lived in the lower apartment. The second house from the left (pictured above) is the home of Mike Belowich. School Street runs between these two homes.

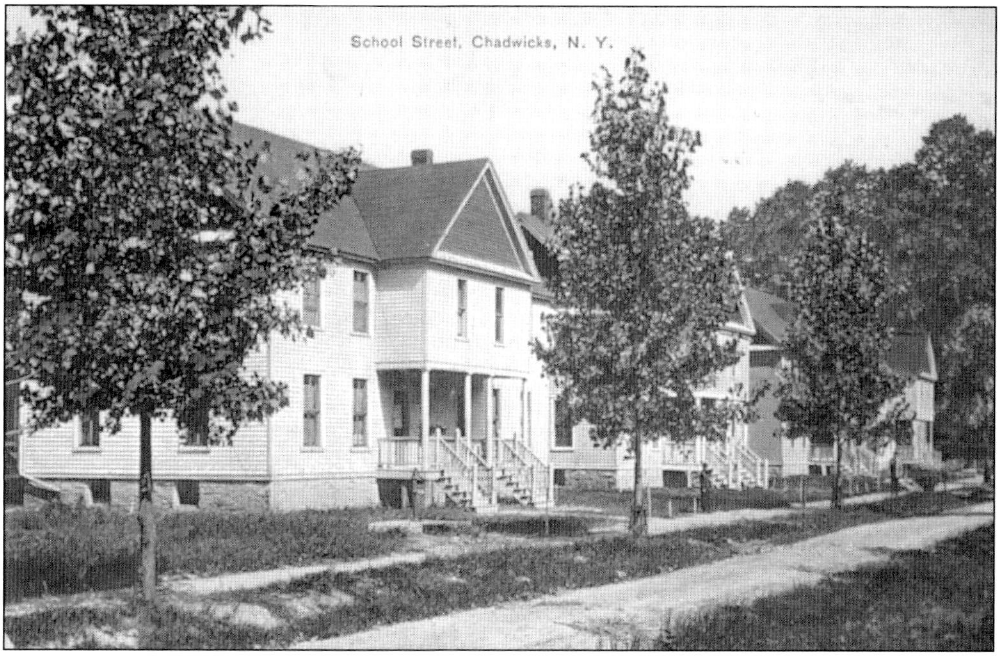

School Street, running north from Elm Street, was logically named for the school erected there in the early 1900s. Spacious two-family homes, built by the mill, lined the west side of the street with the schoolhouse on the opposite side. In the 1930s and 1940s, old movies were shown at the former school; for reasons unknown and perhaps best left unexplored, it was called "The Old Rat Hole."

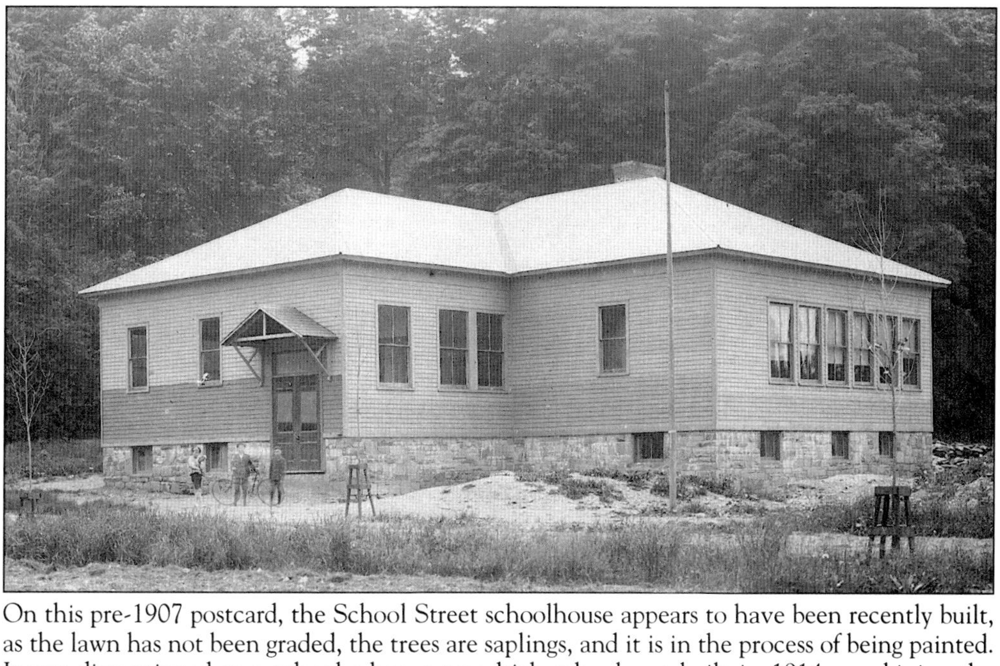

On this pre-1907 postcard, the School Street schoolhouse appears to have been recently built, as the lawn has not been graded, the trees are saplings, and it is in the process of being painted. It was discontinued as a school when a new high school was built in 1914, combining the Chadwicks and Willowvale schools. The building still stands, with a second story added, and is now an apartment house.

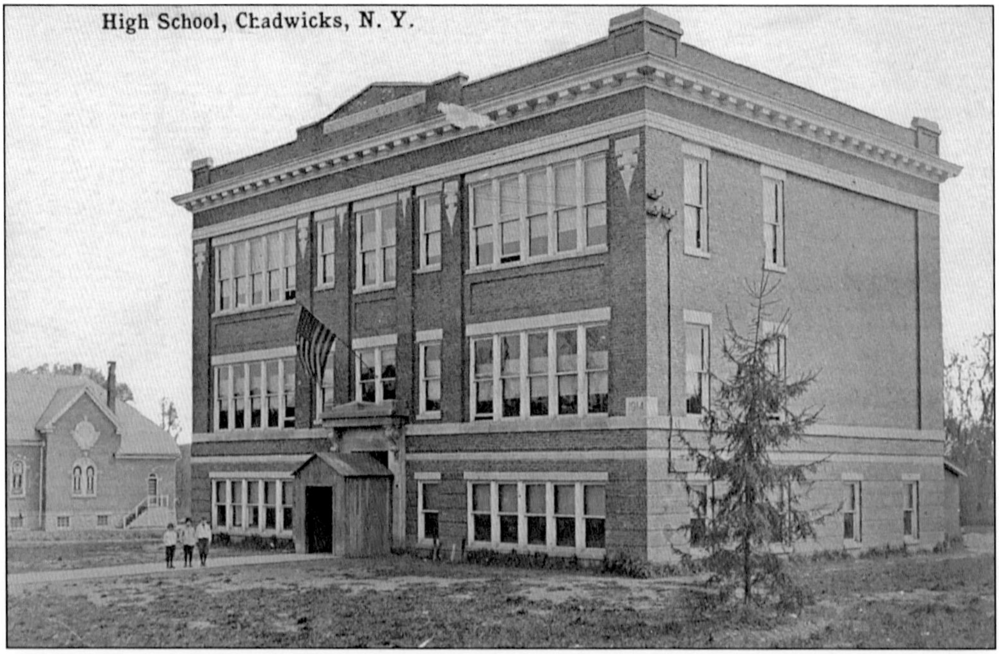

The Chadwicks School, built in 1914–15, graduated its first class of two boys and seven girls in 1922. A source of social activity as well as an educational institution, the school was a focal point of the community. The annual senior class play, trips to Albany and Washington, D.C., and music lessons provided the alumni with a learning experience as well as fond memories. Mary E. Daly was the principal and an exceptional algebra teacher at Chadwicks for half of its 70-year life.

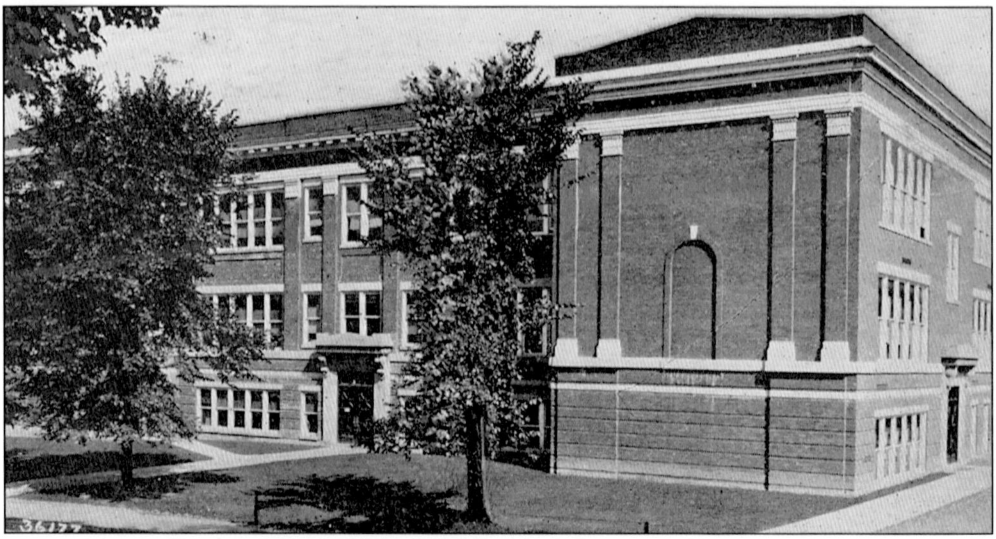

Increasing enrollment necessitated the building of additions at each end of the school in 1930. A one-story addition was added in 1973. By the 1980s, however, enrollment had declined, and Chadwicks merged with the Sauquoit Central School District. The last to graduate from Chadwicks was the Class of 1984. Sauquoit initially used the school for seventh- and eighth-graders, but in 1990 the building was sold. Subsequently, the old Chadwicks High School was a fitness center, and is now occupied by the Word of Life Christian Church.

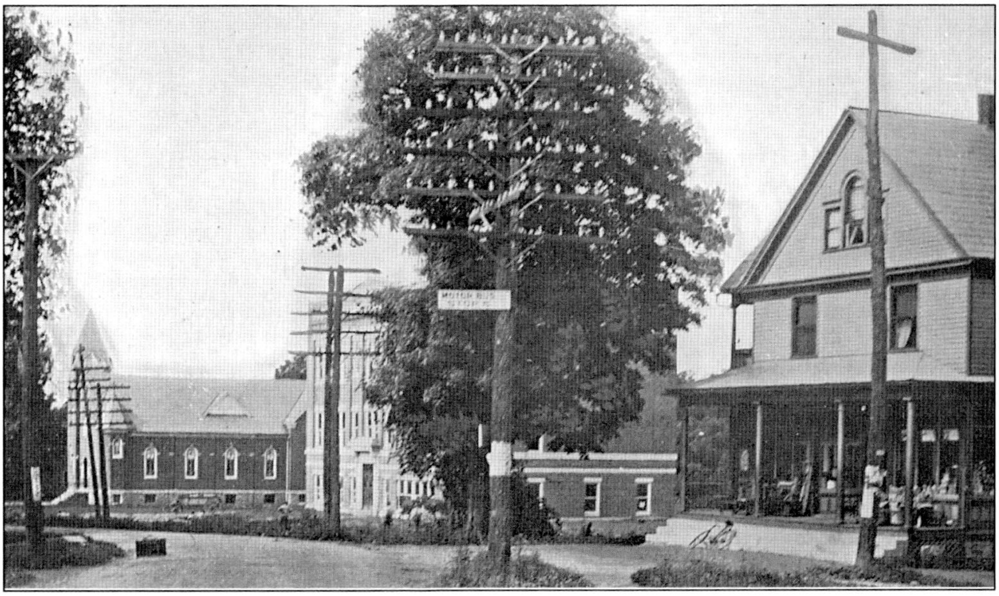

This was called Jones's Corner in the 1930s and 1940s, after the proprietor of a general store that occupied the northeast corner of Elm and Main Street. The new Chadwicks High School, before its additions, stands next to St. Anthony of Padua Catholic Church. In later years, c. 1920, Warren Fisk's Funeral Service and residence was built between the school and the store. In 1930, St. Anthony's Church constructed a rectory to the right of the church.

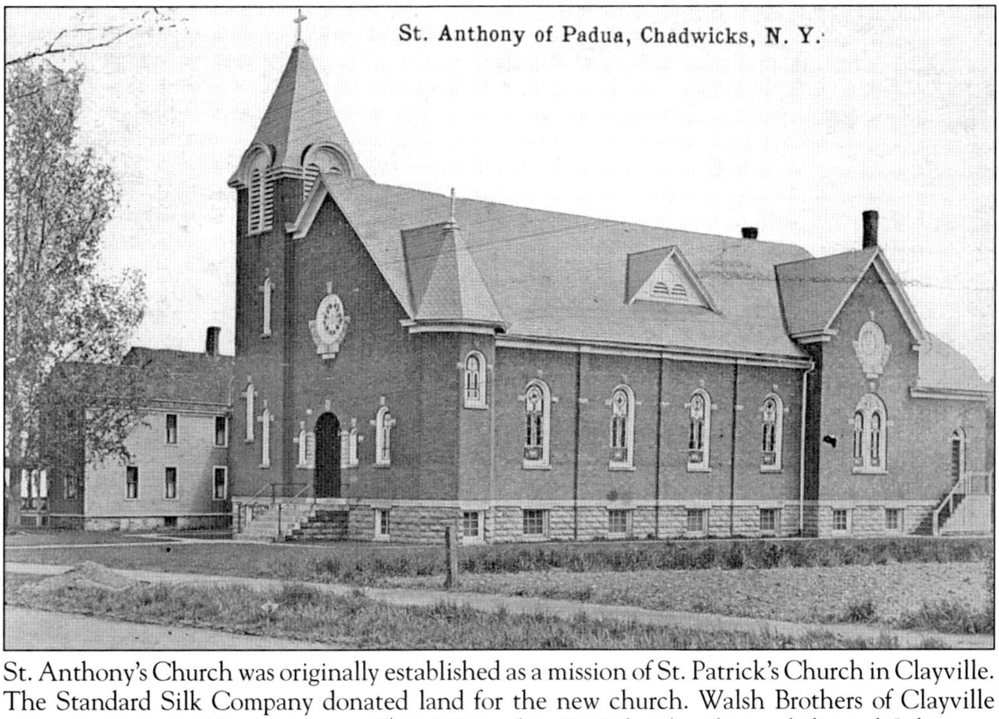

St. Anthony's Church was originally established as a mission of St. Patrick's Church in Clayville. The Standard Silk Company donated land for the new church. Walsh Brothers of Clayville constructed the building at a cost of $10,000, and in 1908 the church was dedicated. It became independent of St. Patrick's Church in 1928, and Rev. John Walsh served as pastor. In 1959, a convent was established in the former LaQuay home next to the church.

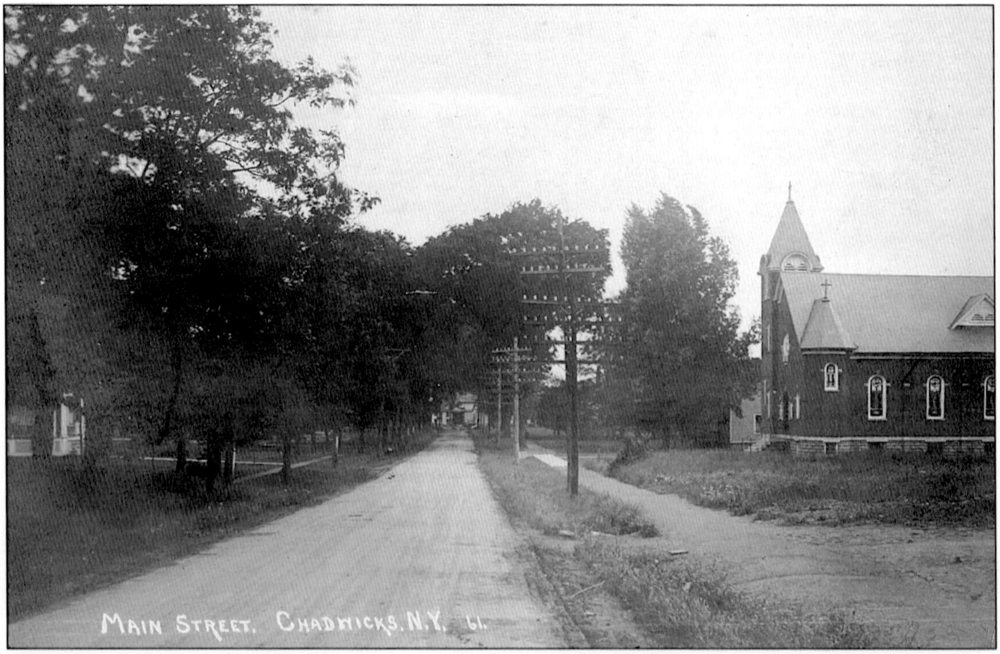

This view looks toward Willowvale on what has variously been known as the Bridgewater Turnpike, Main Street, Route 8, and now Oneida Street. St. Anthony's Church is on the right. Just a little north of the house that is next to the church is the line that marked the boundary between Chadwicks and Willowvale.

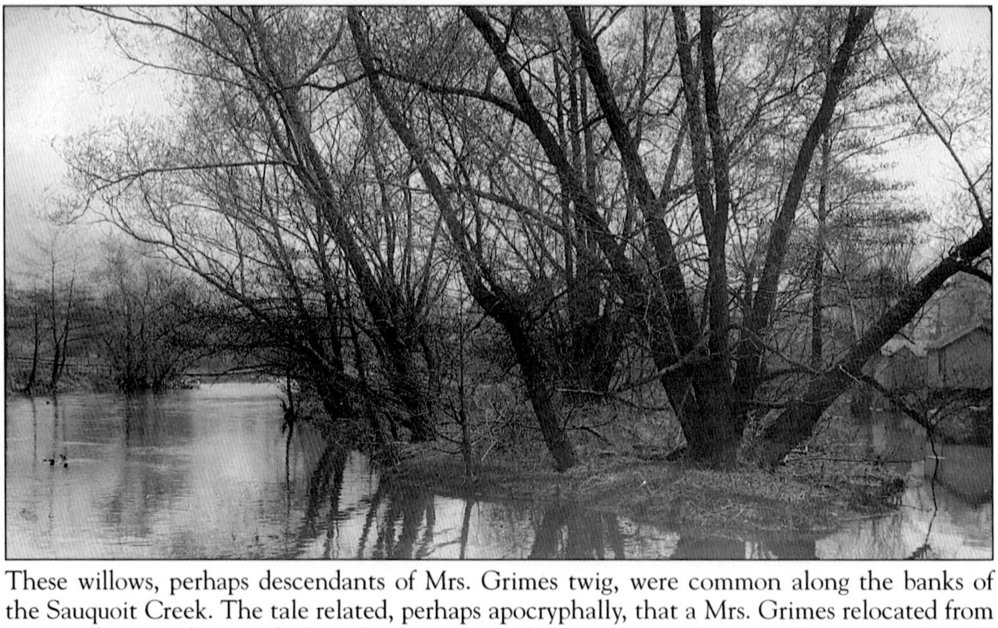

These willows, perhaps descendants of Mrs. Grimes twig, were common along the banks of the Sauquoit Creek. The tale related, perhaps apocryphally, that a Mrs. Grimes relocated from Pepperell, Massachusetts, by horseback in 1791. She cut a sprout from a willow tree at her old homestead to use as a riding crop, and on her arrival at her new home in Willowvale, stuck the willow in the ground, which sprouted and grew into a tree. Other sprouts were cut from the original tree and planted throughout the valley. (Although the postcard identifies this scene as Chadwicks, it is believed to be Willowvale.)

Six

WILLOWVALE

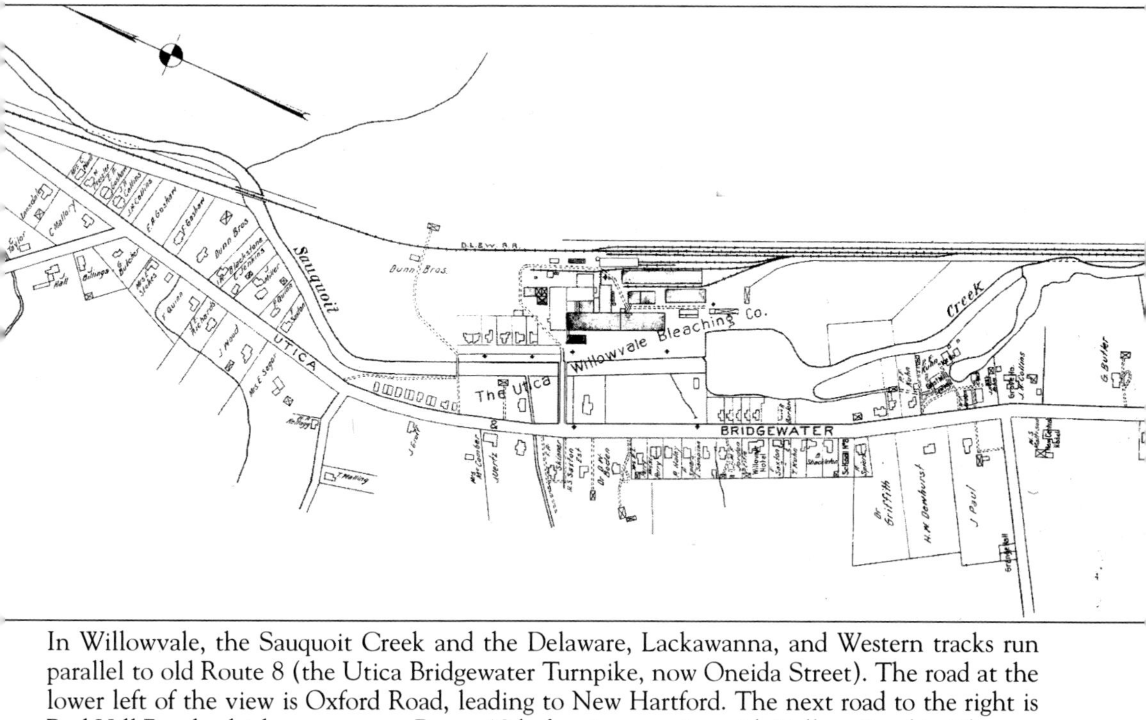

In Willowvale, the Sauquoit Creek and the Delaware, Lackawanna, and Western tracks run parallel to old Route 8 (the Utica Bridgewater Turnpike, now Oneida Street). The road at the lower left of the view is Oxford Road, leading to New Hartford. The next road to the right is Red Hill Road, which runs west to Route 12 before intersecting with Kellogg Road in Clinton. The road on the right is Grange Hill Road, the site of the Grange Hall in 1907. It was later occupied by the American Legion, before they moved to the former Valley Inn/Pine Lodge site. The Grange is now a woodworking shop.

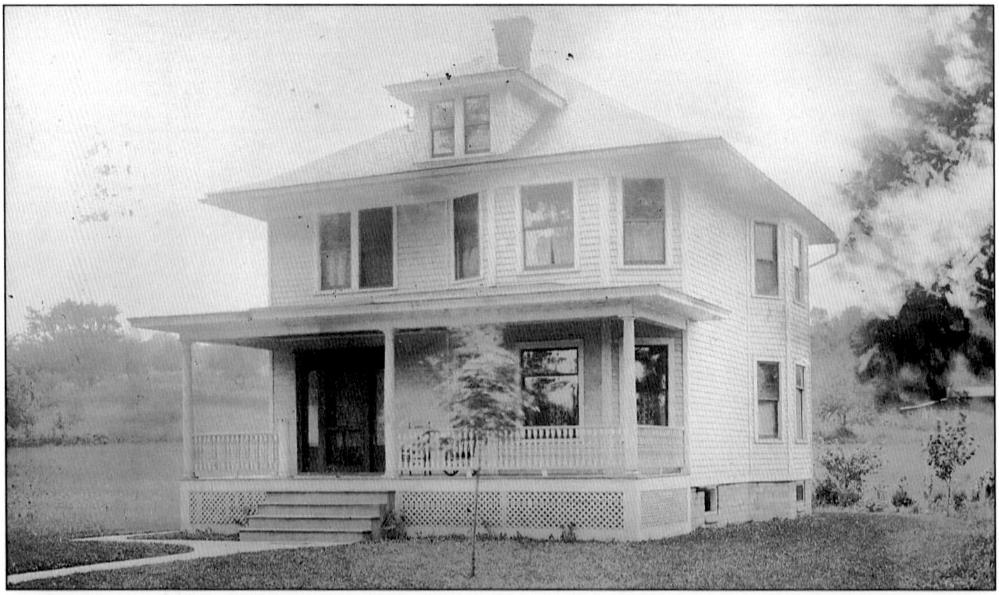

A vintage postcard purchased in Parsippany, New Jersey, found its way back to the Sauquoit Valley area. It had been sent to a woman in South New Berlin, New York, and was signed by Ola (Colwell), the resident of this Willowvale home, c. 1915. Later, the Colwells built another house next door, and their former home became a rooming house. In the 1920s, George Richards boarded here and was employed by Ola's husband, Frank Colwell, in his barbershop.

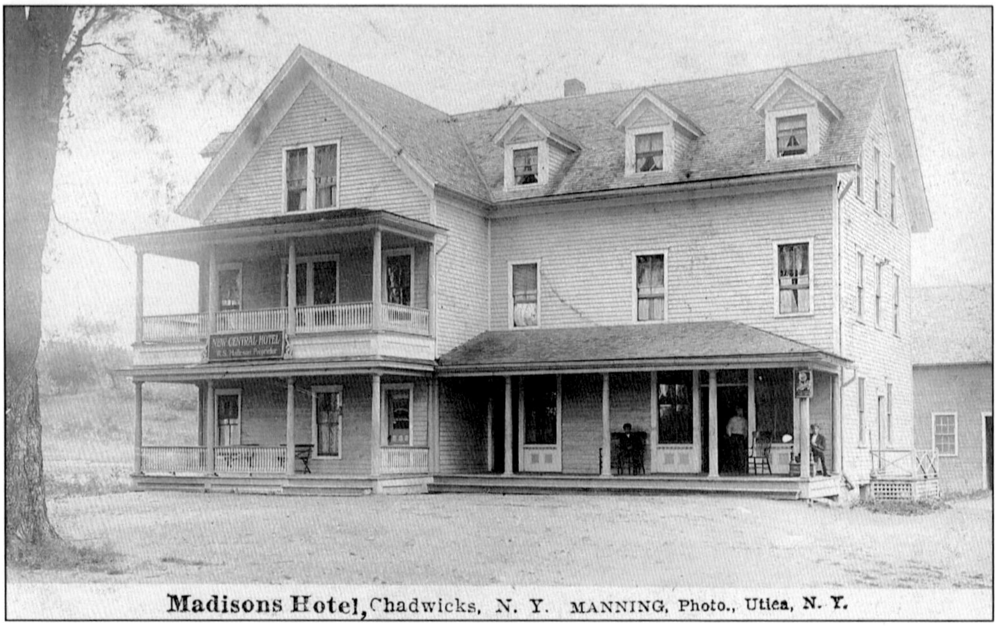

The Matteson (not the Madison) Hotel in Willowvale (not in Chadwicks) later became the Hotel Willowvale. In 1907, it was the New Central Hotel. W.S. Matteson, the proprietor, charged $1.50 per day for rooms and all modern conveniences: electric lights, excellent cuisine, and a livery. Owned by Lawrence and Louise Pavese in the 1940s and 1950s, it still stands on the West side of Oneida Street. It is next to an automobile sales and service station of more recent vintage on the corner of Grange Hill Road.

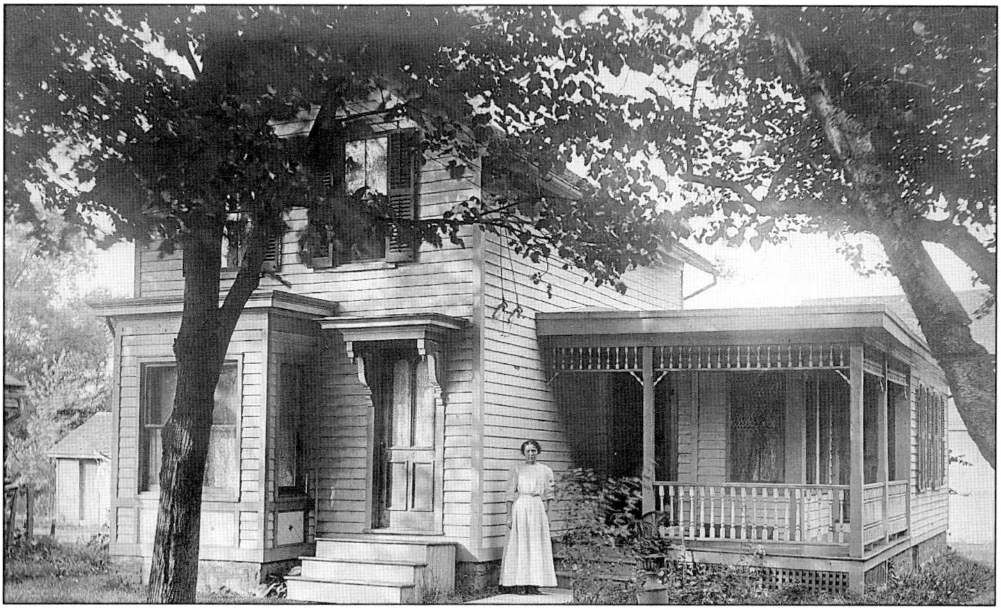

Ella Cavanaugh poses for a traveling photographer in front of her home on Oneida Street (then Main Street). Ella and two relatives, Mrs. Frank Green and Agnes True, lived next door to the Richards family home, the corner of which is visible on the left. The building on the left in the back, now torn down, was a garage, which had been turned into a playhouse for the Richards children. The home, with some alterations, still looks today much as it did then.

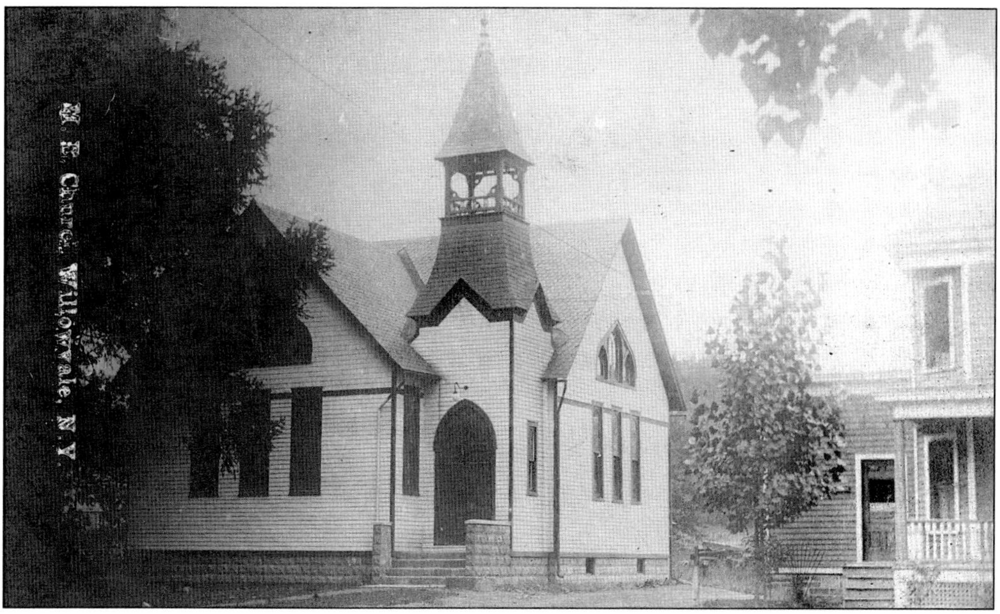

Until 1995, when its congregation merged with the Sauquoit United Methodists, this was the Willowvale United Methodist Church, erected in 1907. Due to a dwindling membership, it was leased and then sold to the Faith in Christ Fellowship. Between 1919 and 1920, the foundation was raised to make room for Sunday school rooms and a kitchen. While building the church, the congregation met in the old schoolhouse (later the home of Thomas Flynn). The office and residence of Dr. and Mrs. E.M. Griffith is on the right.

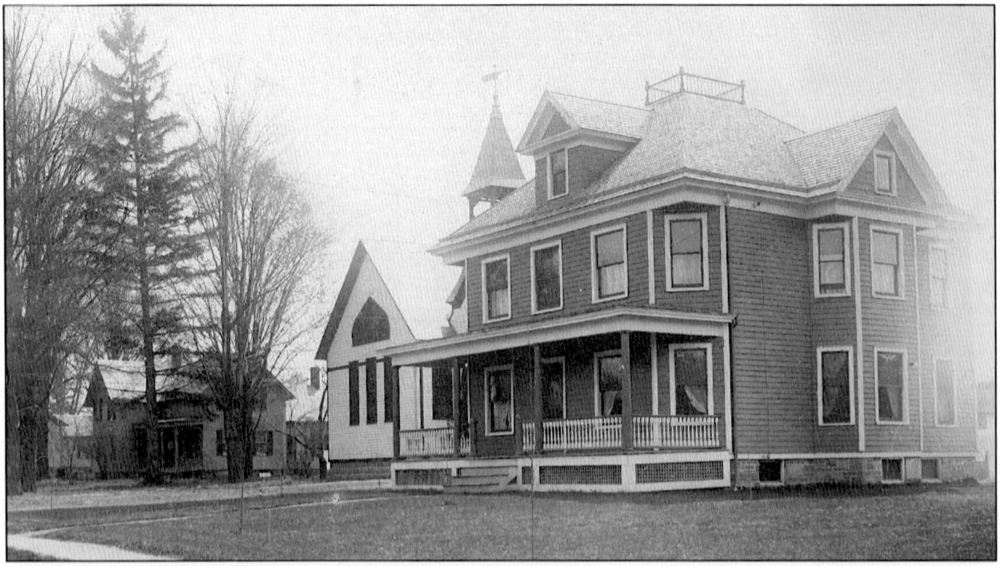

Dr. Edwin Griffith's residence and office later served the same purpose for Dr. David Rosendale. Dr. Griffith, who made house calls, delivered many of the valley's babies. He began his practice in the early 1900s and served until his death in 1946. In 1915, Dr. Griffith was chairman of an elaborate "Community Christmas Entertainment" held in the silk mill in Chadwicks. This event concluded with a processional to the community Christmas tree at Ononda Club Park in Willowvale at the corner of Bleachery Avenue.

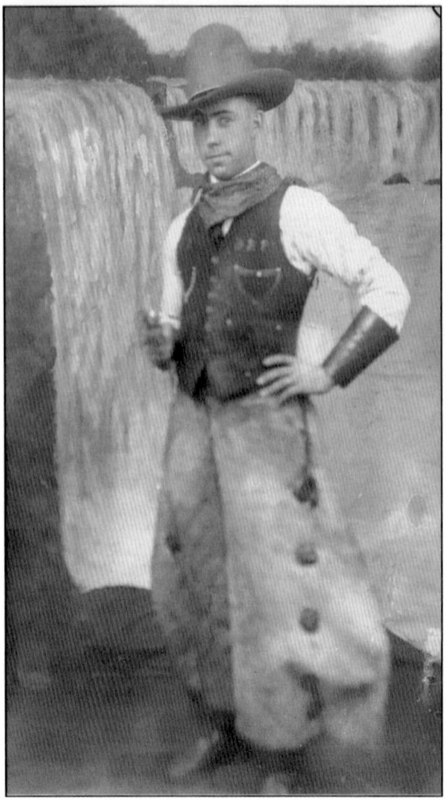

The Wild West meets Niagara Falls. From *c.* 1902, freelance photographers began to take photographs of small towns and their inhabitants. Tourist spots offered "real photo" postcards for souvenirs. The background in this *c.* 1926 postcard taken in Buffalo, New York, reflects that area, but the costume is more appropriate for the Wild West. The "cowboy" is George Richards (the author's father). He was a barber in Willowvale for 56 years; the photograph was taken while he was attending barber school in Buffalo. The barbershop that he built still stands on Oneida Street, across from Dr. Griffith's former residence.

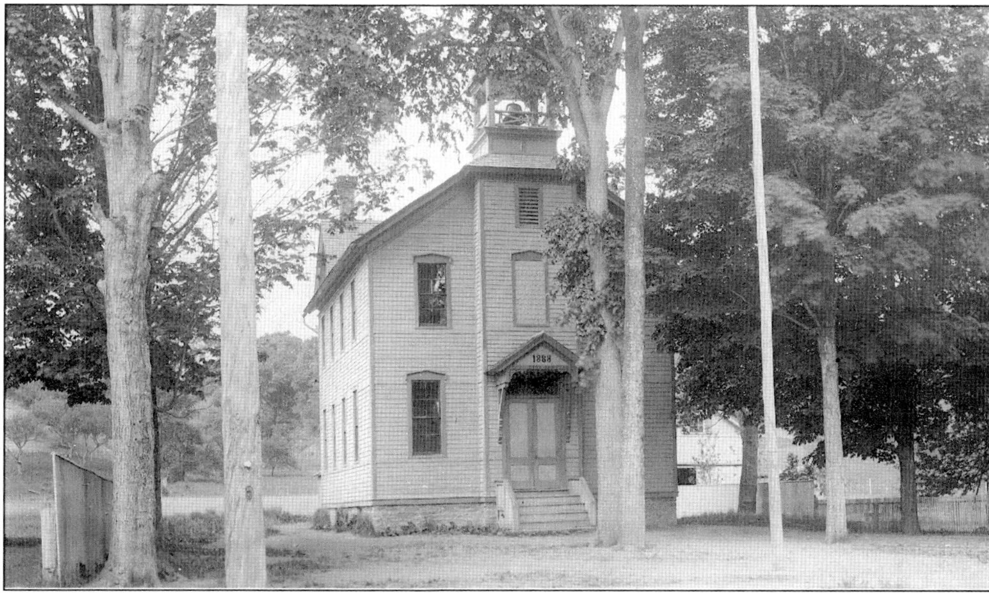

The present-day brick school structure built in 1914 in Chadwicks replaced this Willowvale School and the School Street School in Chadwicks. Once a girl's club for Willowvale Bleachery employees, it was converted in the 1930s into a two-family house, occupied on one side by Edward and Florence Murray and, on the other, by Thomas and Regina Flynn and their families. Mr. Flynn purchased the house in the early 1950s when the bleachery moved. Located on Oneida Street (Old Route 8), it is west of the present Route 8 Arterial.

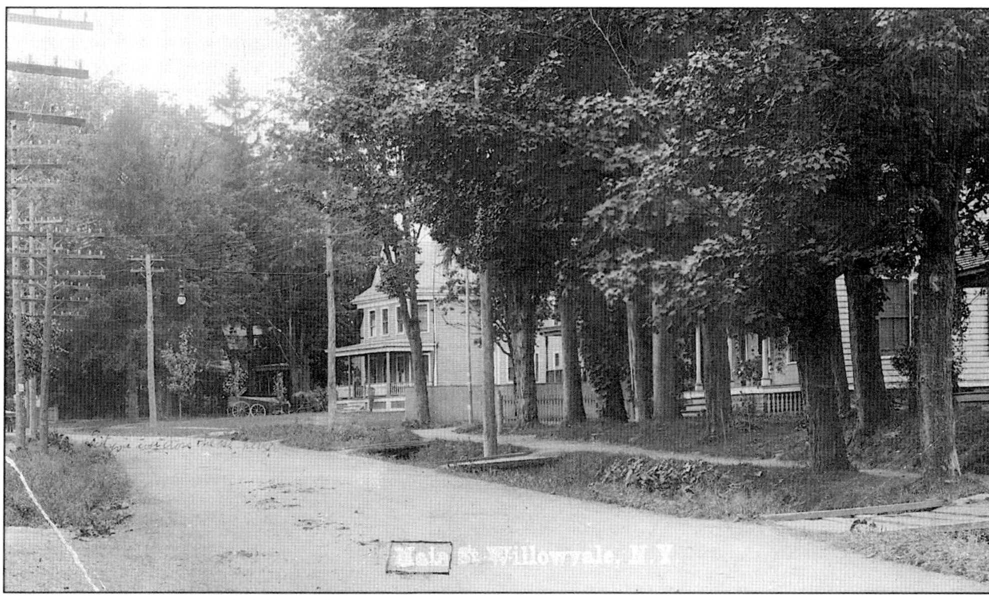

This view shows Dr. Griffith's house on the left and the Irving and Martha Edwards residence on the right. The area shown in this picture is across the road from the old George Richards barbershop and Irving Edwards's Body Shop, which was formerly the site of Townsend and Waddell's Service Station. In the center is a small corner of the present Raymond and Martha Groff home. Between this residence and the Edwards's home, is the building (not visible) that was once the Willowvale Schoolhouse.

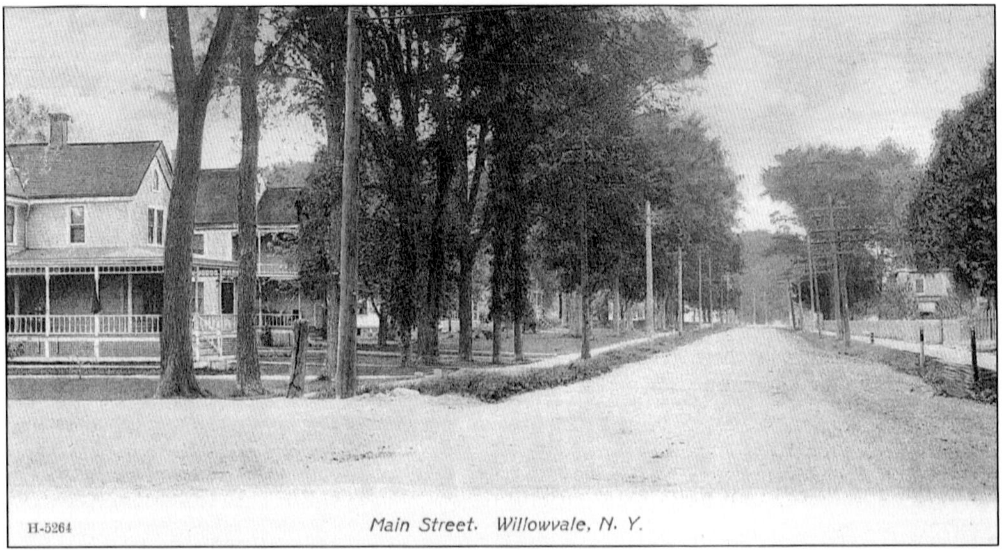

The fence on the right of this view provides a clue to its location, since it can be seen in the next postcard of the Reagan and Hart Store. On the left is what was the home of the Clifford Dougherty family from 1932 to 1955. This home had earlier been the home of Jesse and Lillian Richards Dougherty, Clifford's parents. It is presently the Callahan residence. The dirt road, later paved and widened to about twice its early width, now passes much closer to the houses. Next to the Doughertys was the Kuhn family residence.

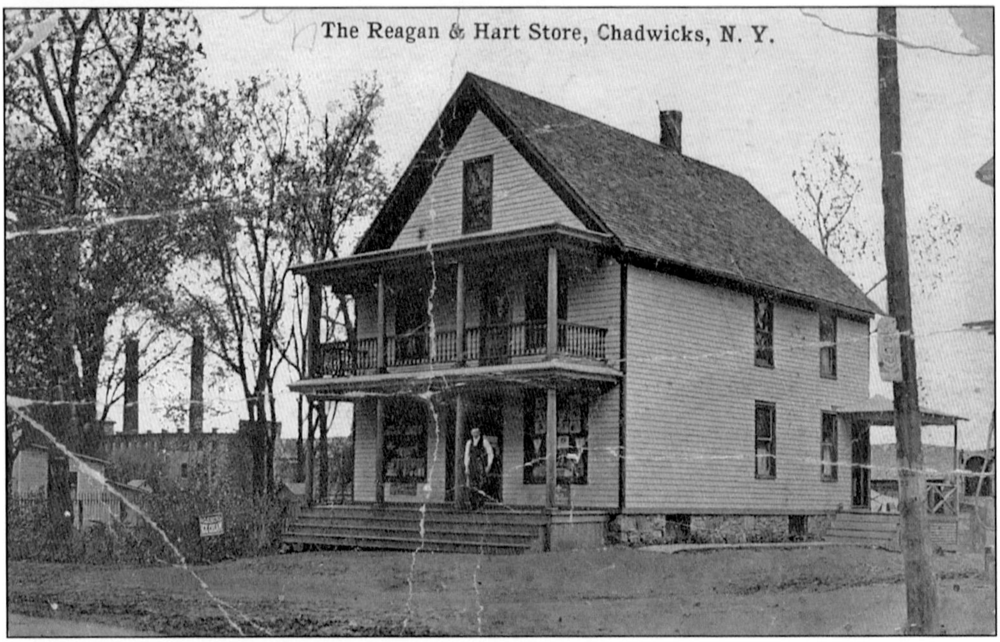

Although the postcard indicates Chadwicks, this store was actually located in Willowvale. The proprietors were James Reagan and his father-in-law, Thomas F. Hart. In the 1940s, it was a tavern called the Valley Inn. It later was enlarged and became Pine Lodge, a bar, restaurant, and dance hall. Purchased in 1981 by the American Legion Edward Clonan Post No. 1000, it now provides catering facilities and Friday night fish fries. Many additions make the building unrecognizable today. The Willowvale Bleachery is in the left background.

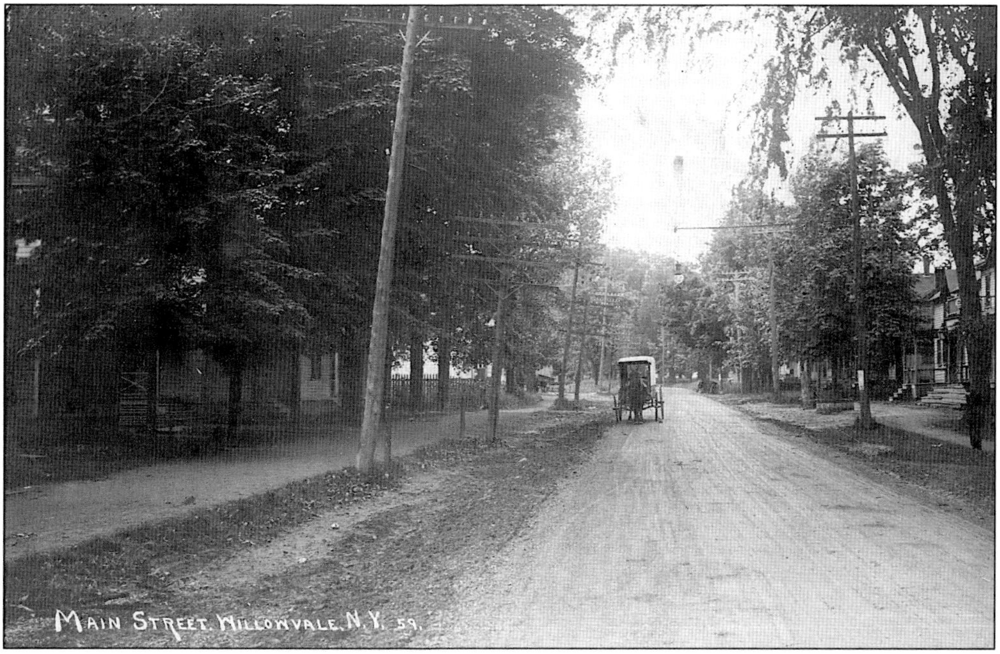

A horse-and-buggy plods down the narrow dirt road on Main Street, *c.* 1917, pulling a deliveryman on his daily rounds. Daily deliveries were routine, since food spoiled quickly in iceboxes. Although the poles are evidence of the availability of electricity, modern electric refrigerators were still rare. A 1924 catalog featured only iceboxes. In 1933, a Montgomery Ward catalog had one electric and one kerosene model refrigerator for sale. The steps to what was once the Old Spain Hotel are visible on the right.

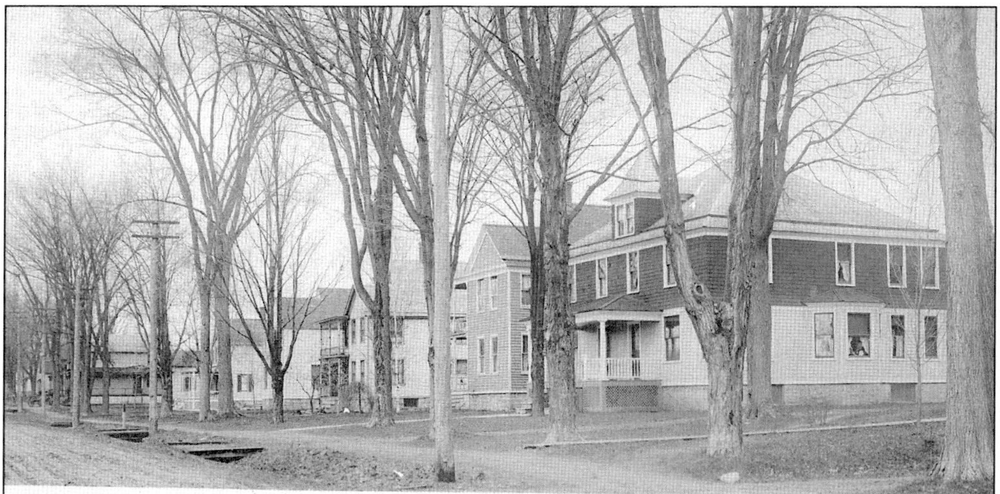

Main Street. Willowvale, N. Y. Manning....Pho., Utica,N.Y

Another Manning postcard is of the west side of Main Street. At the far left is the Old Spain Hotel, now razed, and on the right, several residences, including George Burns's home and store, and the Spears/Dr. Rower home, with the two story porch. In the 1940s and 1950s, George Burns operated a drug store and soda fountain here. A typical teenage hangout complete with a jukebox, the amiable proprietor allowed the teenagers to carve their initials on the wooden booth tables. This postcard dates to *c.* 1906. (From the collection of Tom Schafer.)

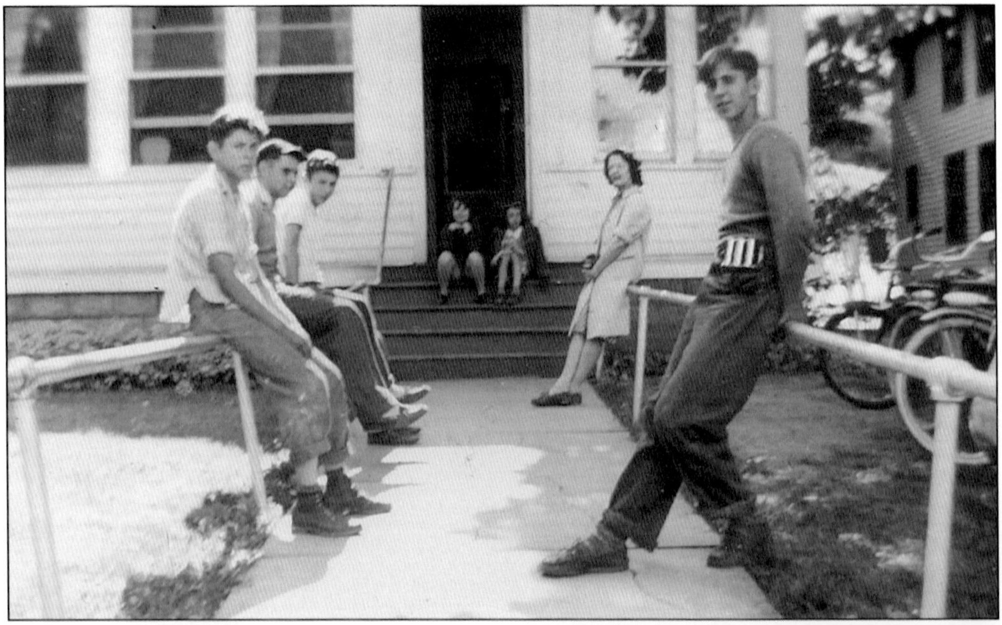

Marian Richards (Jones), who worked at the soda fountain as a teenager, snapped this photograph of a typical day at George Burns's store. The boys lined the iron rail fence to girl-watch, much to the discomfort of the girls. Shown are, from left to right, Raymond Shephard, Edward Bogan, (perhaps) Tony Billman, Miriam Clifford (Llewellyn), and Calvin Nicholas, sporting a coin container on his belt. Nicholas' newspaper bag hangs from the bicycle's handlebars. On the steps, from left to right, are Geraldine Burns (the proprietor's daughter), and Evelyn Richards (Edwards).

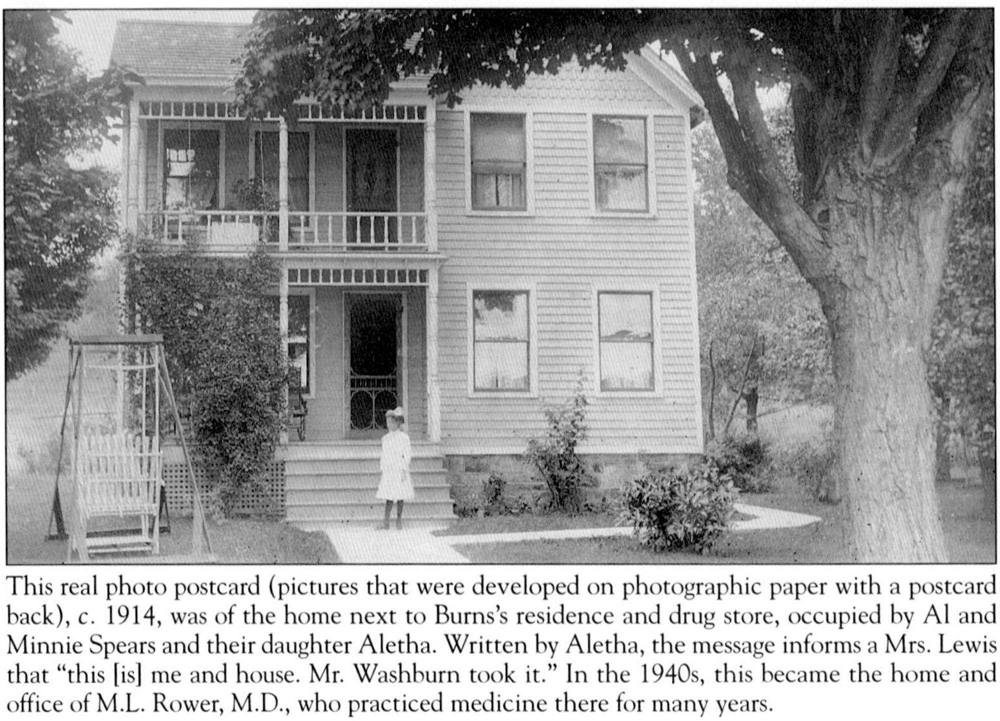

This real photo postcard (pictures that were developed on photographic paper with a postcard back), *c.* 1914, was of the home next to Burns's residence and drug store, occupied by Al and Minnie Spears and their daughter Aletha. Written by Aletha, the message informs a Mrs. Lewis that "this [is] me and house. Mr. Washburn took it." In the 1940s, this became the home and office of M.L. Rower, M.D., who practiced medicine there for many years.

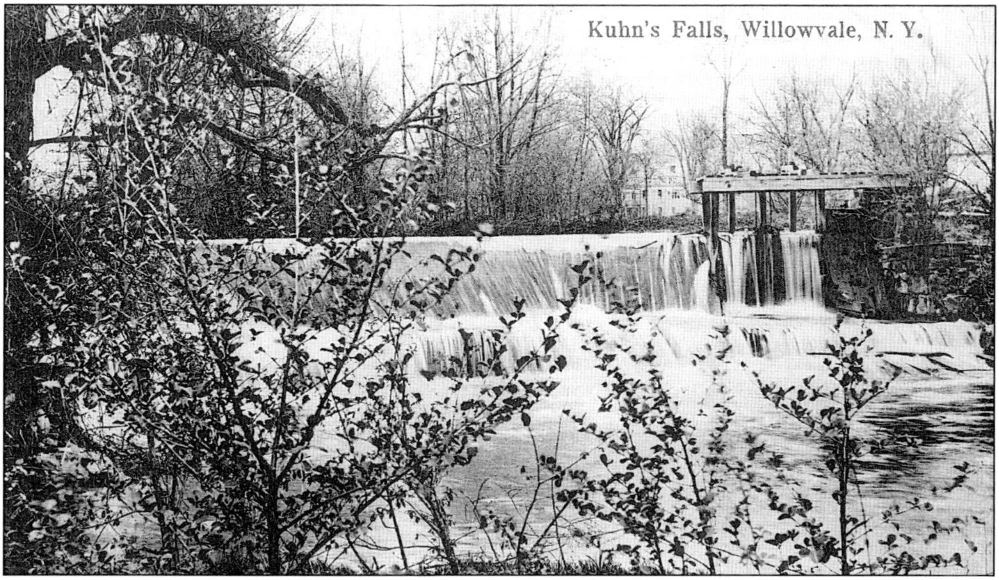

Kuhn's Falls—where was it? This postcard image, c. 1914, reprinted in the "This Week in History" column by Audrey Lewis in the *Utica Observer Dispatch* of March 5, 1990, engendered a still unresolved debate about its location. Some residents declared it was behind the present Willowvale Fire Department on Oneida Street. Others claim it was located further upstream near Kuhn's Sawmill. The majority of residents who responded to the newspaper piece believed that the falls were behind the fire department.

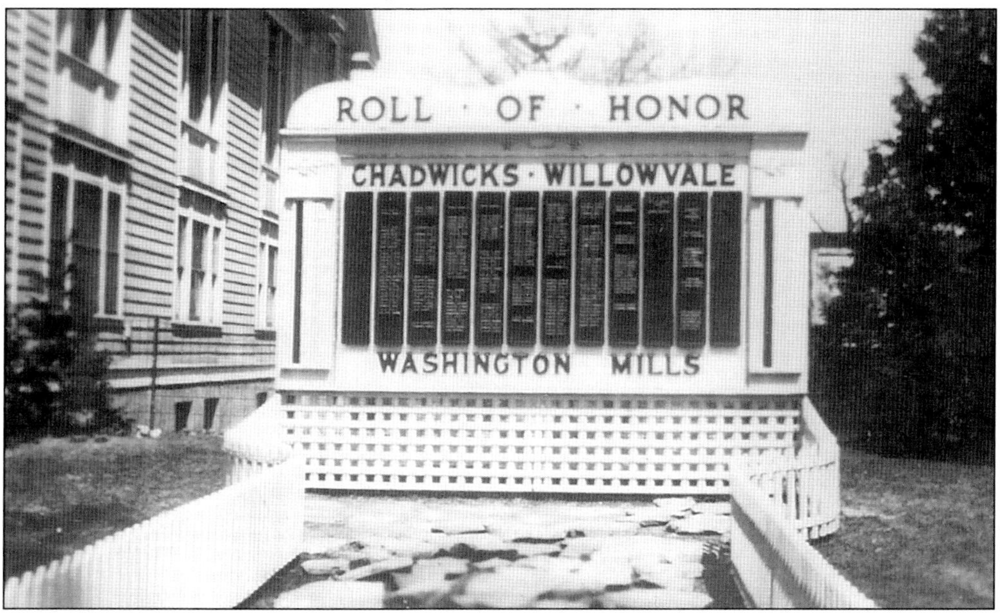

This photograph shows the WWII Honor Roll, sponsored by the Willowvale Fire Department, and dedicated on Easter Sunday, April 8, 1944. Music was provided by the Chadwicks High School band, conducted by student Joyce Richards (Shephard), who substituted for the ailing music teacher. The board was placed next to the Willowvale Bleachery Clubhouse, now the site of a pizza parlor. The committee responsible for it was Joseph E. Richards, Byron Jones, William Hull, Thomas Atwell, and Earl Mathews.

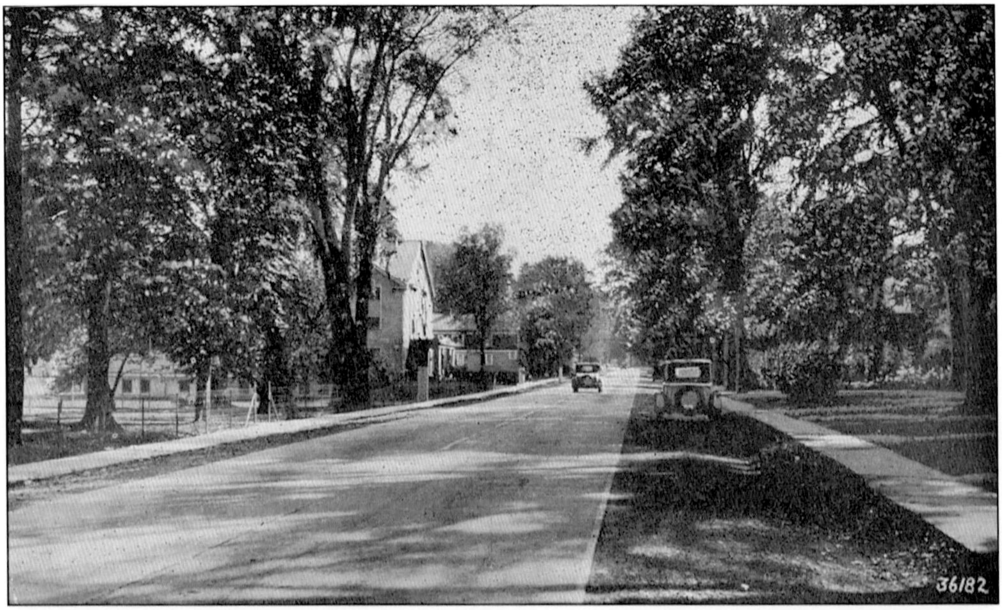

The Willowvale Bleachery employee clubhouse (left) was built in 1922. The three-story building had clubrooms with card tables, shuffleboard, ping-pong and pool tables, bowling alleys, and a spacious auditorium. The Willowvale Fire Department also was housed in the building. The building was the victim of a 1922 flood, and a fire in 1926; it was rebuilt and served the community until the bleachery moved out of the area in 1952, deeding their property to Syracuse University. In 1954, it was sold to Casab's Supermarket.

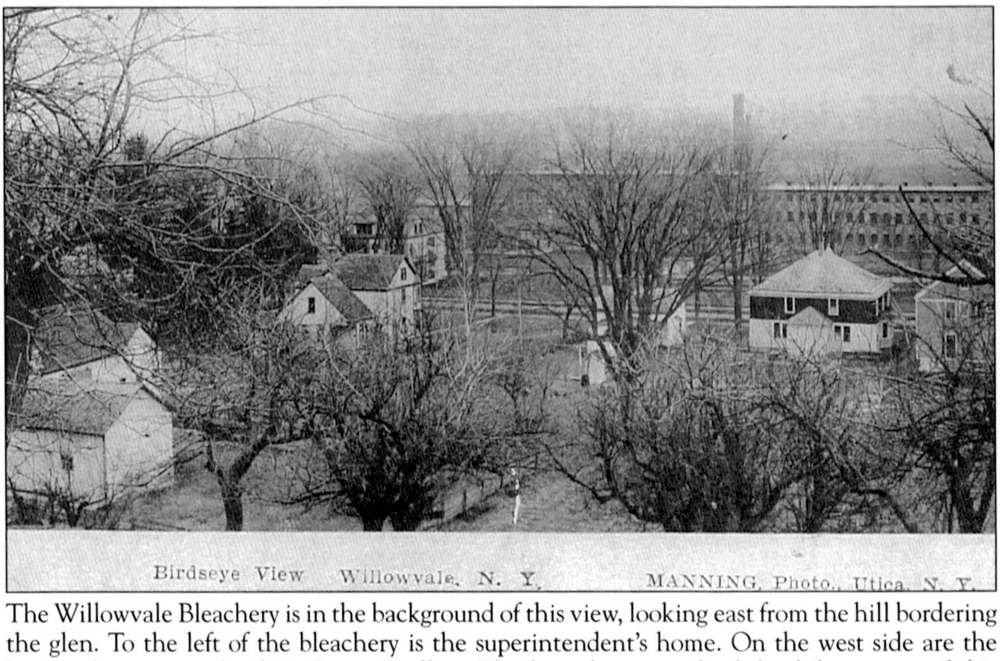

The Willowvale Bleachery is in the background of this view, looking east from the hill bordering the glen. To the left of the bleachery is the superintendent's home. On the west side are the homes that are north of Dr. Rower's office. The large home to the left of the center of this picture was once home to LeRoy and Gladys Farrow; it is currently owned by the Patrick Kress family. (From the collection of Tom Schafer.)

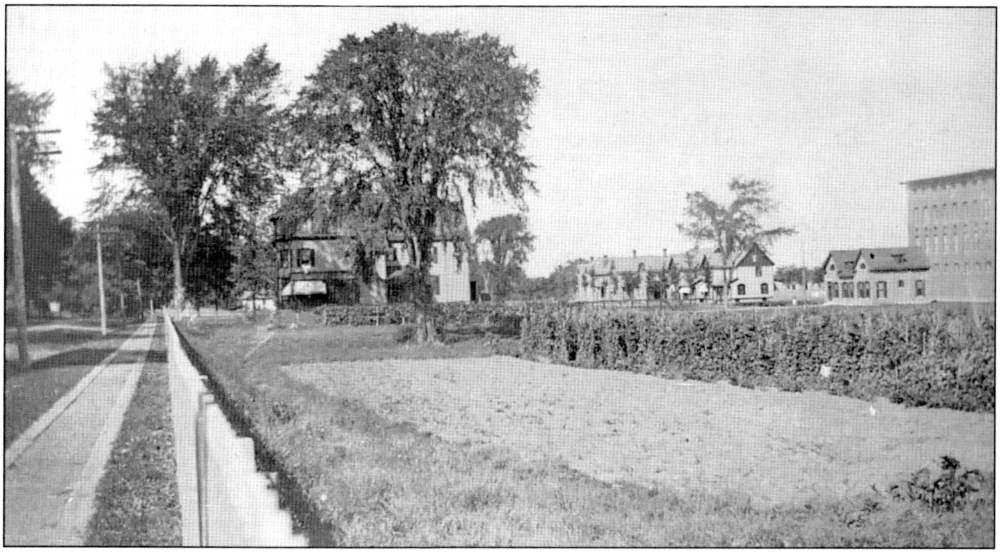

On the corner of Bleachery Avenue and Main Street stood the three-story home of the bleachery's superintendent. This home is located behind the large elm tree, *c.* 1907. Home of the Suplee family in the 1930s and 1940s, it was later converted into an apartment house. The first row of company houses on Bleachery Avenue is to the right of the center. This postcard photograph was taken prior to the construction of the clubhouse in 1922. The area in the foreground was once the site of a foundry and Colt firearms shop.

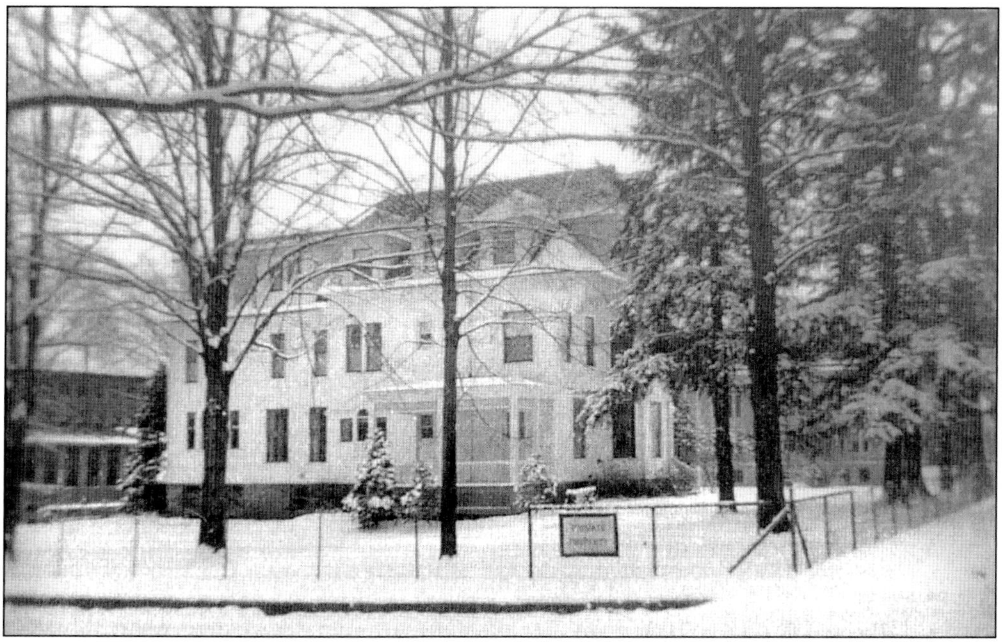

Prior to 1935, when it became the bleachery superintendent's home, this hosue was the Ononda Club, a boarding house for employees of the Willowvales Bleachery. This house had been remodeled into apartments when this photograph was taken in 1948. The victim of a fire in the 1950s, it was razed. The land was purchased by the owner of Casab's Supermarket and a diner was erected on the site. The Chadwicks Shopping Center was built in the mid-1950s adjacent to to diner and attached to the clubhouse (food market).

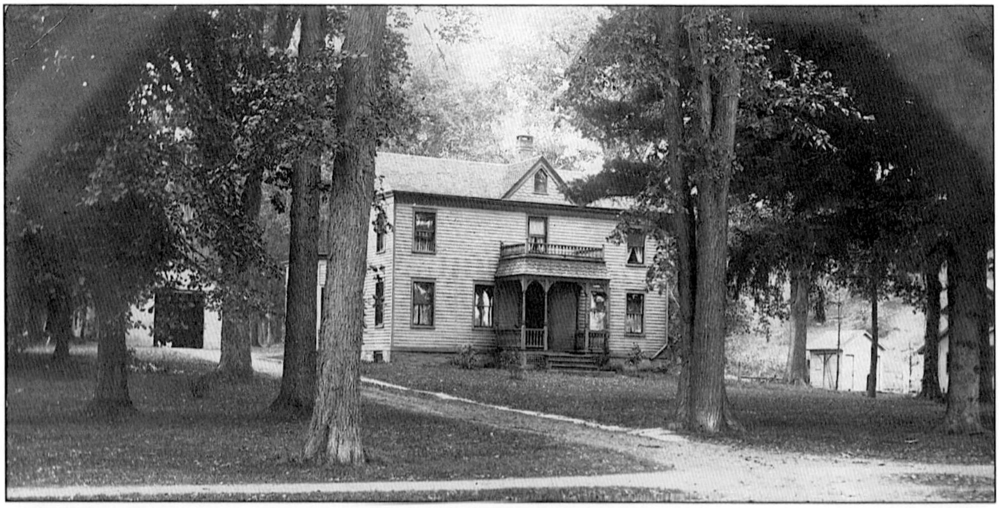

Called the Glen House because of its location just south of the Willowvale Glen entrance, this property was conveyed to Emily Holt Rogers in 1837 by her parents. Emily Holt married Amos Rogers, the son of Oliver G. Rogers. Oliver's father (also Amos) established a machine shop in Willowvale in 1818 near the corner of present-day Bleachery Avenue. In the mid-1940s, the home was occupied by the Clifford family. In 1949, it was purchased by Edward and Florence Murray. The current occupants are the Prichard family.

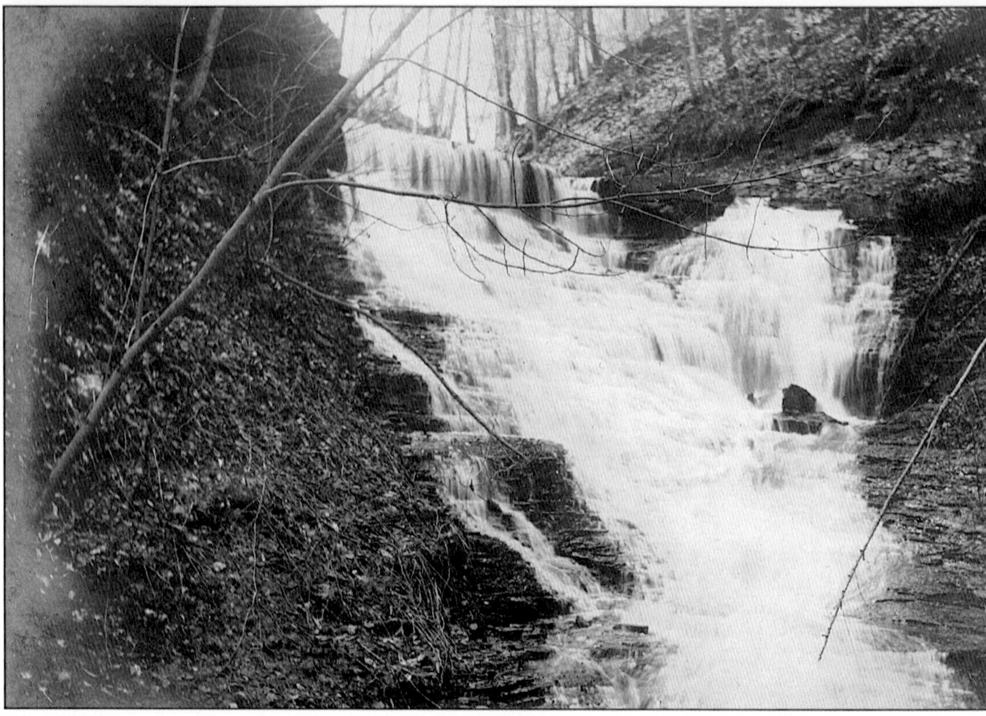

The Willowvale Glen was at one time named Roger's Glen after Amos Rogers, Oliver G. Rogers's son. In the mid-1800s, he spent many hours laying out the paths and erecting stone walls to retain the side slopes. He quarried the stone for the walls from the glen and performed much of the labor himself. A tranquil spot of natural beauty, it was a source of pleasure to many valley residents.

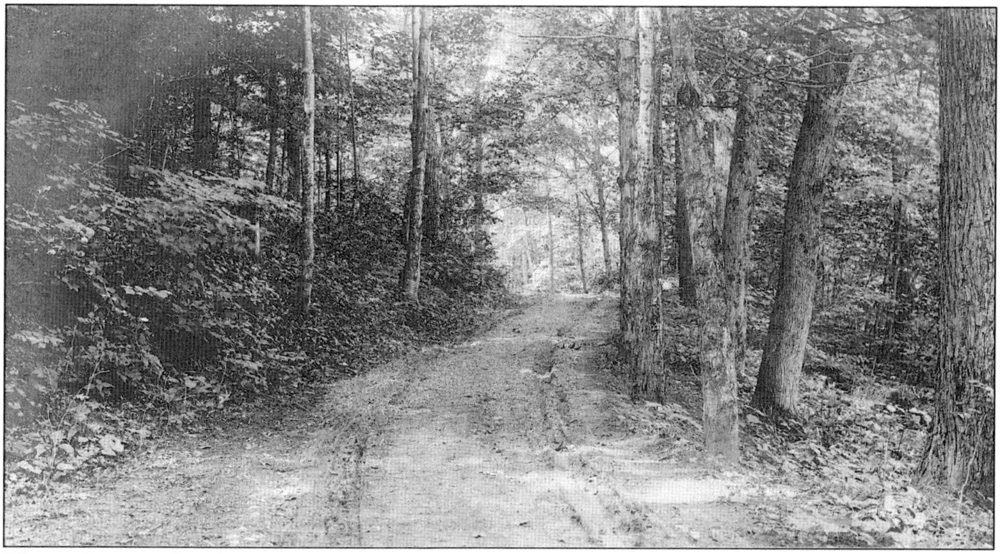

The paths into the glen provided easy access to nature's beauty. It was a favorite hiking spot for neighborhood children, and a trek was made there each spring after the snow had melted. In the glen, hikers could enjoy the mayflowers, violets, and myrtles that grew there in abundance. Deeded to Syracuse University in 1959, it was later sold to private owners who maintain a home and an animal sanctuary nearby.

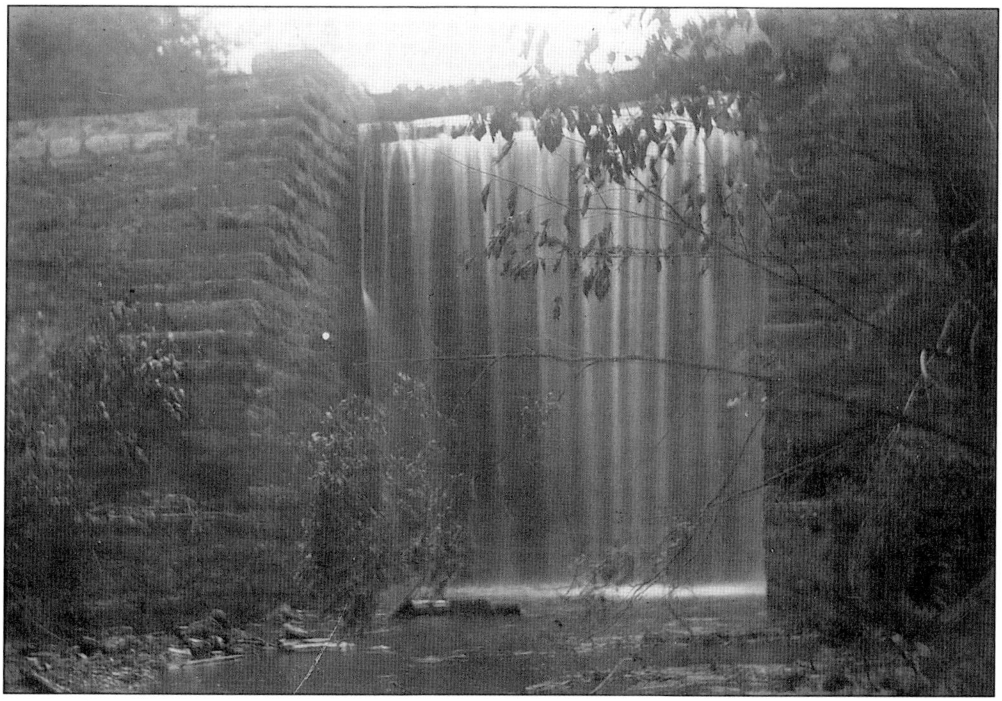

Pictured is one of the three falls in the glen, created when the Utica Willowvale Bleaching Company purchased the site. In 1881–82, a man-made reservoir, which was needed to facilitate the bleaching process, was created to furnish waterpower to the textile manufacturer. As the need for water grew, two additional reservoirs were erected in 1890 and 1905, changing the natural aspect of the glen.

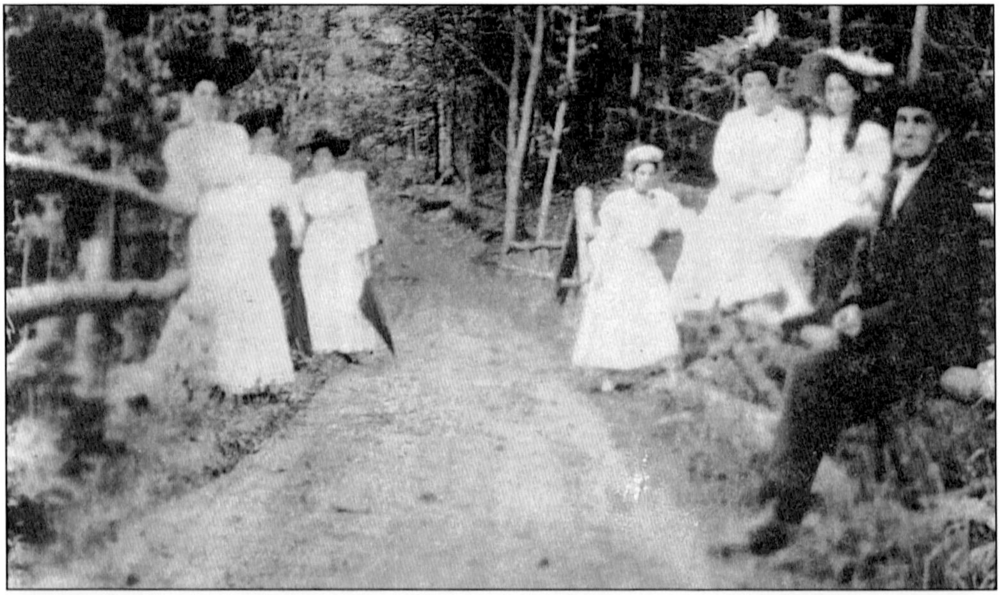

Considered the area's Niagara Falls, the Rogers or Willowvale Glen was a favorite spot for a summer stroll. This photograph from a Chadwick family album records members of that family enjoying the scenic area. No date was recorded, but the clothing indicates that the scene is from the late 1800s or early 1900s. Today's hiking garb would be a startling contrast to the long dresses and hats of that era. (From the collection of Tom Schafer.)

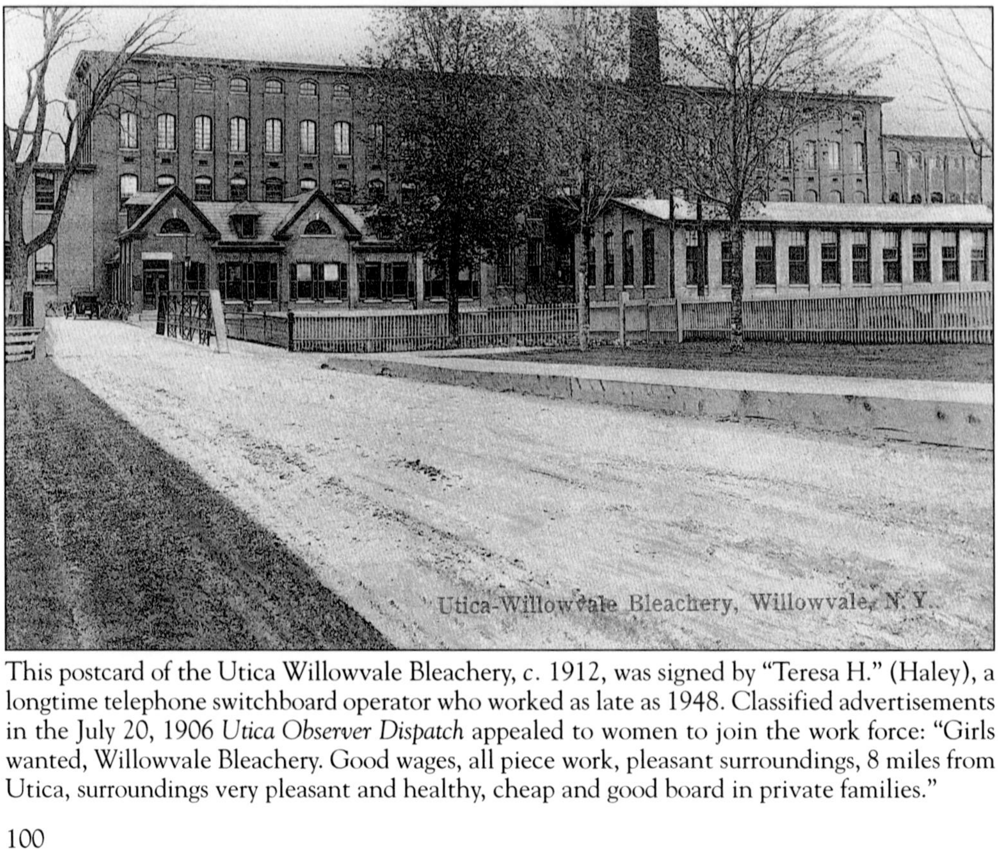

This postcard of the Utica Willowvale Bleachery, c. 1912, was signed by "Teresa H." (Haley), a longtime telephone switchboard operator who worked as late as 1948. Classified advertisements in the July 20, 1906 *Utica Observer Dispatch* appealed to women to join the work force: "Girls wanted, Willowvale Bleachery. Good wages, all piece work, pleasant surroundings, 8 miles from Utica, surroundings very pleasant and healthy, cheap and good board in private families."

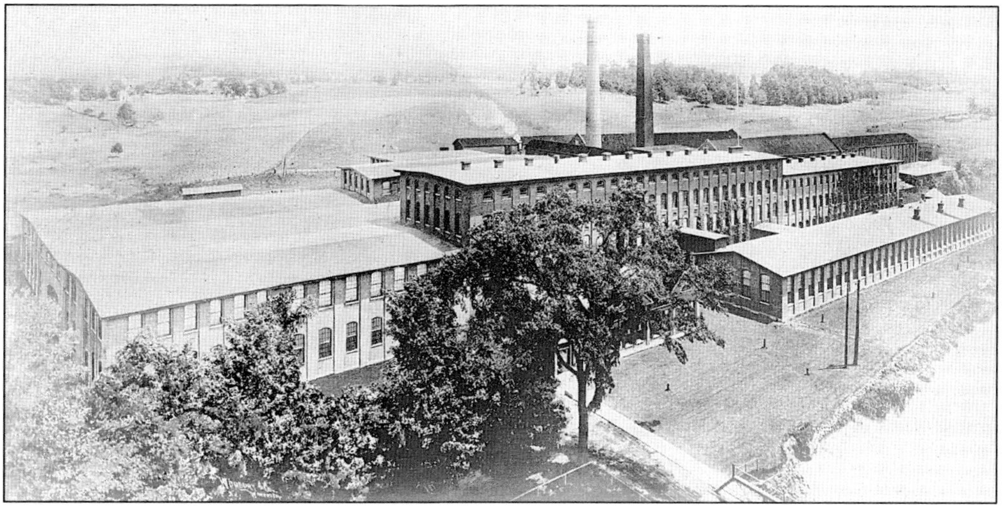

In a 1922–23 book printed for the Utica Gas and Electric Company, the Utica Willowvale Bleachery is pictured with the following caption: "These manufacturers realize that to get maximum efficiency, they must surround the workers with everything conducive to health and that sufficient recreation and amusement out of working hours is essential. To that end they have established the Willowvale Club and other social centers for their employees. This, together with good homes and living conditions, can have but one result: good work through goodwill."

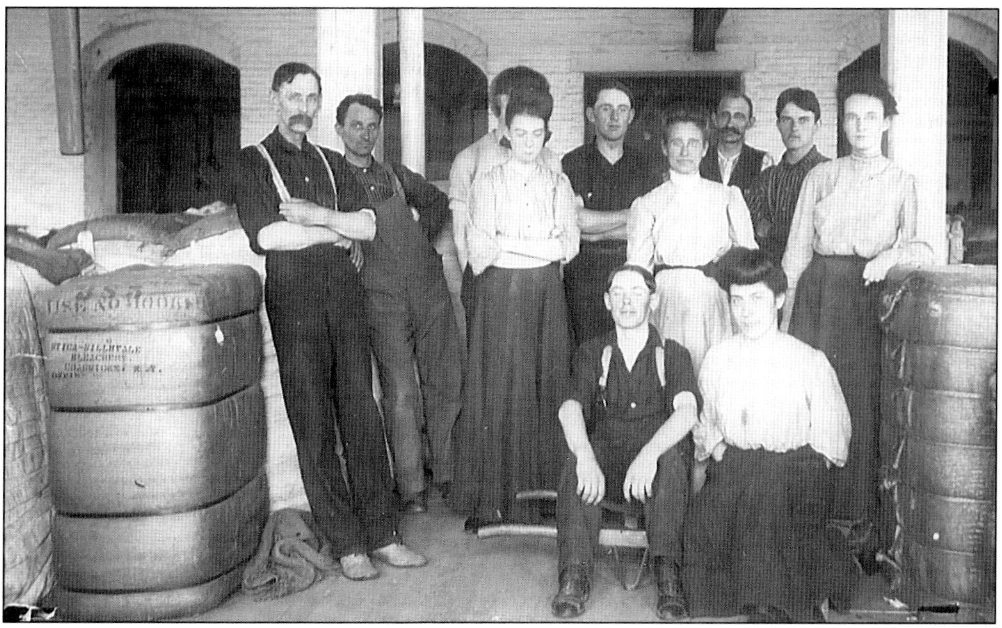

The Brown Room was named for the large bales of raw brown cloth. The ends of the cloth were sewn together to make a long, continuous sheet that was run through the bleach to whiten it. After being plaited in bins, "sheet tearers" tore the cloth by hand into various sizes, tearing by hand to keep the sheets square. The sheets were folded and sent to the Sewing Room for hemming, then to the Folding Room. Charles Mallory, father of current Willowvale resident Rollin Mallory, was the foreman, the second man from right in the back. (From the collection of the New Hartford Historical Society.)

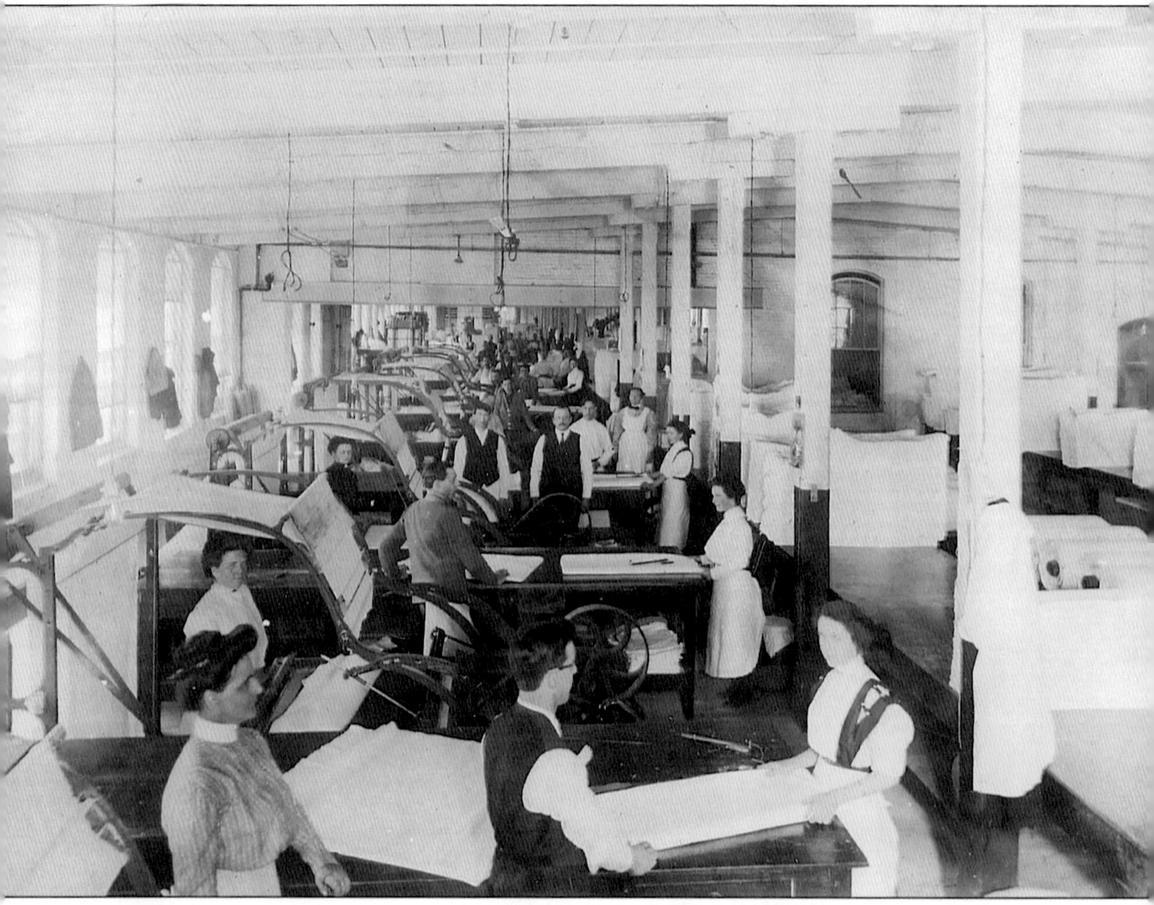

Pictured is the Folding Room at the bleachery. Machine-folded sheets were taken from the frames and sent to be inspected before being ironed, folded, labeled, and packaged. A division of the Utica and Mohawk Cotton Mills, the mill continued manufacturing sheets, pillowcases, table linens, and other cotton goods until 1952, when they left the area. Many of the Willowvale Bleachery buildings have been razed. The front office building and portions of the plant, occupied by the Remet Corporation in the 1980s, now houses Mohawk Communications Limited. One of the founders of the Willowvale Bleaching Company, which was established in 1880 on the banks of the Sauquoit Creek, was George W. Chadwick Sr., the son of John Chadwick. George was the president and general manager until his death in 1885. George was one of the originators and a member of the board of directors of the Oneida National Bank of Utica. He was also a promoter and director of the Utica, Chenango, and Susquehanna Railroad, and one of the incorporators and president of the Sauquoit Valley Cemetery Association. (From the collection of the New Hartford Historical Society.)

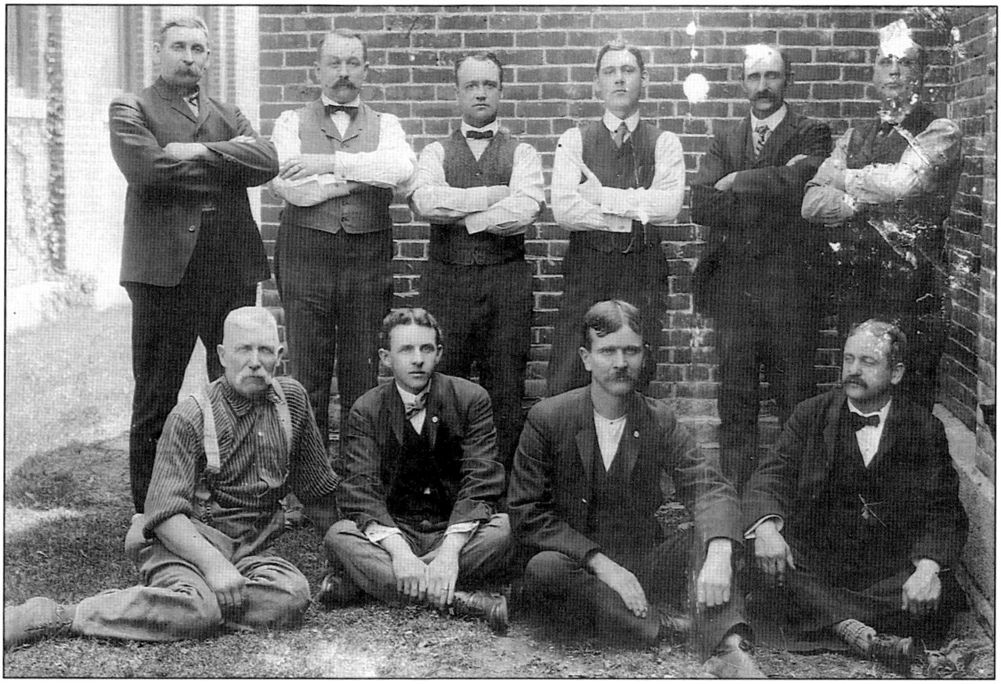

This undated photograph of Willowvale Bleachery foremen is probably from the very early 1900s. Identified by Rollin Mallory are, from left to right, as follows: (front row) Albert Richards, Clarence Brooks, Dennis Haley, and George Chadwick Jr.; (back row) Bion Shackleton, Mr. Jenkins, Frank Green, Mr. MacManus, Charles Mallory, and John Urtz.

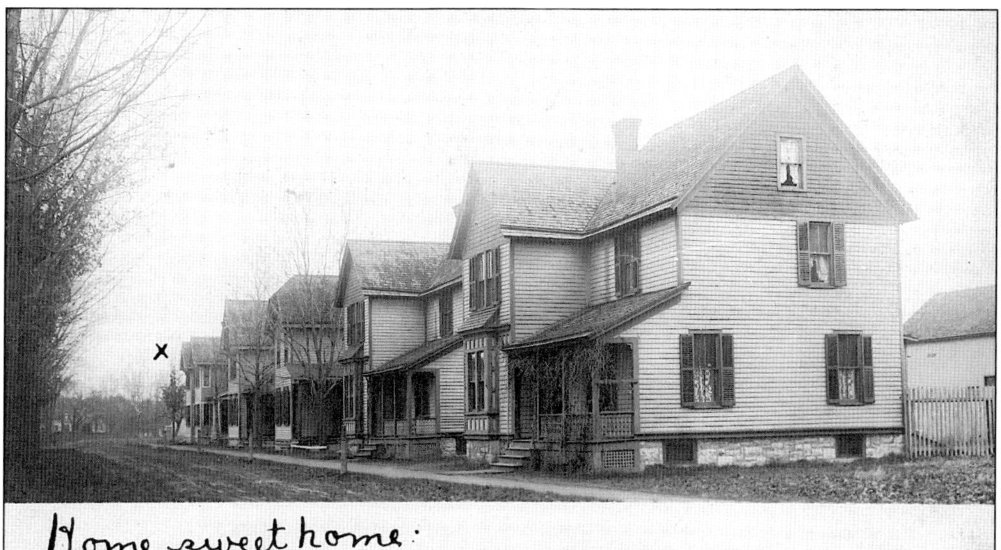

The homes on the east side of Bleachery Avenue are typical of the housing provided by the mill. Spacious, comfortable homes were an employee benefit that is uncommon today. Rented to employees at nominal fees, many of these residences were sold to the occupants at generous prices when the factories moved in the early 1950s. The house on the right is currently home to the Warren and Linda Mundrick family. A factory storage barn (at right) is still standing.

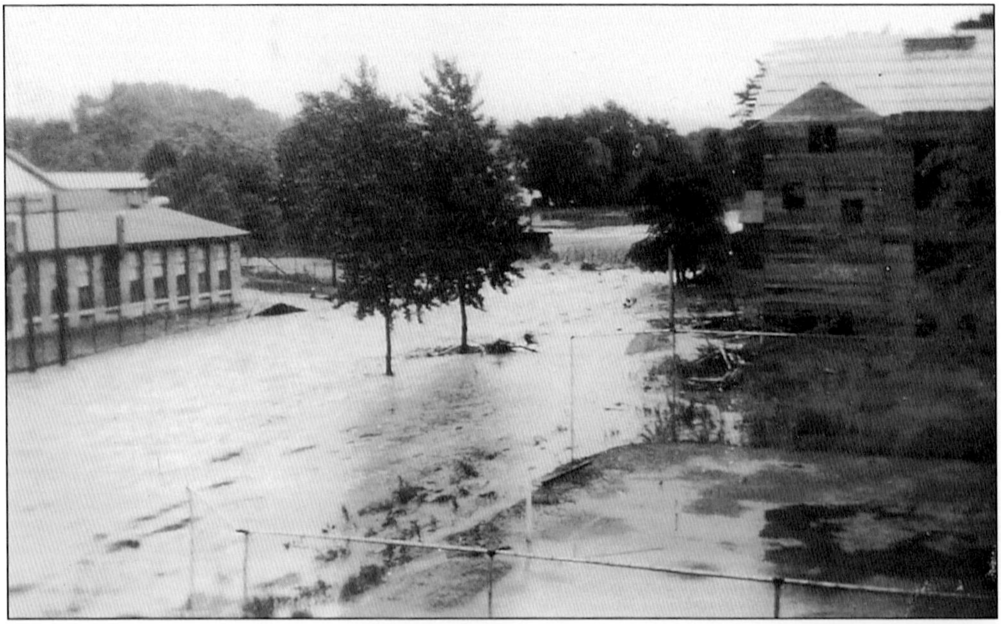

On April 11, 1922, the Sauquoit Creek flooded as the result of a heavy spring snowstorm followed by torrential rains. The swollen stream washed out dams along its route. On the right in this photograph is a side view of the Willowvale Bleachery clubhouse under construction. The tennis courts are on the bottom right. The overflowing stream filled the bleachery's buildings, causing a loss of thousands of dollars. (Courtesy of Bill Welty.)

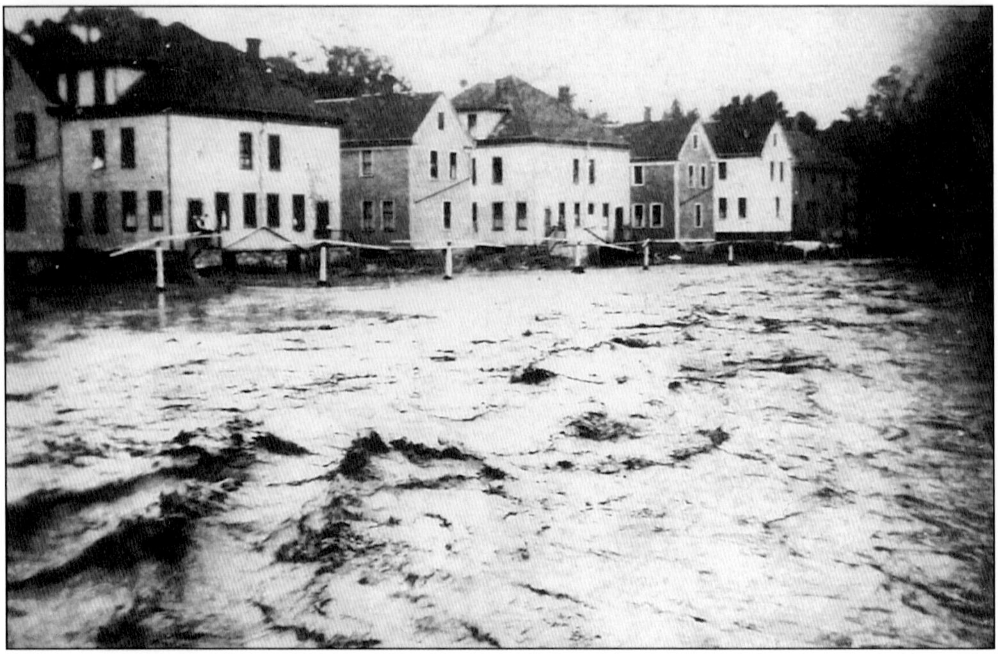

The area behind the homes on Main Street (the front views of which are seen on the top of page 106) is inundated by the swollen creek waters. Note the clothesline reels with water half way up the center poles. Because of the flood, the bleachery and residents along the creek built high stone walls to restrain future flooding. (Courtesy of Bill Welty.)

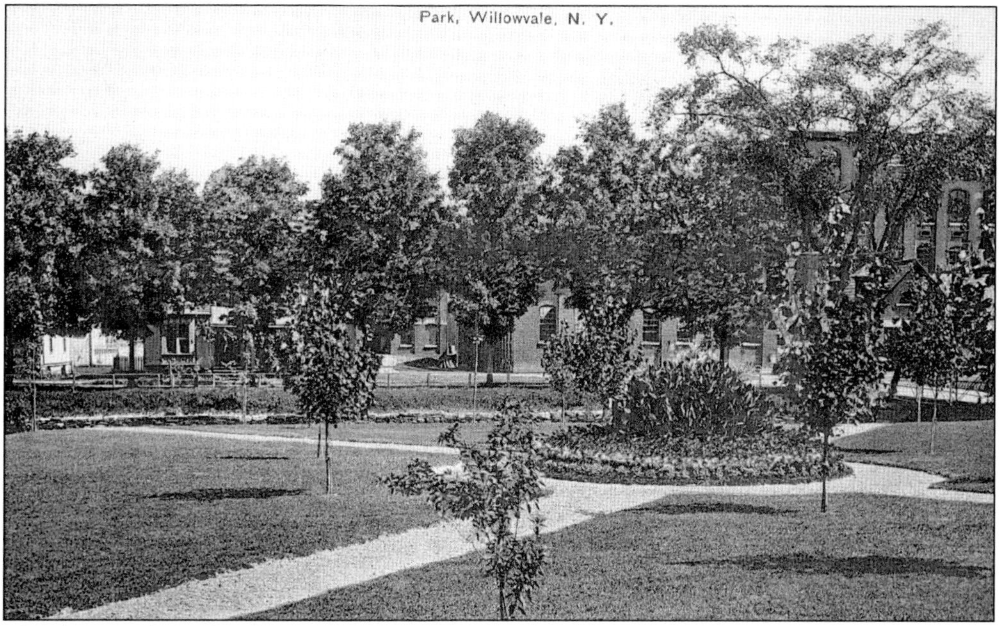

Bleachery Park (earlier known as Ononda Park) at the northeast corner of Bleachery Avenue, once a site of footpaths and flowers, is today a vacant lot. Behind it can be seen the bleachery, and to the left, the first row of mill housing. The Sauquoit Creek flows between the park and the factory. The park was the destination for the processional in 1915 to the Community Christmas Tree, a grand finale to the program of music and recitations held at the Standard Silk Mill in neighboring Chadwicks.

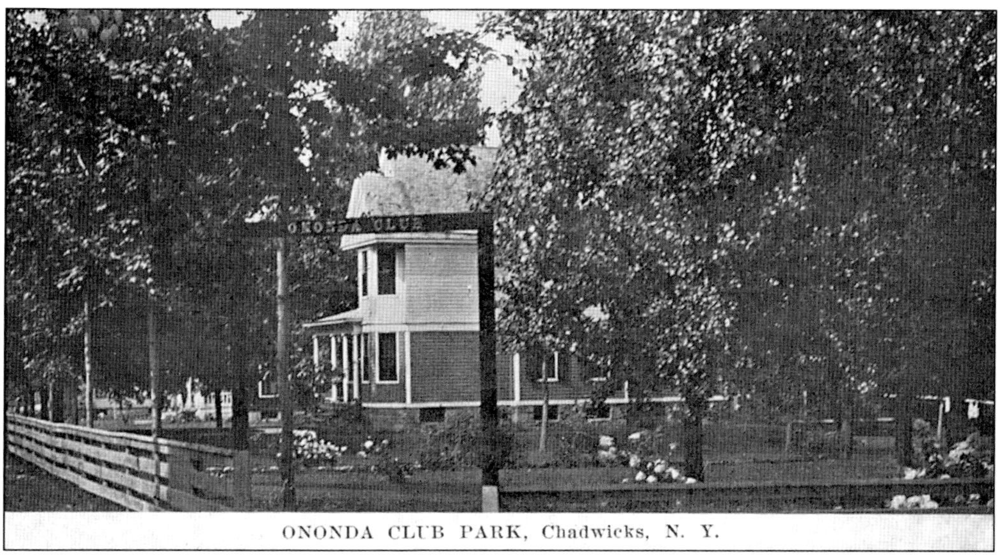

Ononda Club Park (in Willowvale, not Chadwicks) was on the opposite corner of Bleachery Avenue (house shown on page 97), across the avenue from the park. The house pictured here was a residence of the bleachery supervisor. For the past 60 years, it has been the home of E.J. Peters. Beyond this house is the former home of Andy Scheffer—the scourge of under-16-year-olds who tried to sneak into the Bleachery Clubhouse. Next to that is the home of Avis Shaw, the school music teacher. Shaw's home was later the home of the Dan and Mary Daly family.

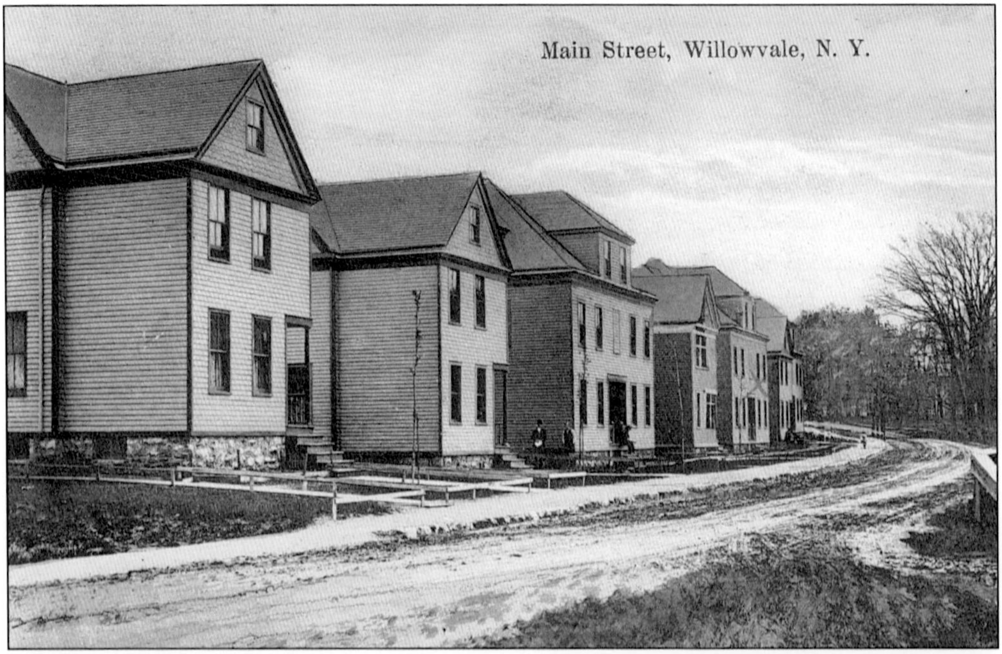

Another row of bleachery houses, c. 1912, appears to have just been built. The wooden frames are not yet removed from newly planted lawns or freshly cemented sidewalks. Interspersed with the single-family dwellings are two double-family dwellings. This area on the east side of present-day Oneida Street, below Bleachery Avenue, was once called "Finnegan's Row" for reasons undetermined.

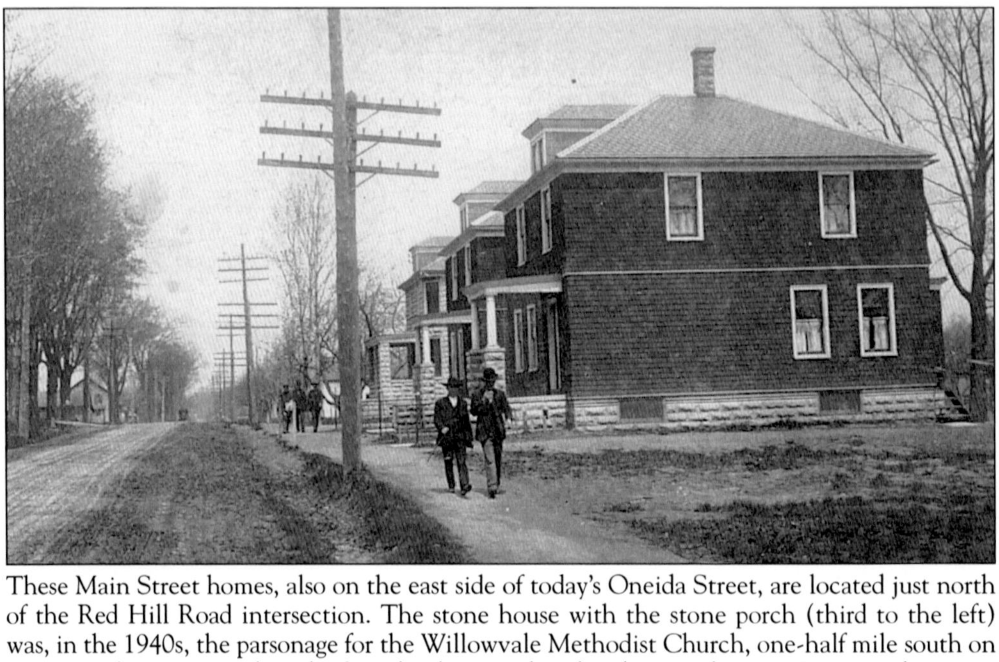

These Main Street homes, also on the east side of today's Oneida Street, are located just north of the Red Hill Road intersection. The stone house with the stone porch (third to the left) was, in the 1940s, the parsonage for the Willowvale Methodist Church, one-half mile south on Route 8. The stone porch at the front has been replaced with a wooden one. In 1908, the writer of the postcard indicates that these were the residences of Mr. Smith, Mr. DeBee, and Mrs. Shephard. (From the collection of New Hartford Historical Society.)

Seven

WASHINGTON MILLS

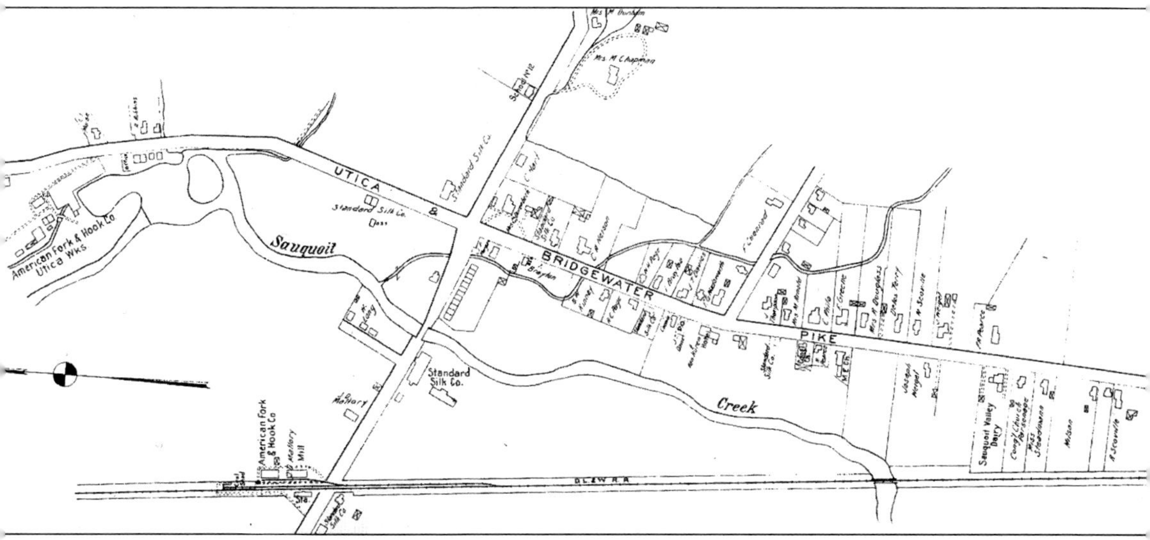

Entering the Utica Bridgewater Turnpike near the center of the map is Kellogg Road to the west and Chapman Road to the east. To the right of Chapman Road is Mallory Road, across from the apartment house that is the surviving section of the VanKurran Hotel. Crossing under the highway near the boundary between Willowvale and Washington Mills, the Sauquoit Creek here is west of the Utica Bridgewater Turnpike (now Oneida Street).

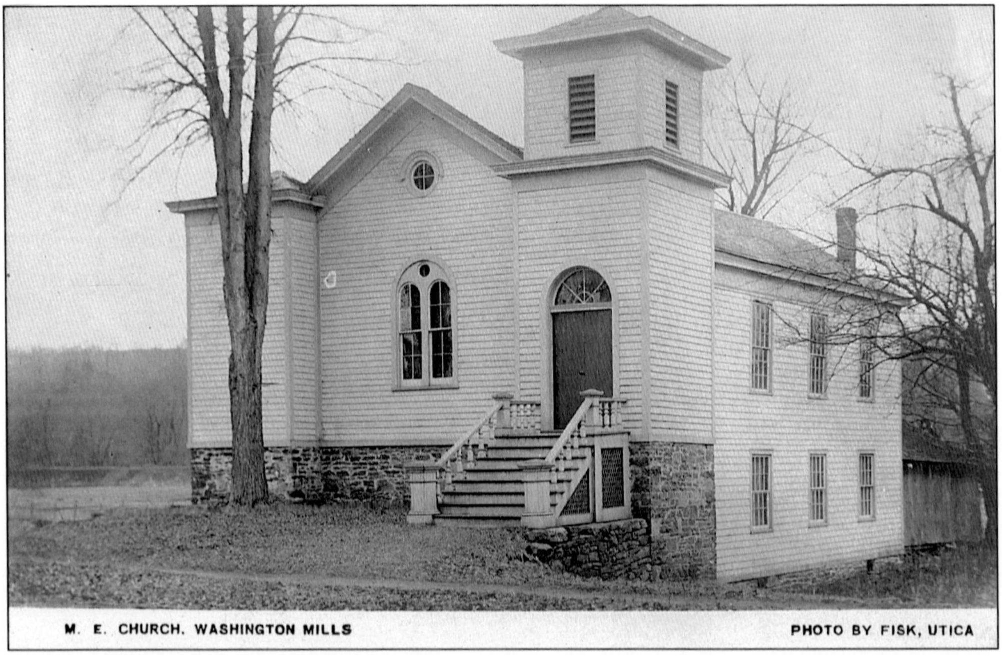

This church edifice once housed the Methodist Church in its earliest years, the 1860s. Located at 3839 Oneida Street, the building has subsequently had various business uses: Halligan and Roberts Feed Mill, Bitteker's Bakery, Everett Hall's sign business, a snowmobile sales store, and a computer shop. The building is currently vacant.

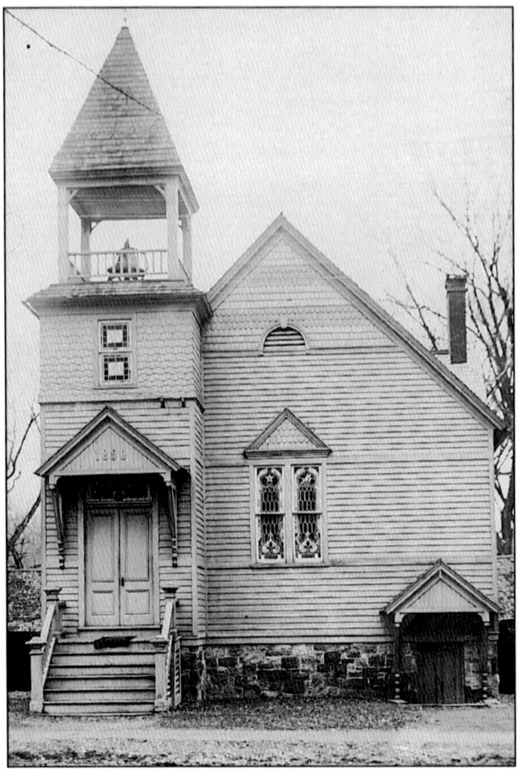

The Congregational Church, built in 1890, was used as such until 1972. In 1891, the congregation adopted the name Messiah Congregational Church. The church stood on Oneida Street where the Valley Garage is today until the church burned in 1974. Merging with the United Church of Christ in 1960, the name was changed to Messiah United Church of Christ. In 1967, a new church was erected across the street and slightly south of the early church.

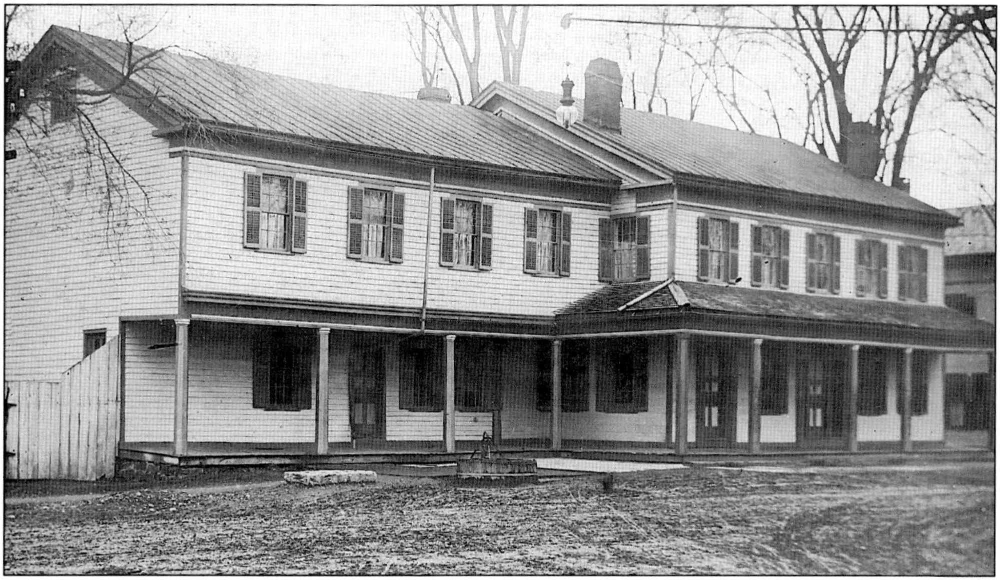

The VanKurran Hotel was directly across from Mallory Road. The watering trough in front furnished fresh spring water, which was piped in from high up on Mallory Road. Lewis Smith, a longtime Washington Mills resident, relates that as a boy of about five, he expressed a desire to see somebody dunked in the watering trough. Obligingly, Mr. VanKurran lifted Lewis and deposited him in the trough. The left half of the building was torn down in 1940, and the remaining part is today an apartment house.

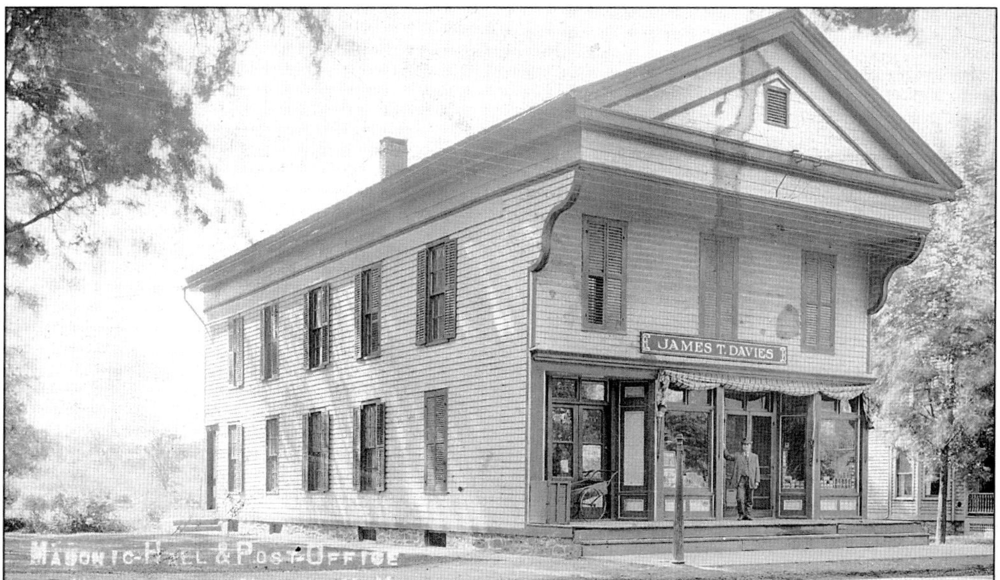

In the late 1800s and early 1900s, when J.T. Davies (likely the gentleman on the porch) was the owner and postmaster, this building housed the post office and the Masonic Hall. From 1930 to the 1950s, Mr. and Mrs. Stanley Champ (of Champ's Market) were the proprietors. Mrs. Champ was also the postmaster from 1933 to 1943. Struck by fire in 1952, the store was badly damaged, but was rebuilt by Mr. Champ. Presently, it is a candy store with a body shop in the back. An apartment occupies the second floor.

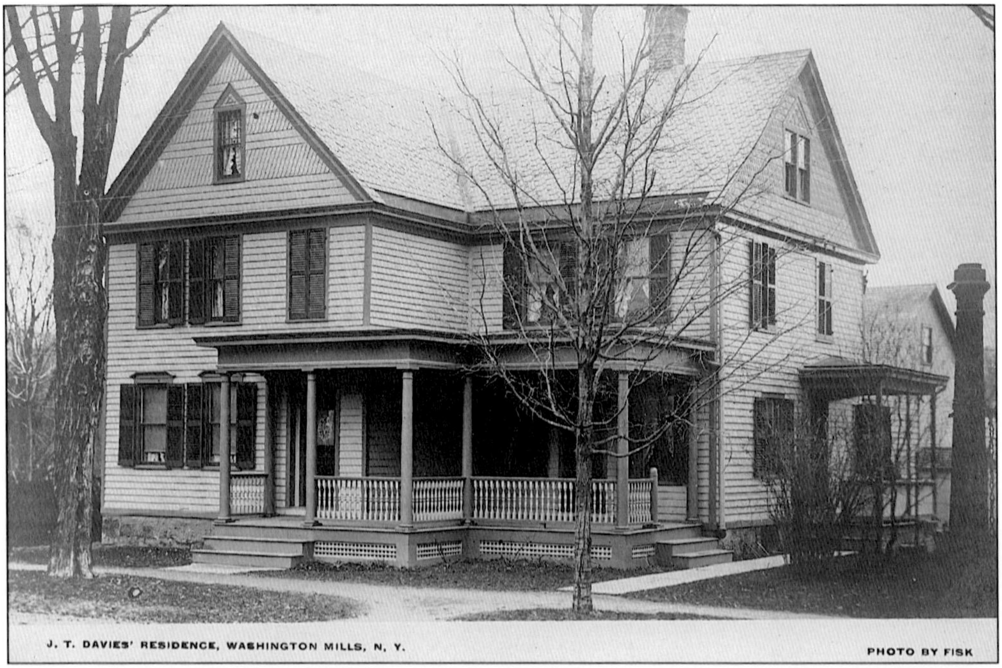

The J.T. Davies residence was the home of the proprietors of the general store across the main road. It is located on Oneida Street, two doors north of the intersection with Mallory Road. The large front porch has been removed and the house extensively remodeled over the years, giving it a completely different appearance today.

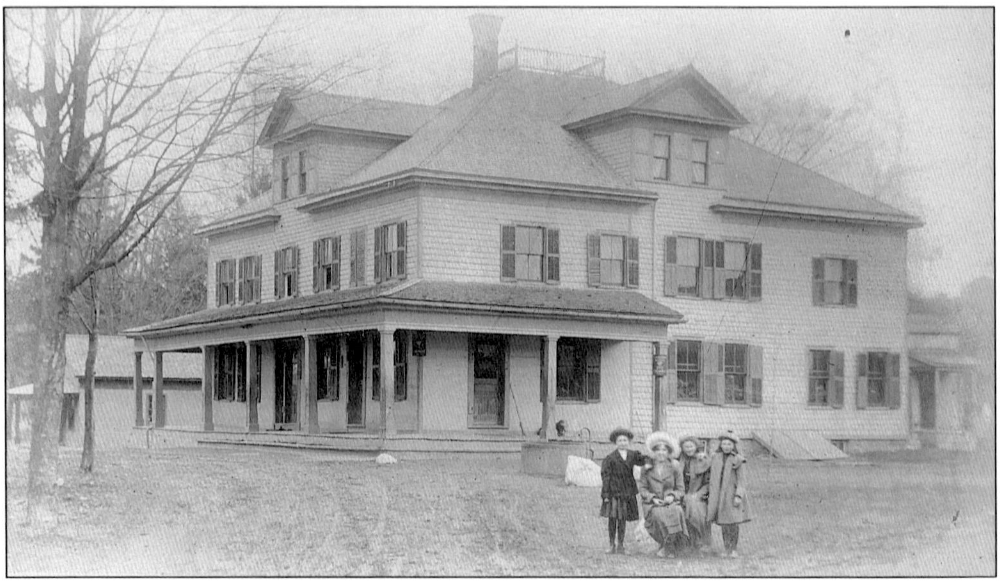

The Durrenbeck House was a hotel located at the intersection of Chapman Road and Oneida Street, where the MacDonald's restaurant now stands. At one time, Charlie Gage ran an Amoco gas station on the corner in front of the building, and Ken's Grill occupied part of the former hotel. The woman seated is Mrs. Durrenbeck, the proprietor of the hotel who reportedly ran a very "high class establishment." Her three children pose with her in this photo postcard taken c. 1907.

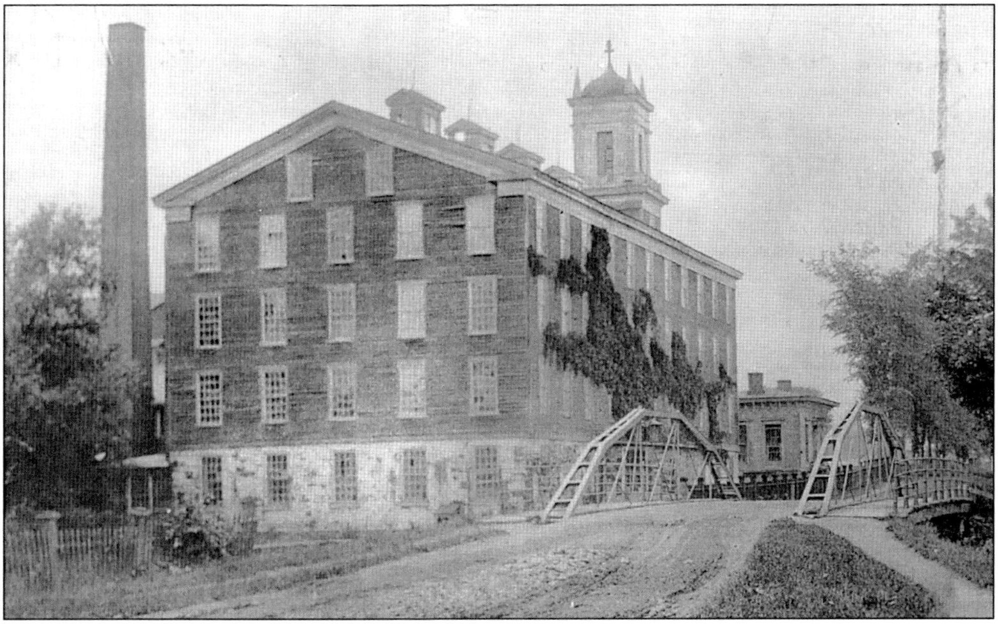

Two hundred employees of the Stewart Woolen Mill on Kellogg Road in 1873–74 worked from 6:30 a.m. to 6:30 p.m. (5 p.m. on Saturdays). Closed in 1880, the mill was torn down *c.* 1905 and material was taken to Chadwicks to use in building mill houses. Left standing, the small office section on the right was once the Crane's Nest, a tearoom operated by Jessie Bowers. Some of the outer buildings were used by the New Hartford Town Highway Department until they were torn down in 1968 to make room for the Sauquoit Valley Arterial. (From the collection of the New Hartford Historical Society.)

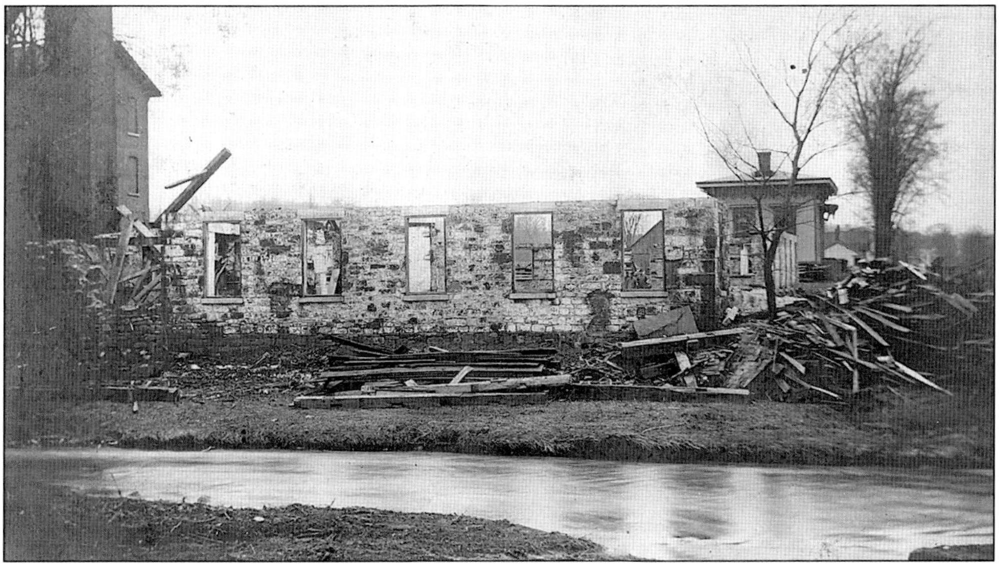

The New York Silk Company was located on the west bank of the Sauquoit Creek on Kellogg Road. After two mills were destroyed by fire, Frederick Hollister rebuilt and painted his mill in with a checkered pattern. Thus the nickname of Checkerville was born. Hollister' new large frame mill was called Washington Mills, and this became the official name for the village. By the late 1870s, the mill was owned by the A.T. Stewart estate of New York.

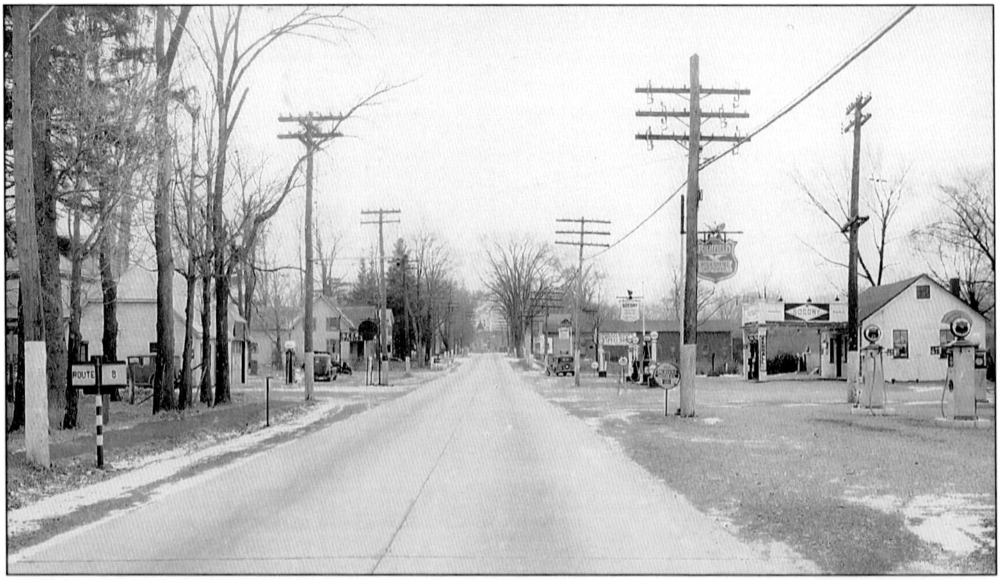

The intersection of Oneida Street, with Kellogg Road to the west (right) and Chapman Road to the east (left), is the hub of Washington Mills. Out of sight at the northwest corner is Hart's Richland gas station. This also housed the Washington Mills post office. Thomas Roy Hart served as the postmaster from 1943 until 1963. On the southwest corner in the 1950s was the Little Chateau, a restaurant operated by Ken and Ruth Prentice; the building is now home to Tony's Pizza. The site of the Shell gas station is a MacDonald's restaurant. (Courtesy of Lewis Smith.)

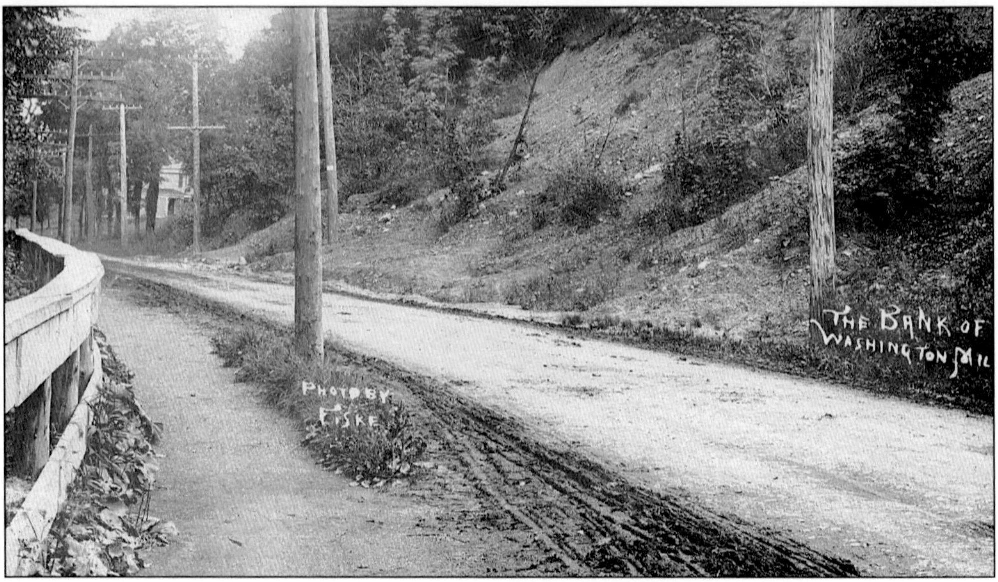

Although a tranquil scene, Hoe Shop Hill on today's Oneida Street was actually a beehive of activity. On the east side of the Sauquoit Creek, across the road from the embankment shown, was the site of a hoe factory. Henry H. Babcock and Charles B. Brown began the business. In 1871, Porter Huntley and Mr. Babcock became owners; in 1887, the firm became Lewis (Ladd J. Lewis of Sauquoit) and Babcock, forerunners of the Utica Tool Company. A small shopping center and a residence is now located where once the old hoe shop stood.

Eight

NEW HARTFORD

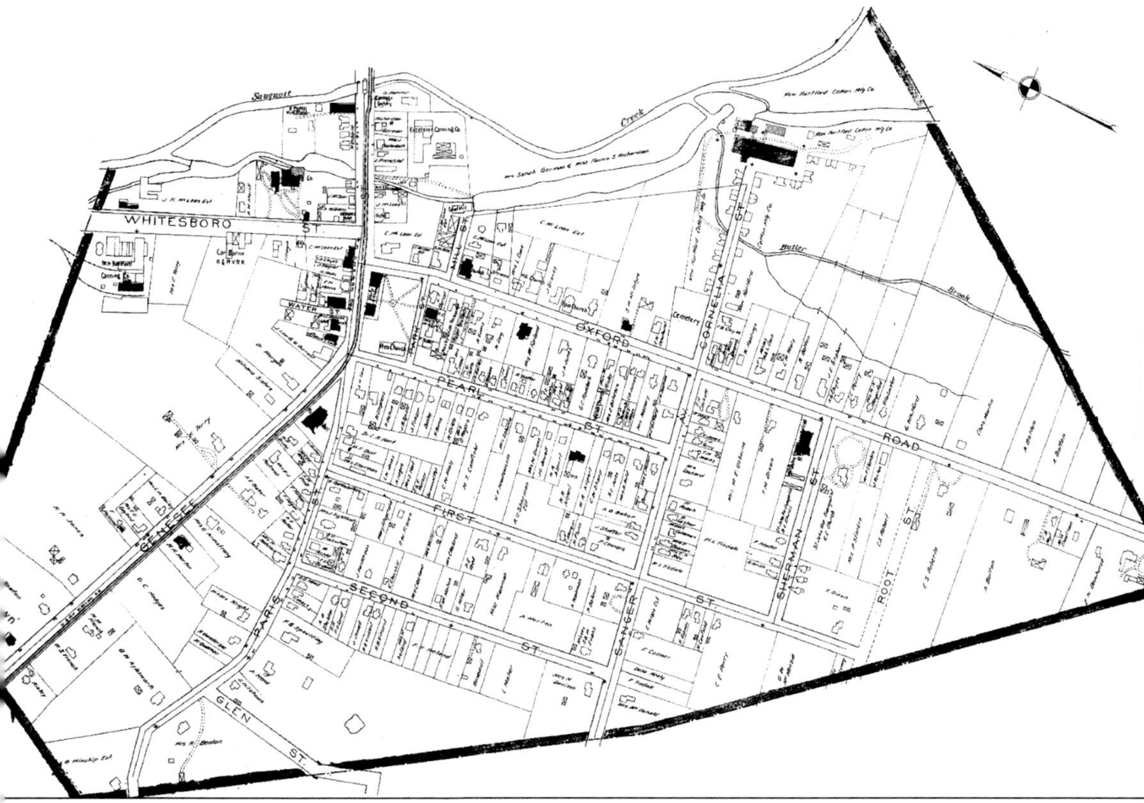

Whitesboro Street to the left is today's Campion Road. Cornelia Street off Oxford Road, now Daly Place, was named for longtime school teacher and guidance counselor Eloise Daly, who was the sister of the former Chadwicks school principal, Mary E. Daly. On the northwest corner of Oxford Road and Sherman Place (right center), there is now a church parking lot that once was the site of St. John's Roman Catholic Church. A new church was built on the southwest corner. The home there, used as a parsonage for the church, was formerly U.S. Vice President James Schoolcraft Sherman's family home.

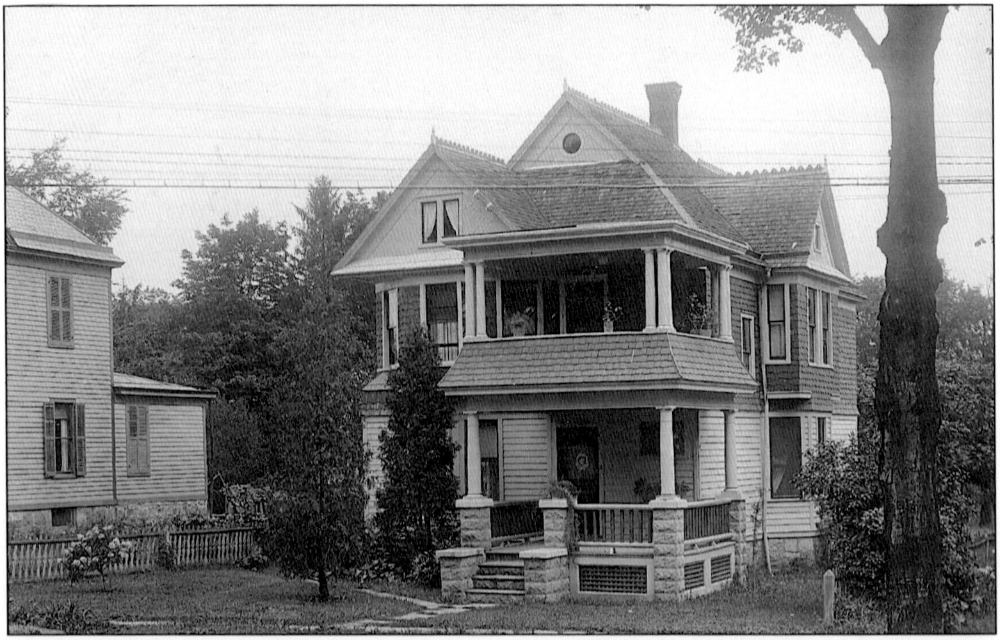

This Oxford Road two-family home, c. 1911, was once Edgewater Nursing Home. In the 1950s, it was an apartment house. Located several doors away from the recently built New Hartford Public Library, the house has not changed much except for the addition of numerous trees that give it a more secluded appearance. Early maps indicate that Oxford Road was first named South Street.

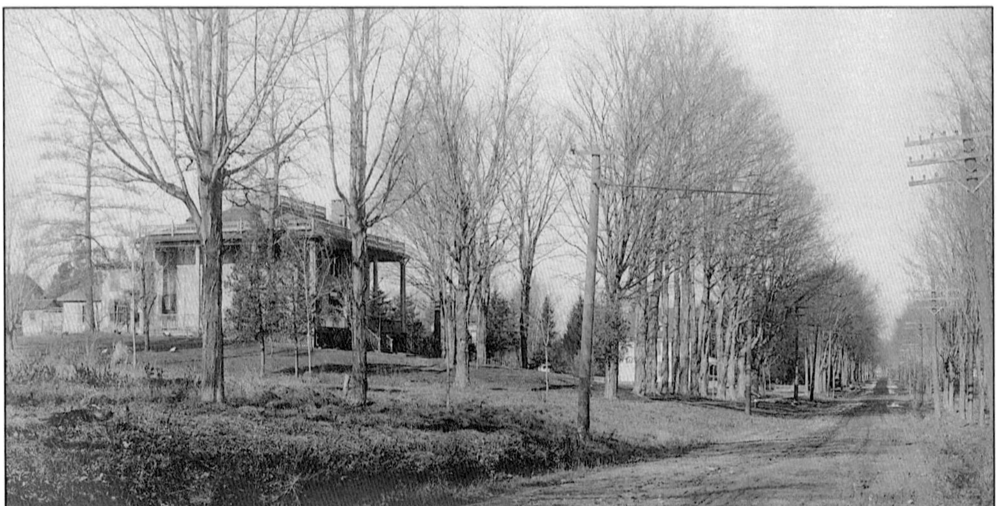

A beautiful Colonial-style mansion is perched atop a hill on Oxford Road. Although the date and builder are disputed, it may have been built c. 1793 by Jedediah Sanger, who founded the village in 1788. It was a wedding gift to his daughter, Sarah, who married John Eames. Others say it was built in 1830 by Walter Eames, Sanger's grandson, to replace an earlier home on the site given to his parents by Judge Sanger. Trees from the surrounding forest were used for porch pillars, and seven fireplaces graced the interior.

The original St. John's Catholic Church, built in 1885, was located on the opposite corner of Sherman Place and Oxford Road, the site of the present-day church parking lot. Groundbreaking for a new church with a seating capacity of over 1,000 people took place on August 22, 1964 and was dedicated in 1966. It is on the site where U.S. Vice President James Schoolcraft Sherman once lived. (Sherman was vice president from 1908 to 1912 under President Taft.) This home was used for a rectory until it was razed to make room for the new church.

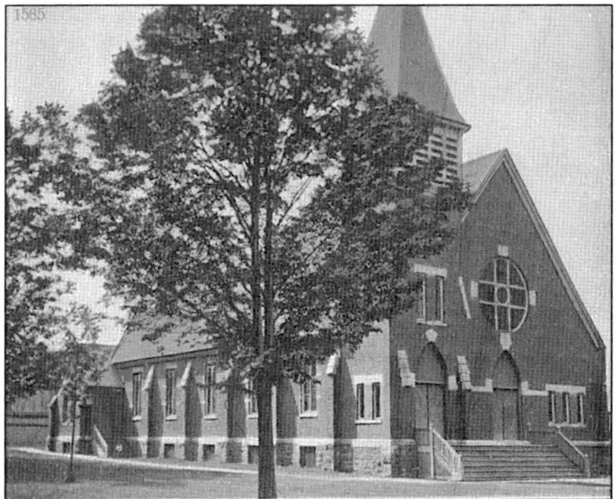

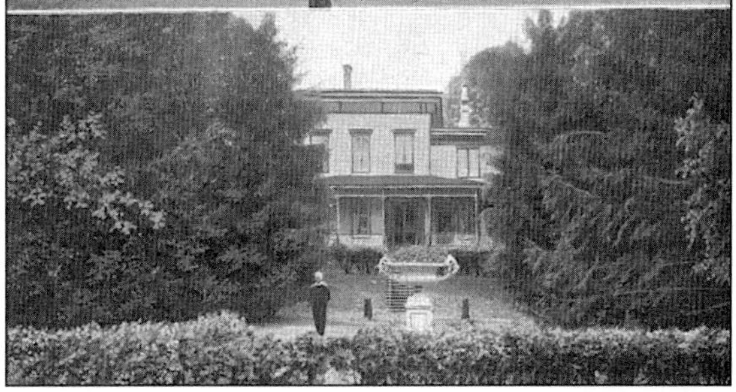

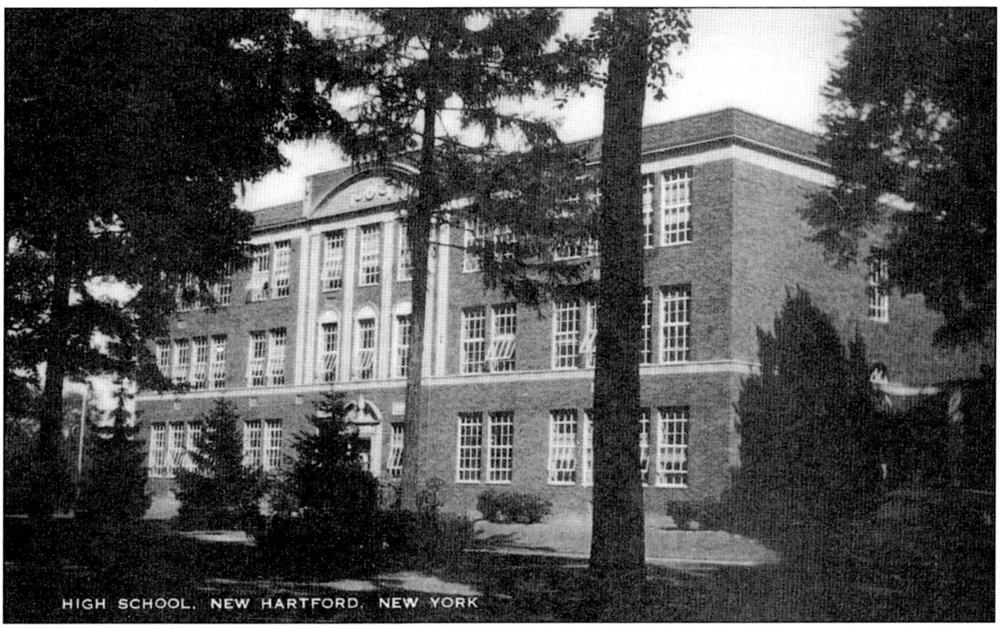

New Hartford High School opened to students in 1932 at a cost of $250,000 and with a capacity of 600–700 students. Lockers replaced coatrooms, and the newspaper reported that modern conveniences of the school included a telephone, radio, heat, and ventilation. It was planned to make enlarging practical; in 1952, an adjoining elementary school wing was added. To handle the rising school population in subsequent years, additional schools were built on Clinton Road, Higby Road, and Chapman Road.

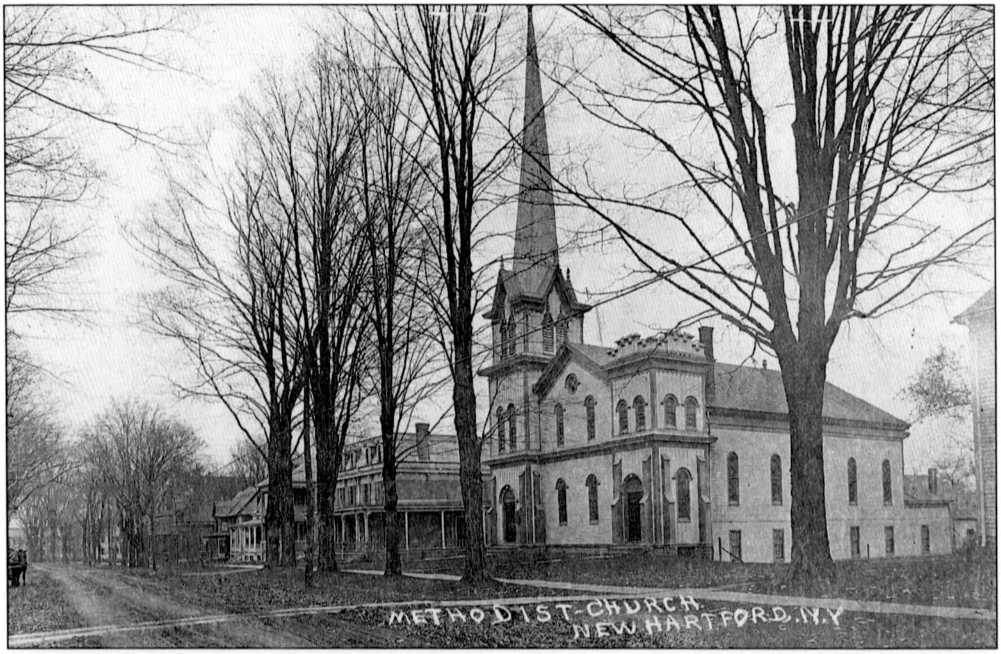

The Methodist Society's first church was built in 1841 on South Street (Oxford Road.) at a cost of $3,000, which included the parsonage. It was moved to an adjoining lot after the new church with its soaring steeple was built in 1868–69 at a cost of $13,786. In 1961, the Methodists built a new modern church at 105 Genesee Street. The Players, a community theater group formed in 1912, took over the church in 1962. An unfortunate fire of suspicious origin in May, 1999 nearly leveled the structure, and it was subsequently razed.

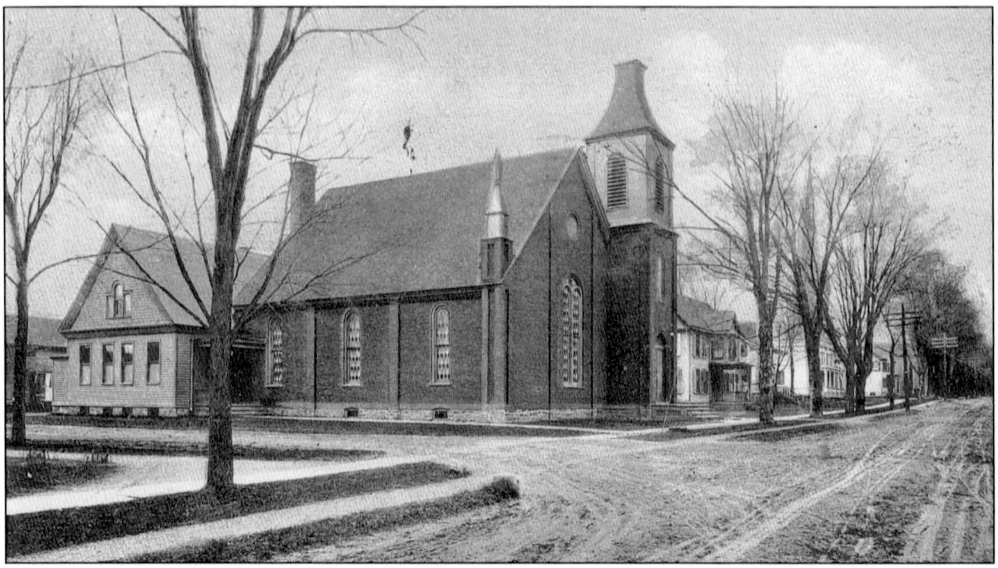

The Baptist Church, revived and reorganized in 1855, met with little success in the early years. A small church at the corner of Campion Road and Genesee Street was used for 30 years. In 1884, the church removed a house from the corner of Mill Street and Oxford Road; they moved it next door for a parsonage and built a new church at a cost of $4,500. It was dedicated in 1885. This building still houses the New Hartford Baptist Church.

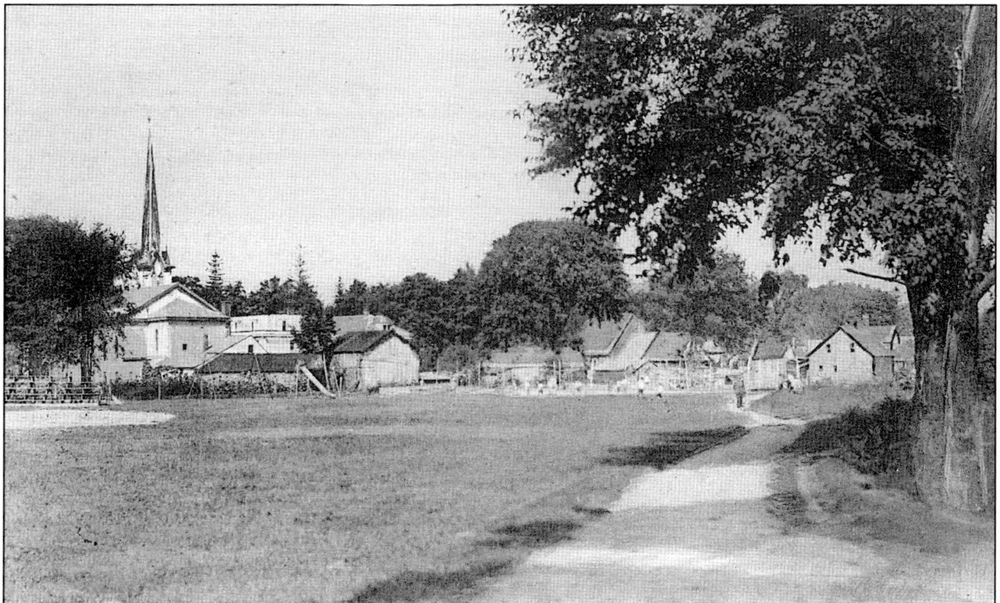

PLAYGROUNDS, NEW HARTFORD, N. Y.

Located on the east side of Oxford Road, behind the Baptist and Methodist Churches, was a community playground. In addition to the usual slides, swings, and seesaws, the playground's tennis courts were flooded in the winter to provide a skating rink. In 1979, the New Hartford Recreation Center was built in this area. It featured an ice rink for figure skating and ice hockey in winter and various community activities in the summer.

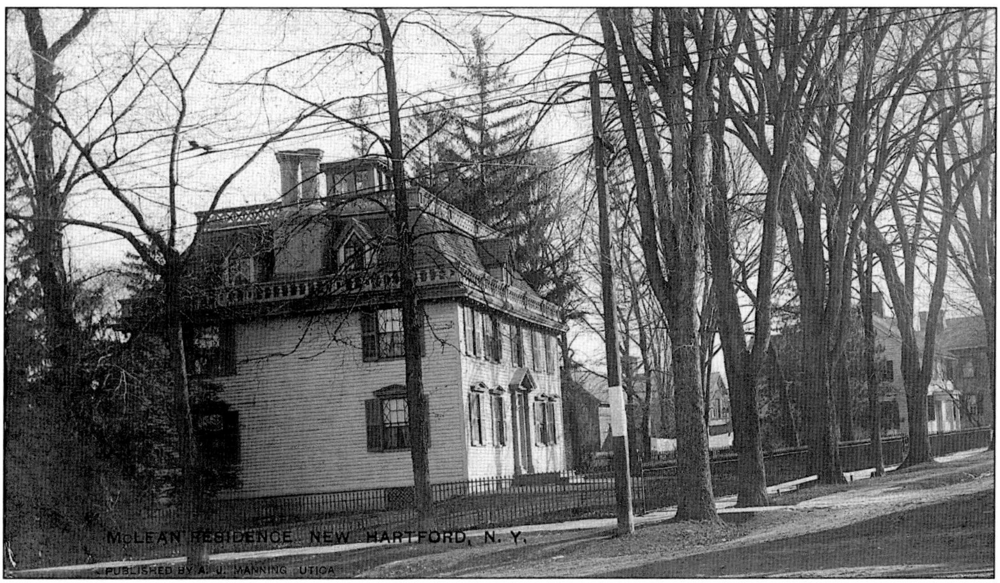

Judge Jedediah Sanger's first residence after his log cabin was this house on the corner of Genesee Street and Oxford Road, facing the village green. In later years, it was known as the McLean house. The McLean estate sold some of the property to the Masonic Lodge, who tore the house down to build a temple. Later purchased by Oneida County, it became the offices for the County Agricultural Department. The corner portion of the property has been a drug store, soda fountain, and a shoe store. It is now occupied by the New Hartford Florist.

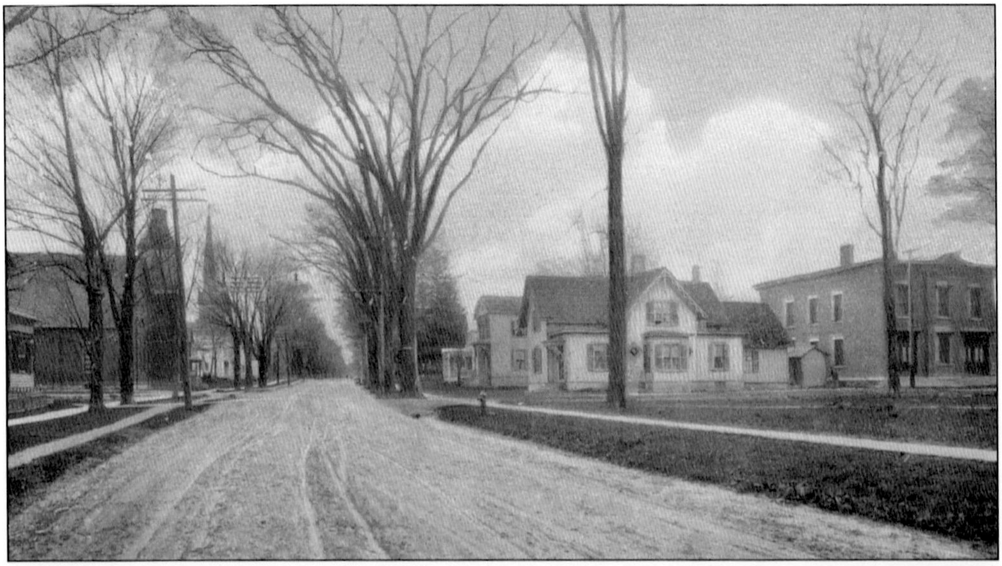

In 1906, New Hartford changed South Street to Oxford Road because it went south and connected with Old Route 8, then on to the Oxford Turnpike. The Gothic-style house on the right, once known as the Brennan house on the corner of Park Street, was moved to the Cassville area. Two adjoining homes were razed to permit the fire company to build a new facility. The building behind the house was formerly the fire department, organized in 1901. Earlier this structure had been a school.

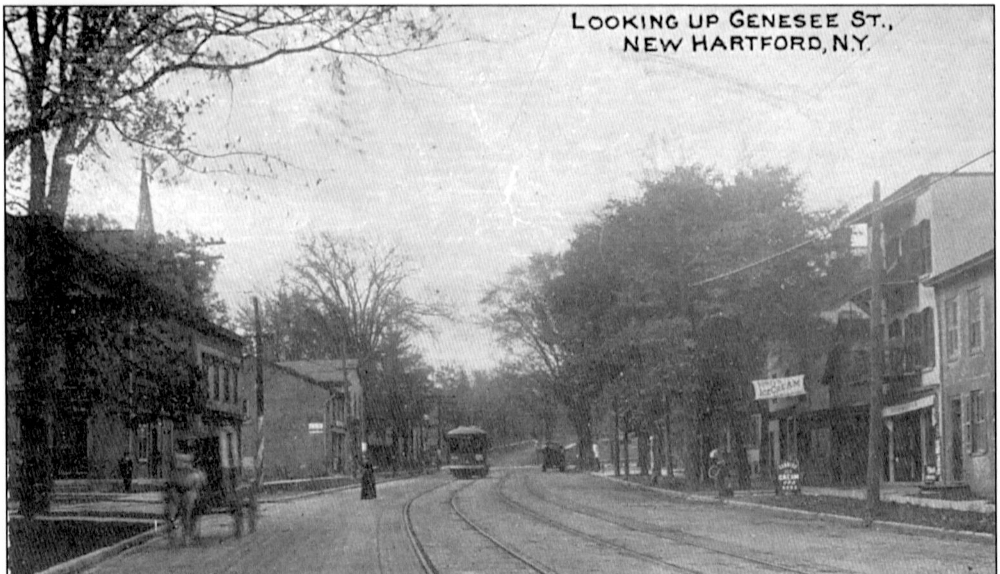

The Utica-to-Clinton trolley line that ran through New Hartford was opened in 1901. The final run was in 1936, and the tracks were taken up in 1941. Genesee Street, also known as the Seneca Turnpike and State Route 5, was a major east-west route. Jedediah Sanger, village founder and benefactor, was influential in getting the road routed through New Hartford in 1800. Until the Erie Canal opened in 1825, New Hartford was larger, more prosperous, and had more industries than Utica.

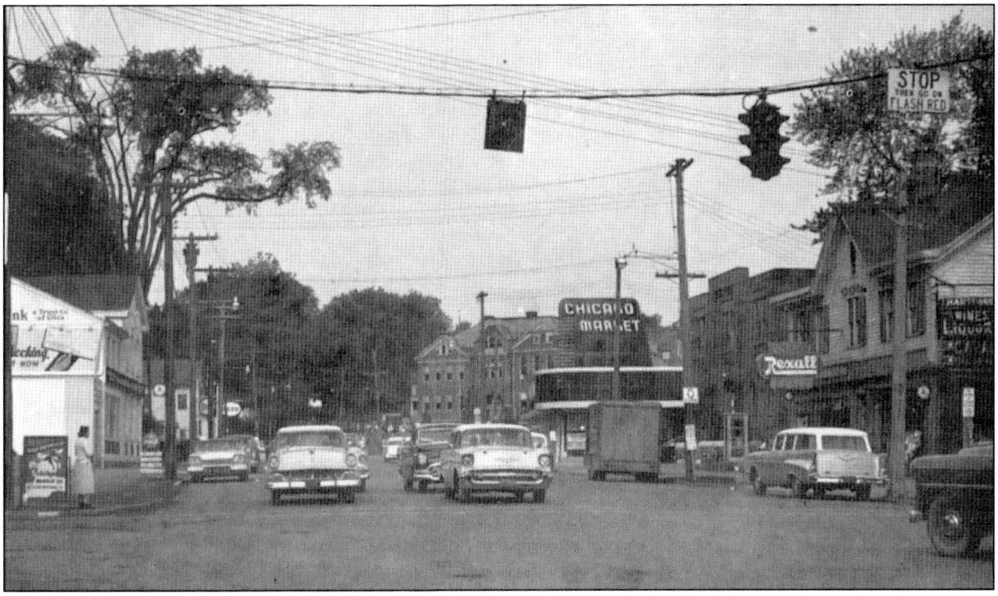

On the left is the Oneida National Bank, *c.* 1960s, that absorbed the National Bank of New Hartford in 1946. In its early days, this was the site of New Hartford's first soda fountain, bakery, and confectionery. In 1979, the bank moved across the street to the former Chicago Market location. The vacated bank building was razed for additional parking for the Presbyterian Church. On the right is the former Rexall drug store, now Randall's Pharmacy, and in earlier days the residence of Enoc Morris.

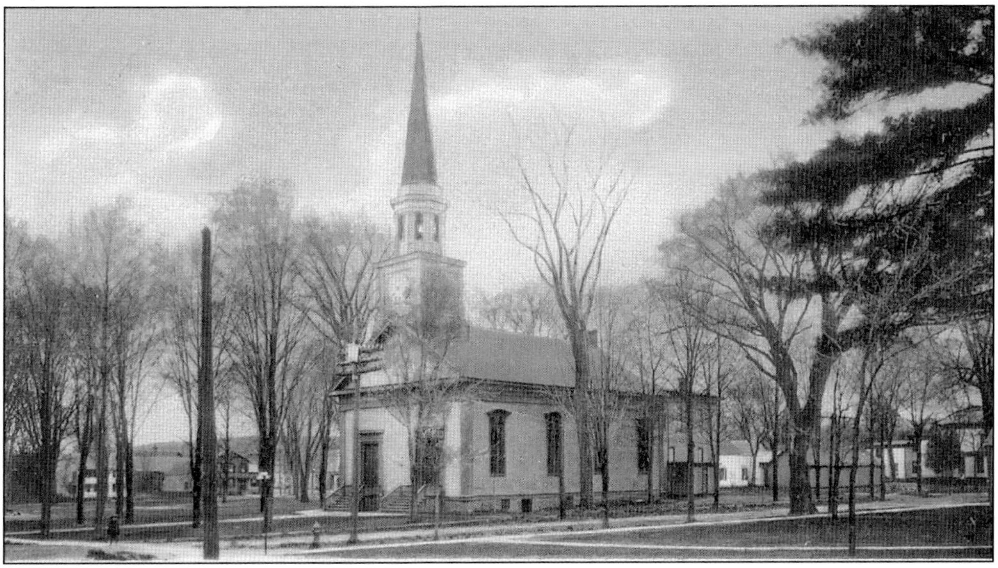

The Presbyterian Church, which was a Congregational Church until 1802, is the oldest in New Hartford. It was built in 1793, although the steeple was not added until 1796 with the generosity of Jedediah Sanger. The clock was added in 1851. The lot was donated by Judge Sanger, as was the lot for St. Stephen's Episcopal Church on South Street. In 1843, seven women and five men of the Presbyterian Church presented a document to the pastor and the congregation stating their belief that slavery was "a serious sin against God, and a flagrant violation of the dearest rights of man."

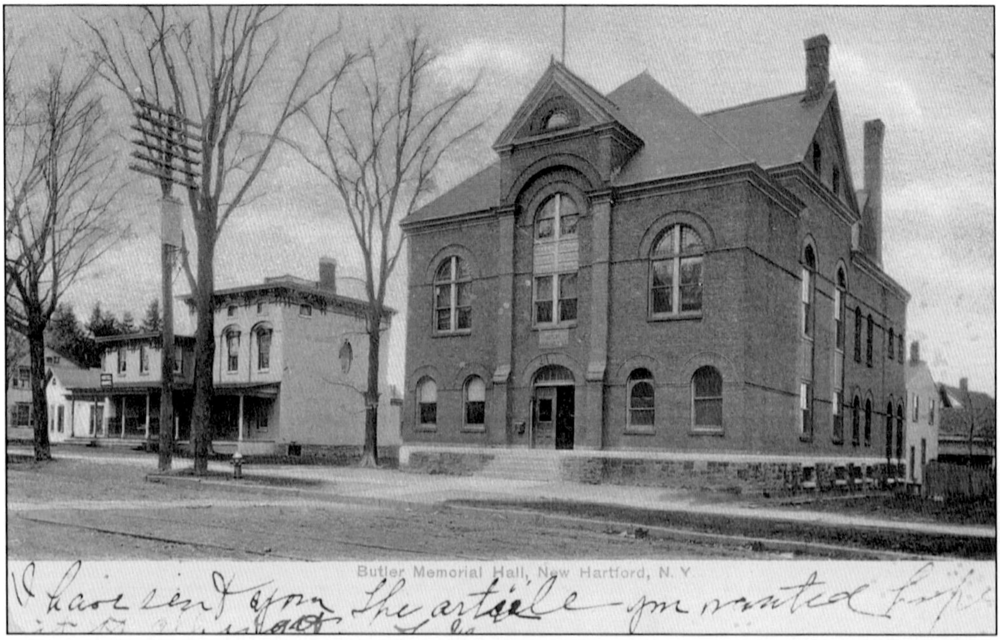

Morgan Butler, one of New Hartford's oldest residents, donated Butler Hall to the village. James Schoolcraft Sherman was on hand for the presentation. Frank Tomaino's "This Week in History" column in the *Utica Observer Dispatch* (April 1995) states that the Chadwicks brass band performed for the May 1890 occasion. The hall provided a post office, library, town and village offices, bowling alleys, an auditorium, and a stage for theatrical offerings. Today, the building still holds the town and village offices. It also furnishes space for the Chamber of Commerce and the New Hartford Historical Society.

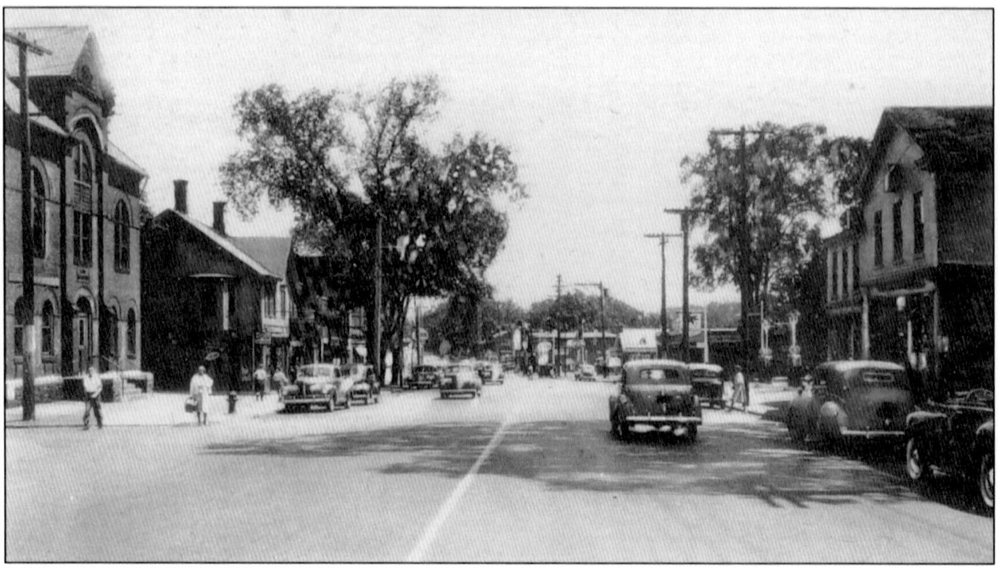

On this *c.* 1930 postcard of Genesee Street looking east, Butler Hall can be seen on the left. Gas stations were abundant—a Sears, Texaco, and a Mobil gas station all operated on Genesee Street near the corner of Oxford Road. The building on the right was later home to the Oneida National Bank.

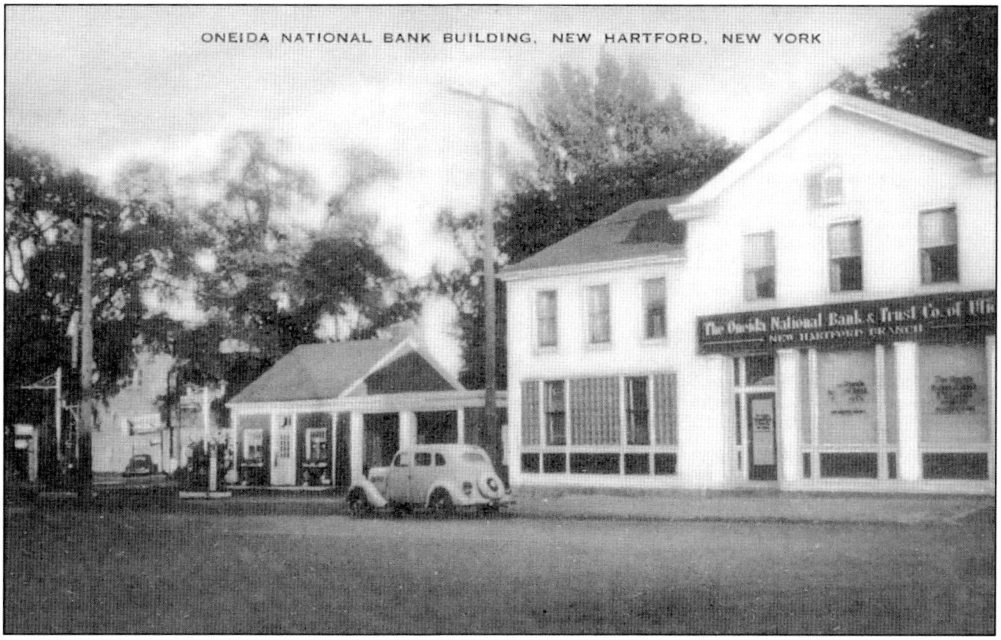

The Oneida Bank of Utica, incorporated in 1836, became Oneida National Bank in 1865. It suffered a rocky start with much ado about the distribution of stock and a theft from their vaults in 1836. The thieves escaped by canal to Rochester. One was traced to Canada, returned to Oneida County, and convicted. His accomplice was never caught. The bank building and gas station were torn down in 1979. A Blimpey's fast food restaurant now occupies the southwest corner of Genesee Street and Oxford Road.

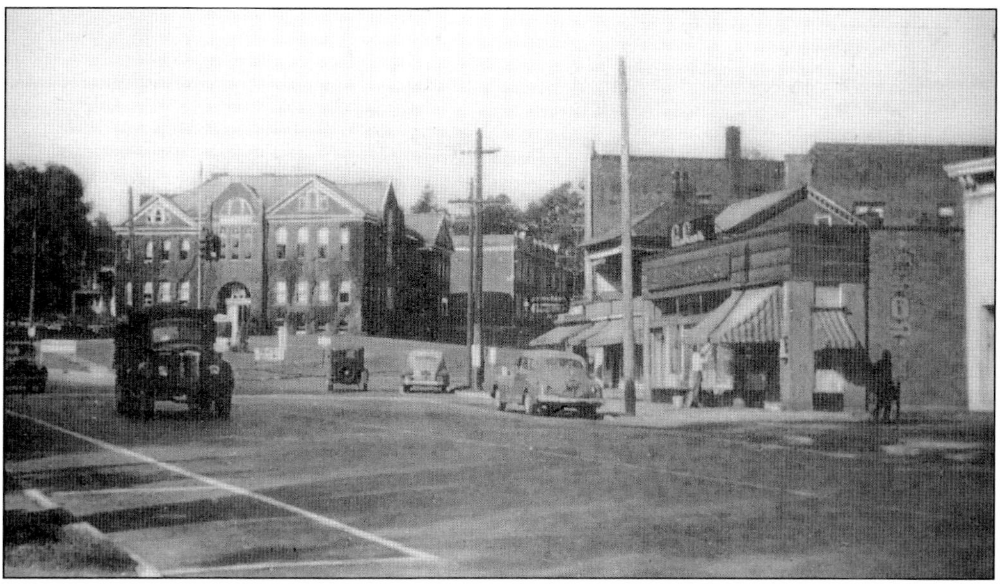

Fisher's Department Store, seen on the right, was a popular 5&10 cent store. Moving a few doors west, it later became a fabric store, but had closed by 1990. The Point School built in 1903 is on the left at the junction of Genesee Street and Paris Road. The addition built in 1921 is visible at the right rear. Since 1982, the building has been a senior citizen apartment complex. It also housed the New Hartford Public Library from 1976 until 1999.

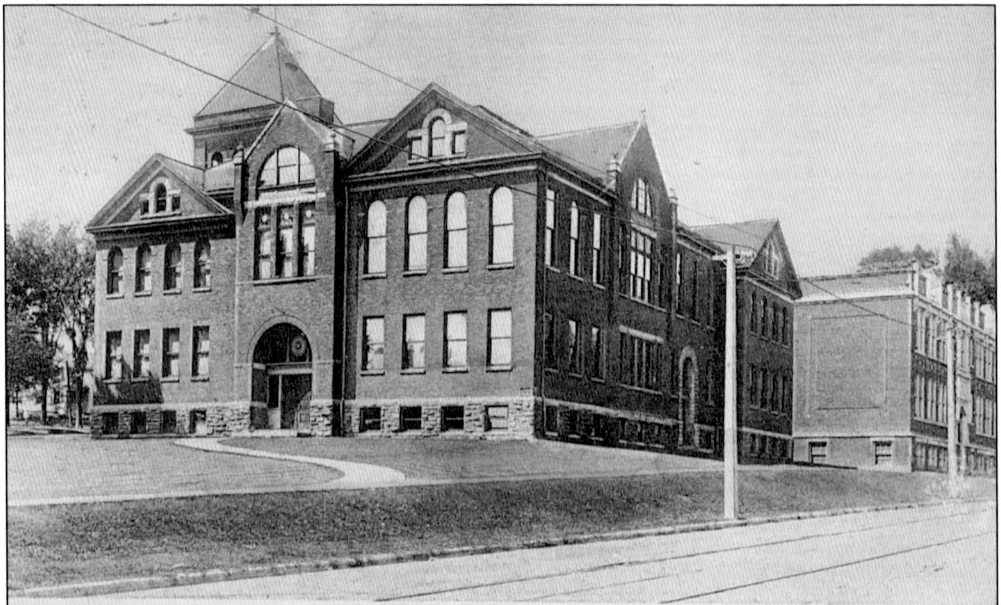

HIGH SCHOOL, NEW HARTFORD, N. Y.

Built in 1903, this red brick school of Romanesque design was the New Hartford High School, built to accommodate 600 students. The second floor featured an assembly hall, study, and recitation rooms. The 1921 addition doubled the capacity of the school and added a gymnasium. Earlier the site of a Sanger family mansion, and later occupied by the Eames and Golden families, it was from 1878 to 1883 the Home School for Girls. In 1900, a disastrous fire resulted in the demolition of the mansion.

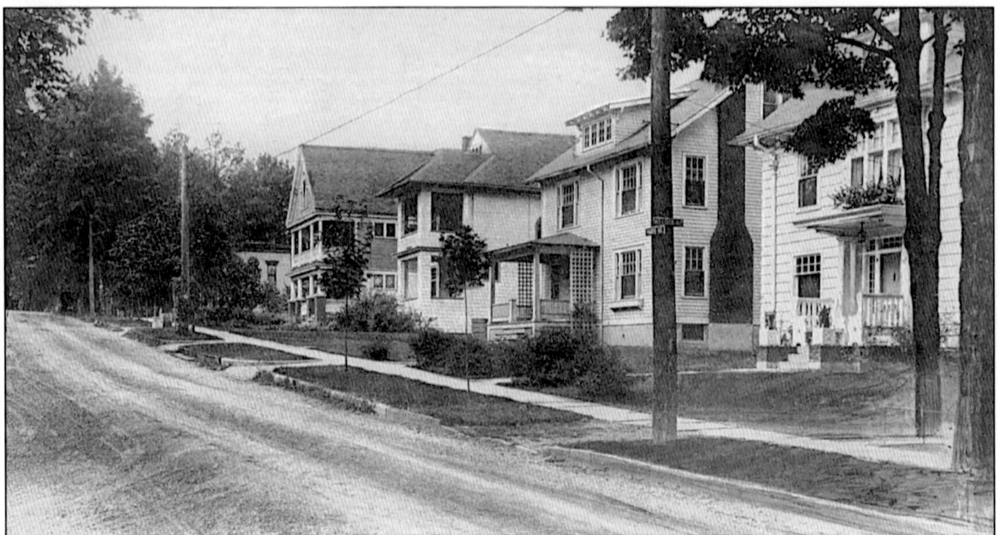

PARIS STREET, NEW HARTFORD, N. Y.

Multiple- and single-family dwellings grace Paris Street, which was called Paris Road or Old Paris Road in later years. A very early route to Clinton and Paris Hill, the Seneca Turnpike replaced it in 1800 as the main thoroughfare through New Hartford. The trellises on the porch of 36 Paris Road remain intact. Except for the contemporary colors, these homes look very much as they did on this 1930s postcard.

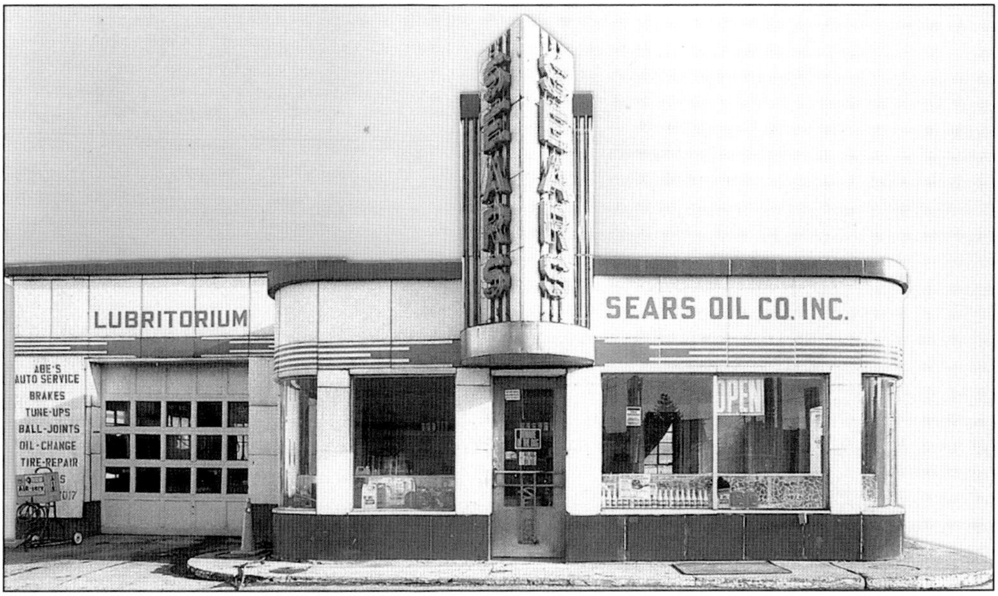

Considering it a historical landmark and architectural gem, preservationists were unable to persuade the Sears Oil Company of the value of this 1936 gas station. A rare example of Art Moderne, it was built in a streamlined, functional style that was popular in the 1930s and 1940s. It was torn down in 1988 and donated to the New York State Museum in Albany, where it is awaiting reconstruction in a transportation exhibit. A modern Citgo service station now occupies the site. (Jeff Milstein photograph.)

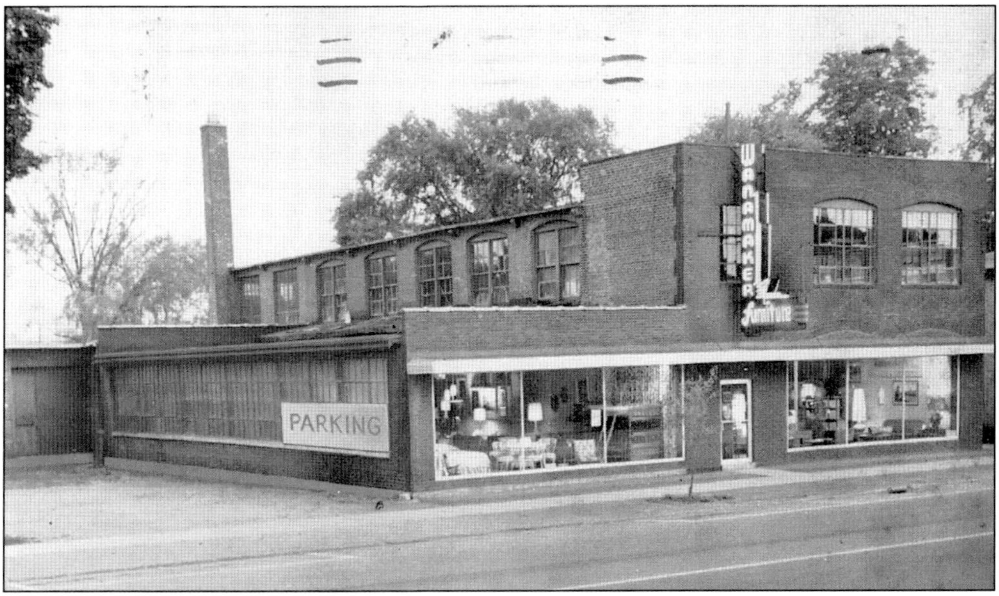

A chair company formed in 1916 by E.E. Wanamaker and partners relocated to New Hartford to a lane called 42nd Street, near Casa Too Mucha restaurant. In 1945, the store became retail only, and dining room and bedroom furniture was added to their line. Wordie Wanamaker followed his father in business and was, in turn, succeeded by his son, Robert. The store went out of business in 1974. The All-American Fitness Center occupied the site for a time. It is now home to the Uptown Grill, recently relocated from Utica.

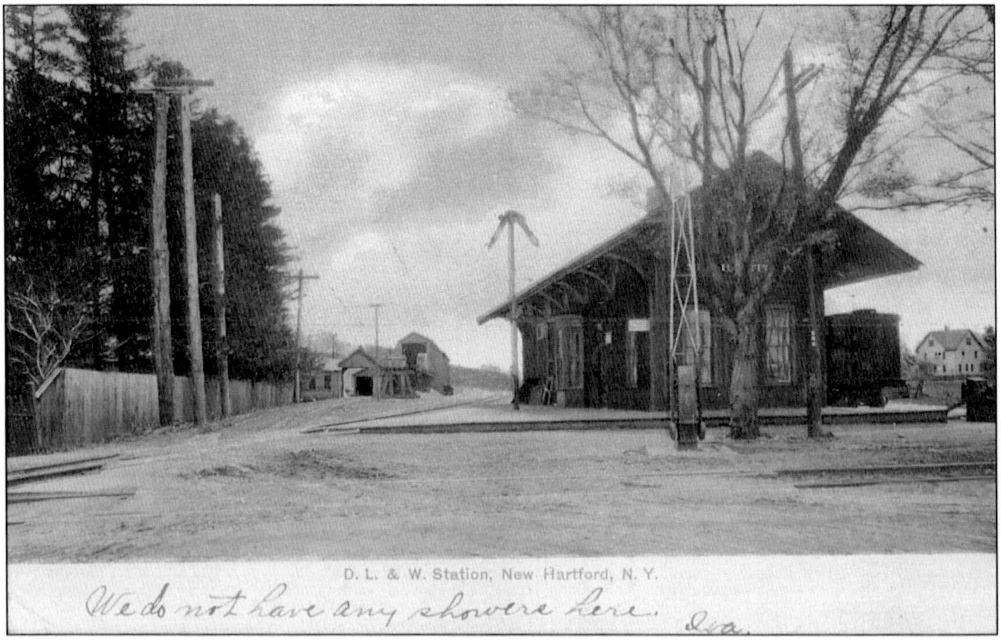

The New Hartford train station on the DL&W Railroad, erected in the early 1900s, has undergone numerous transformations. It is currently an insurance agency, but in the 1960s, a children's clothing store called the Balloon Shop occupied the premises. This area, once in New Hartford village, is now in Utica because of boundary changes.

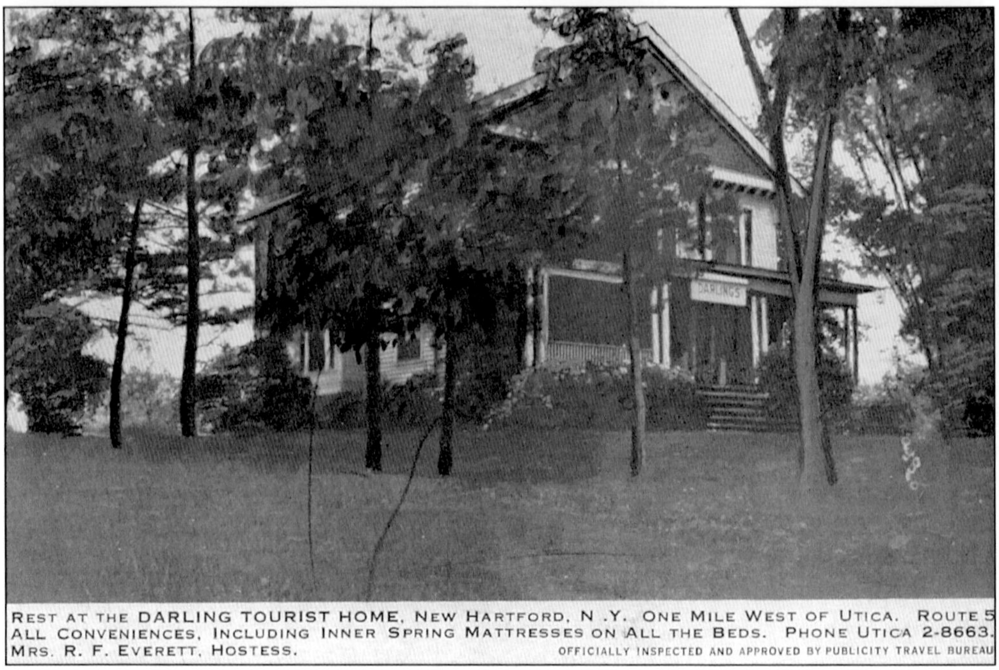

The Darling Tourist Home, once a welcome stop for weary travelers, sits between Routes 12 and 12B on Route 5 (Genesee Street or Seneca Turnpike) across from Utica National Insurance Company and east of Sangertown Mall. Situated on what was once farmland, it is now a residence at the hub of an intersection of three busy state roads.

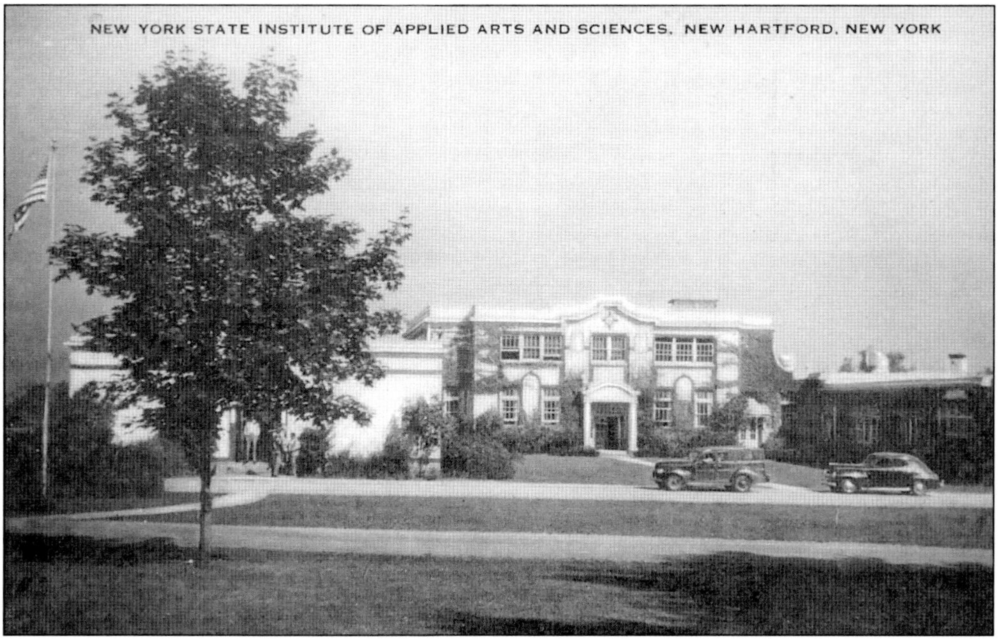

The private Country Day School on the Seneca Turnpike was established in 1921 on the site of the old Yahnundasis clubhouse, located where the Wedgewood apartments are today. After the school's closing, New York State refurbished the building and opened the New York State Institute of Applied Arts and Sciences in 1946 as a two-year technical school. In 1950, it became part of the State University of New York and was renamed the Mohawk Valley Technical Institute. In 1959, a new college was built on Sherman Drive in Utica and, in 1960, it became Mohawk Valley Community College.

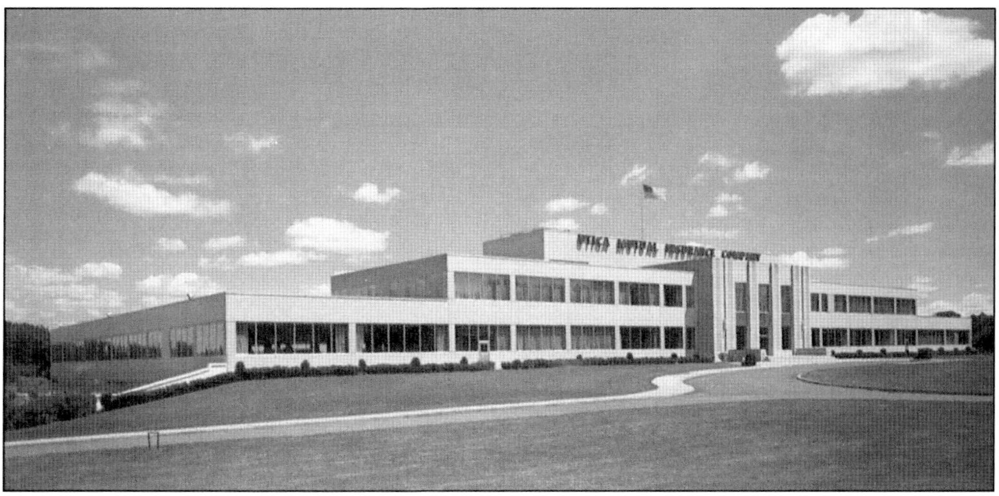

Established in 1914, the Utica Mutual Insurance Company was formed by a group of Mohawk Valley businessmen. It originally provided workmen's compensation, mutual property insurance, and casualty insurance. It was first named the Utica Mutual Workmen's Compensation Insurance Corporation. After adding other lines of insurance, the name was changed to the Utica Mutual Insurance Company and later Utica National. By 1951, this new home office was built, and the firm became a multiple lines company and one of the area's largest employers. In 1969, an addition was erected next to the home office structure.

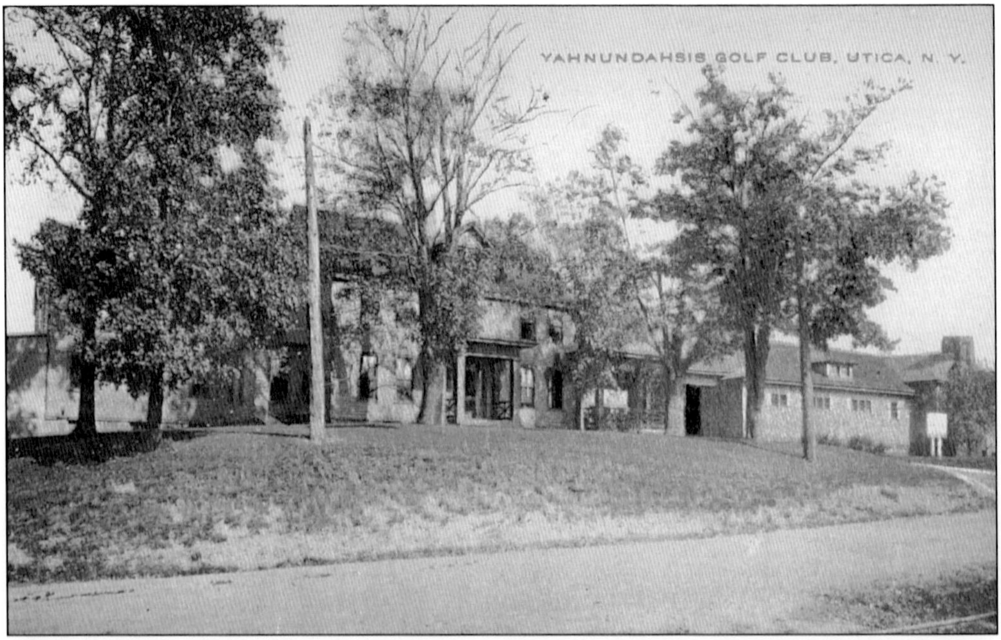

The Yahnundasis Golf Club was organized in 1897. It erected its first clubhouse for $728 on Proctor Boulevard (now in Utica, then in New Hartford.) In 1905, they moved to Seneca Turnpike in New Hartford and, in 1907, opened the remodeled Sherrill farmhouse for use as their clubhouse. This postcard shows that site as it looked in 1913. Although the postcard caption states the location was in Utica, it was in New Hartford.

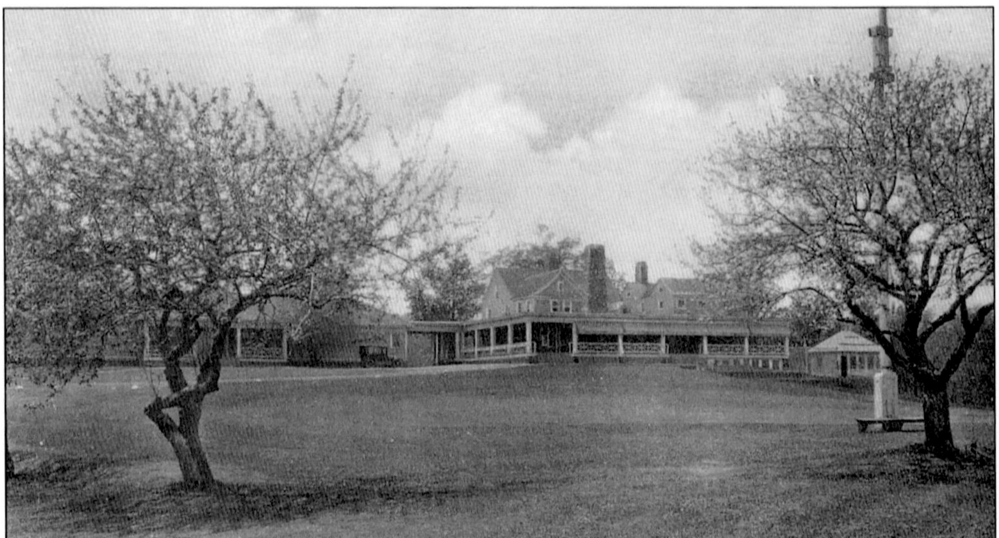

Additions to the Yahnundasis clubhouse were made after their 1905 move to New Hartford, a spot chosen for its accessibility to the trolley line. The site of this first New Hartford clubhouse was sold in 1921 to the Utica Country Day School for their new building. They shared the property while the new clubhouse was being built west of the old one. The golf club moved to the new clubhouse in 1924.

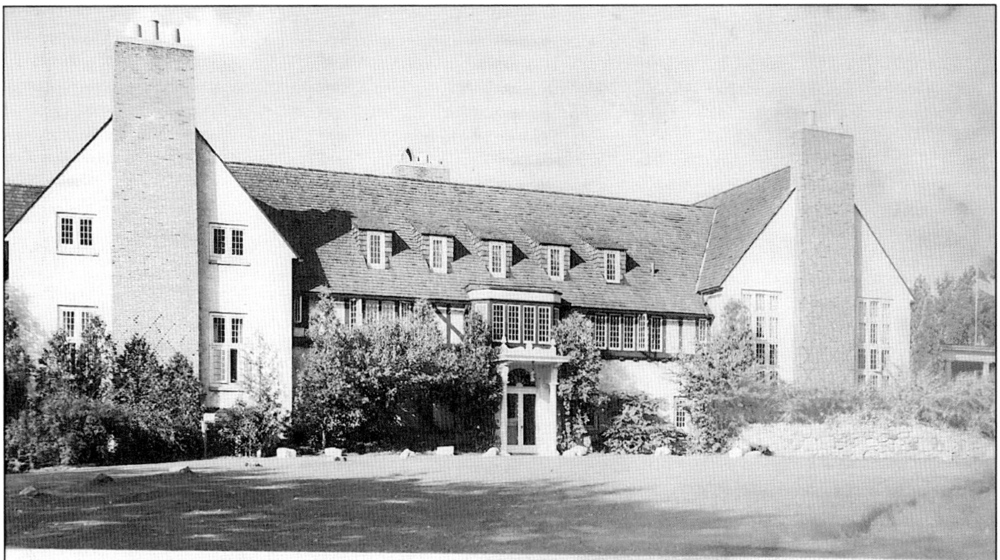

CLUB HOUSE, YAHNUNDASIS GOLF CLUB, UTICA, N. Y.

The 1924 clubhouse is still the home of the Yahnundasis Golf Club. According to the *Utica Observer* of March 13, 1926, the Yahnundasis club purchased an additional 100 acres of an adjoining parcel from the Moore sisters. The plan was to sell building lots from the property located between Genesee Street and the Ontario & Western railroad tracks that ran through their property. Part of the acreage was to be used for tennis courts.

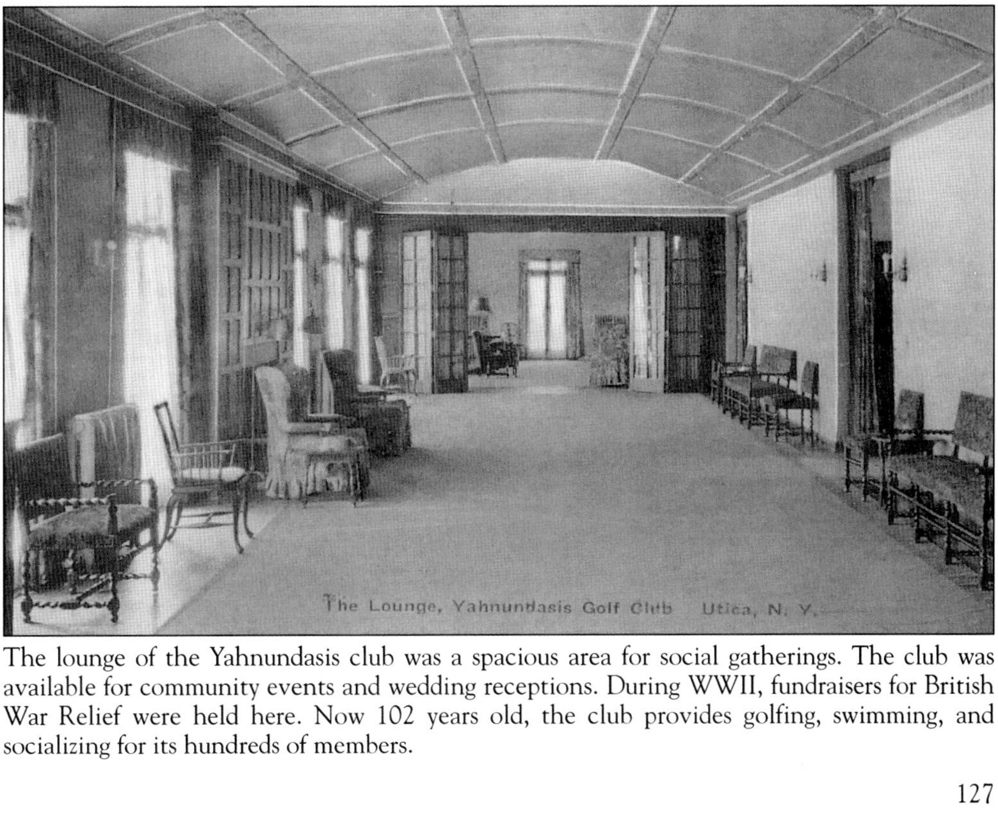

The Lounge, Yahnundasis Golf Club Utica, N. Y.

The lounge of the Yahnundasis club was a spacious area for social gatherings. The club was available for community events and wedding receptions. During WWII, fundraisers for British War Relief were held here. Now 102 years old, the club provides golfing, swimming, and socializing for its hundreds of members.

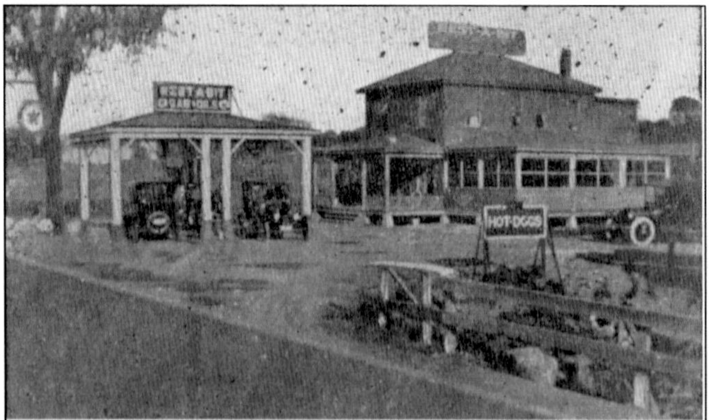

Service Station and Administration Building at Rest-A-Bit Camping Grounds, six miles west of Utica, on Route No. 5. Excellent camping facilities here.

The Rest-A-Bit camping grounds provided all conveniences—from gas and oil for your car, to hot dogs for your family's lunch. The campsites on Route 5 (now 12B) were behind the service station and administration building. This building still stands, as do the cabins to the right. The covered gas pump structure has been moved behind the administration building (now a private residence), and has been enclosed to make an apartment.

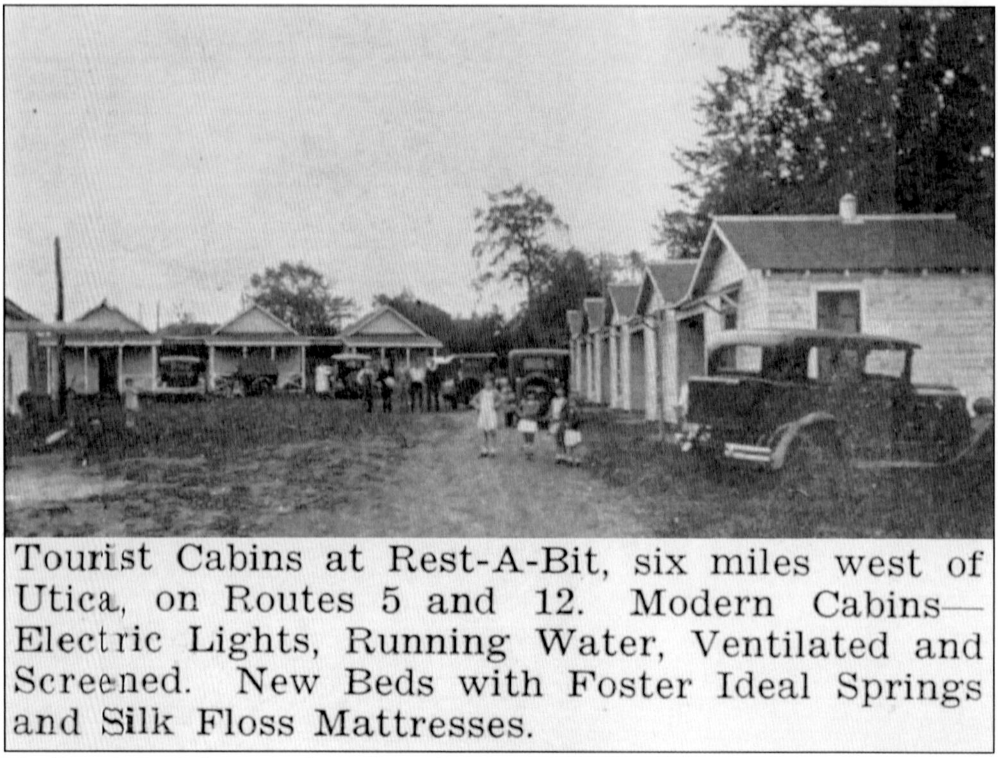

Tourist Cabins at Rest-A-Bit, six miles west of Utica, on Routes 5 and 12. Modern Cabins—Electric Lights, Running Water, Ventilated and Screened. New Beds with Foster Ideal Springs and Silk Floss Mattresses.

The Rest-A-Bit Cabins were located on what is now Route 12B, near the town of Kirkland line. The pre-motel cabins were a popular tourist stop in the 1930s. Taken for granted in the last half of the 1900s, conveniences such as electric lights and running water were novelties that the proprietor W. E. Sloane considered worth advertising. Ventilation and screening were the 1930s version of air conditioning. Most of these cabins remain standing, although some have been joined to make apartments.